THE
FIELD AND FOREST
HANDY BOOK

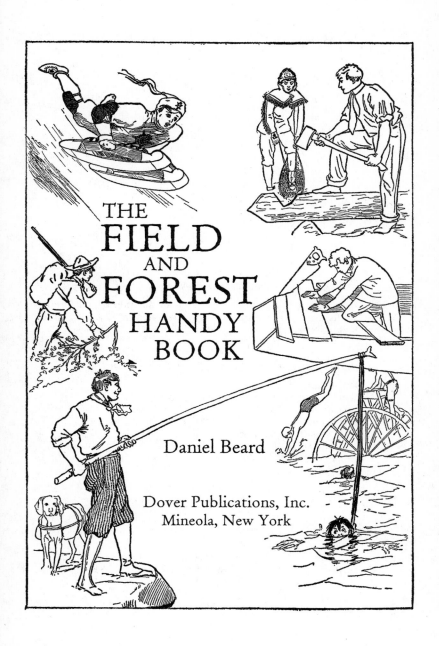

THE
FIELD
AND
FOREST
HANDY
BOOK

Daniel Beard

Dover Publications, Inc.
Mineola, New York

Bibliographical Note

This Dover edition, first published in 2007, is an unabridged republication of the 1912 edition of the work originally published in 1906 by Charles Scribner's Sons, New York.

Library of Congress Cataloging-in-Publication Data

Beard, Daniel Carter, 1850–1941.
    The field and forest handy book / Daniel Beard.
       p. cm.
    Originally published: New York : Charles Scribner's Sons, 1912.
    ISBN-13: 978-0-486-46191-5
    ISBN-10: 0-486-46191-2
    1. Camping—Handbooks, manuals, etc. 2. Outdoor recreation—Handbooks, manuals, etc. I. Title.

GV191.7.B42 2007
796.54—dc22

                                 2007026659

Manufactured in the United States of America
Dover Publications, Inc., 31 East 2nd Street, Mineola, N.Y. 11501

PREFACE

THE purpose of the present volume differs from that of those which have preceded it in the following respect: It is essentially a book for the use of readers who are living, for the time being at any rate, close to Nature in field and forest, men as well as boys, and who desire to make as much a success of their vacation as possible, to know how to meet and overcome difficulties in the simplest way. It is even more extended in its purpose, for it exploits a number of schemes for the benefit of those who have permanent camps or dwellings in field and forest; also for those whose sphere of adventure takes them into the untrodden wilderness. The matter, except where it is expressly stated otherwise, is entirely new and original, and, as the author believes, will prove practically very useful to those for whom the book is designed. The diagrams and their explanations have been made with great care, so as to render them as easily intelligible and as unambiguous as the author can possibly make them.

I am under obligations to Mr. Frederic Vreeland, the young inventor and scientist; Mr. Belmore Browne, artist and explorer; and Col. Brainard, U. S. A., one of the heroes of the Greely Expedition, for effectual aid in solving a number of knotty questions which their several specialties and experiences enabled them to answer in the most successful and practical manner; and also to Mr. Annis of *Recreation*, Mr. Caspar Whitney of *The Outing Magazine*, and Mr. Bok of *The Ladies' Home Journal* for their promptness in returning drawings and matter in time for use in publishing this book.

DAN BEARD.

FLUSHING, L. I., *Oct.* 1, 1906.

CONTENTS

SPRING

CHAPTER I

CHAPTER II

CHAPTER III

CHAPTER IV

WINTER

CHAPTER XXX

CHAPTER XXXI

CHAPTER XXXII

CHAPTER XXXIII

CHAPTER XXXIV

CHAPTER XXXV

CHAPTER XXXVI

CHAPTER XXXVII

SPRING

CHAPTER I

HOW TO MAKE A TAILLESS FILIPINO

Since it is perfectly proper to speak of the skeleton of a kite, there is no good reason why the sticks may not be called the bones of the skeleton. This will suggest good names for otherwise nameless sticks and be found most convenient in describing the structure of a kite. Such being the case, the boys will not think it odd if we now describe

The Bones of a Filipino

We will begin first with the most important in the kite, which we call the

Backbone

This should be made of a sound piece of straight-grained wood, free from knots and blemishes. Make it about one-quarter inch thick, one inch broad, and three feet two or three inches long; see that this bone is of uniform breadth and thickness throughout. With a lead-pencil make the

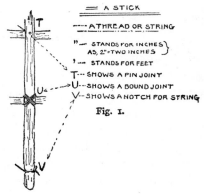

= A STICK

---- A THREAD OR STRING

" — STANDS FOR INCHES
AS, 2"=TWO INCHES

' — STANDS FOR FEET

T— SHOWS A PIN JOINT

U—SHOWS A BOUND JOINT

V—SHOWS A NOTCH FOR STRING

Fig. 1.

mark A on the backbone an inch or two below one end of the spine (Fig. 2), five inches from A mark the point K, twenty-two inches from K mark the top of the fluke at L. Eight and one-half inches from L mark the bottom of the fluke at B (Fig. 2). This leaves a little spare timber at each end of the spine A B, which may be trimmed off when the frame is finished. Lay

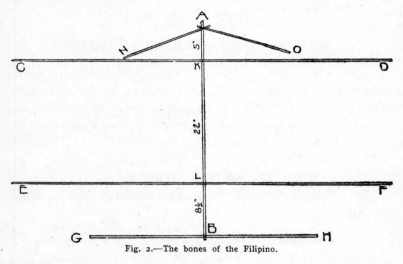

Fig. 2.—The bones of the Filipino.

A B carefully away and select some strong elastic wood from which to fashion

The Ribs

or bowsticks C D and E F.   Make them about five and one-half feet long and much thinner and every way lighter than the backbone A B.   The thickness of the ribs must depend to some extent upon the material used; split bamboo ribs may be made much lighter than may be safe for ribs of pine or similar wood.

The Pelvis,

or fluke-bow G B H, is made of the same material as the ribs and of equal thickness; make G B H about three and one-half feet in length. · All these bowsticks must be of uniform thickness throughout their length, otherwise they will bend in irregular curves, and besides being unsightly will make that abomination —a "lopsided" kite.

The Neck Sticks

A N and A O are made flat like the backbone A B and about fifteen inches long; they are not supposed to bend and should be

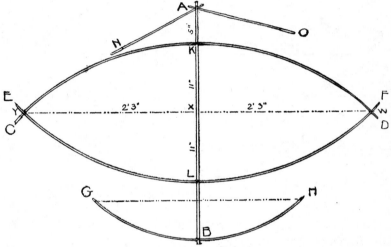

Fig. 3.—The bows and bow strings.

stiff. Make them considerably lighter than the backbone and see that they are duplicates of each other. In choosing wood for the two

Ilium Sticks

select elastic wood similar to that from which the ribs have been cut. Make G P and S H (Fig. 4) of equal length and proportions, otherwise the fluke of the kite will not be well balanced, and like a badly laden boat it will "list to port or starboard" and make a bad sailer.   The iliums need not be as heavy as any of the other bones because the former have no very hard strain to bear.   Having

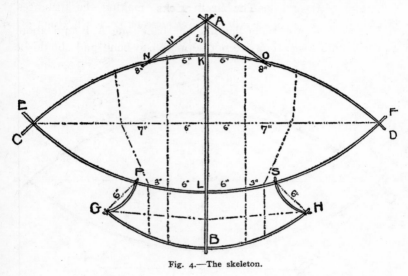

Fig. 4.—The skeleton.

fashioned all the sticks to your satisfaction you may now make the frame or the

Skeleton of the Filipino

With some strong string or shoemaker's "wax-ends" bind the middle of the ribs C D to the point K five inches below A on the backbone stick (see Fig. 2).   In the same manner bind the middle of the second rib E F to the point L, twenty-two inches below B. After securing the rib bones at K and L, lash the ends of the ribs together (Fig. 3).   Adjust the ribs so that the distance from X to Y measures exactly the same as the distance from X to W, then take the pelvis or fluke-bow G B H and bind it securely to the backbone at B and with a string temporarily fasten the ends G and H to the rib E F (Fig. 4). Now string the bows G P and S H and lash them in place, making the distances P L and L S each exactly ten and one-half inches (Fig. 4); leave the bowstrings G P and S H in place until the frame is finished, when they may be removed. The dotted lines show the strings.

After the fluke P G B H S is finished, measure nine inches from centre of spine at K and mark the point N, measure nine inches in opposite direction and mark the point O (Fig. 4); then fasten the crossed ends of the neck bones securely at A and their opposite ends at N and O. Stretch a bowstring from Y to W (Fig. 3), pull this until the wings of the kite are slightly bowed backward, fasten the bowline with a half-hitch at X and securely at Y and W (Fig. 3). In the same manner stretch the bowline G H, making the curve or bow of the flukes equal that of the wings. Next run the stay-lines shown by the dotted lines in Fig. 4. It is now only necessary to know

How to Put a Skin on a Filipino

that you may finish your kite. Spread the paper on the floor, and if it is too small paste enough pieces together to make the skin large enough for the frame; do your pasting neatly, making the seams as narrow as safety will admit; use boiled flour paste for the work, and any light strong paper, the brighter the color the more attractive the kite. After the skin is prepared place the frame over it and weights at X, Y, and Z (Fig. 5); use paper-weights, books, stones, or similar objects for this purpose. Since

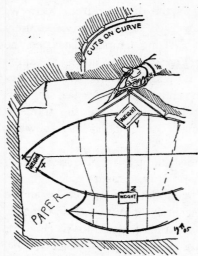

Fig. 5.—How to cut the paper around the framed kite.

you have tightened the bow-strings until there is a slight bow backward of the whole kite, you will not be surprised to find that, when one wing is weighted down, the other will not touch the floor.

With a sharp pair of scissors cut around the kite frame (as in Fig. 5), making notches or slits at each angle and at short intervals (Fig. 6) on the curved lines. When one side is cut shift the X weight to the opposite wing and cut the other side in the same manner, until the pattern, skin, cover, or dress for the kite is finished; then with a towel in your left hand and paste-brush in the right take one flap at a time,

Coat it with Paste,

fold it neatly over the outline frame of the kite and press it gently but firmly down with the towel. When one side is finished transfer the X weight to the opposite side and paste that, after which cut a number of little slips of paper and paste them over the strings on the kite frame at short intervals, thus gluing the strings to the skin of the

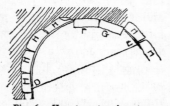

Fig. 6.—How to cut and paste on a curve.

kite. Now add the bright-colored flags to the fluke of the kite
(Fig. 7). When all is dry the belly-band may be attached
by using a sharp lead-pencil and punching small holes on
each side of the backbone at Y and Z (Fig. 8), through which

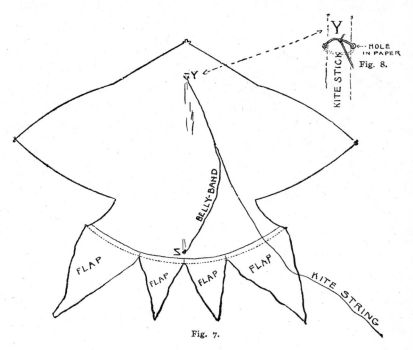

Fig. 7.

string the line for the belly-band and tie it around the backbone, and the kite will be ready for a voyage to the sky to
surprise the birds and cause the boys on your block to stare
in awe-struck wonder at the graceful movements of the first
great Filipino kite which has spread its wings under an American sky.

If you wish, you may transform the Tailless Filipino to

An Owl

by simply painting it with broad strokes of black or brown paint. Take Fig. 9 and set it before you, then with a brush and paint make

Fig. 9.—The Owl

a faithful copy of it. When it is done and your kite is sent aloft, you can be certain that there are no other kites like it except those some other readers of this book are flying. I have tried to make the diagrams of the kites so that the construction may be understood even should the letter-press be lost.

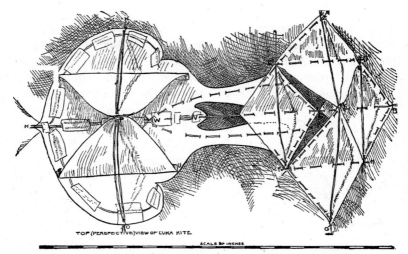

Fig. 10.—Sketch of luna kite looking down on the back of the butterfly.

CHAPTER II

AIR-SHIPS, BROOM STRAW FLYING MACHINES, AND KITES

The Luna Kite,

a perspective top view of which is shown by Fig. 10, looks so complicated that a few words of explanation will be necessary. Fig. 11 shows the pattern of one side of this new butterfly kite. It was first built without the queer appendage on the tail, but I found that it darted around so much that it was necessary to have something to steady it. (It must be understood that when I here speak of the tail of these tailless kites I mean the lower or rear end of the kites themselves and not any long streamers of rags or strings and tufts of paper. So when I refer to the tetrahedron on the tail of the Luna I mean on that part which would be called the tail of the real butterfly's wings.) On the back of the butterfly's wings two other wings are pasted (as may be seen by referring to Fig. 10), and in the sectional view (Fig. 12, S P and R P) these two wings are joined at their tips by a bit of paste and kept in position by the straw (O P N) run through them and the other wings. This straw is held in place by a thread which is fastened securely to one end of the straw and then run around the curve of the kite (O M N) and secured to the other end of the straw at N. Fig. 13 shows a section of Professor Bell's tetrahedron; Fig. 14 shows how to make one with paper and broom straws; Fig. 15 shows the finished box of "cells," and Figs. 10 and 11 show how the cells are pasted to the tail of the butterfly and braced by broom straws. The kite measures twenty-four inches in length and has a spread of wings measuring fifteen inches. If made of brilliant and varicolored paper it makes a beautiful kite.

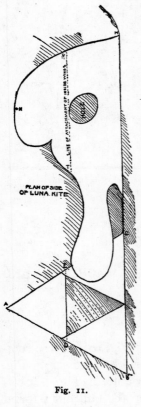

Fig. 11.

Of course it may be built of sticks in place of straws, but the one these diagrams were drawn from was made with broom straws and sent aloft attached to a spool of ordinary thread.

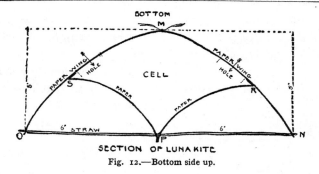

BOTTOM

CELL

SECTION OF LUNA KITE

Fig. 12.—Bottom side up.

In making my experiments for broom straw I used the light, strong writing-paper called textile bond, and found it suited my purpose exactly, but the only reason I used this paper was because it was handy; in fact, it was the first thing which I could lay my hands on, and really no better for the purpose than the cheap yellow paper which comes in writing-pads.

Any Light Paper

that is stiff enough to hold its form when folded will answer the purpose. Tissue-paper will need more straws to hold it in shape and need paste to hold the straws in place; but to build the machines here described one needs only paste for extra wings with straws plucked from the broom behind the kitchen door and paper from the writing-desk; as for tools—a pair of scissors.

But if any of my readers

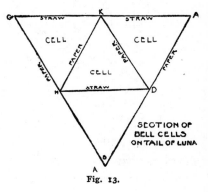

SECTION OF BELL CELLS ON TAIL OF LUNA

Fig. 13.

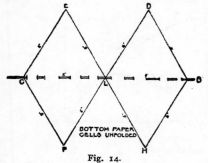

Fig. 14.

are not content with such primitive flying machines, they may use wooden sticks of any reasonable dimensions and cloth in place of paper, and with such material build

A Flying Machine

that can lift a man, and yet this powerful engine will be built on the same principle as the broom-straw air-ship here described:

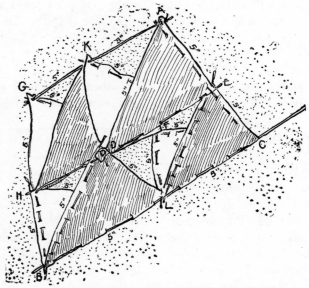

Fig. 15.—The tail box is a bell tetrahedron of cells.

How to Make Equal Lateral Triangles

Take a piece of light-weight writing-paper and cut it into a strip about five inches wide (Fig. 16); fold it lengthwise so as to make a crease in the centre of the paper, as shown by the dotted line G M. Do not make a deep crease, but a light one, just sufficient

To Mark the Centre of the Paper

Now fold the paper cross-wise so as to make a deep crease at E F, then take another small slip of paper and

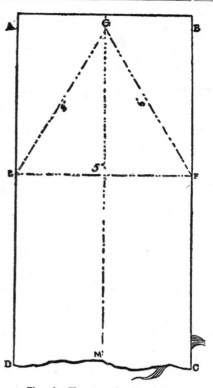

Fig. 16.—How to make the triangle.

Fig. 17.—The paper ruler.

Make a Ruler

of it by folding the strip lengthwise, as shown by Fig. 17; lay this ruler along the crease E F (Fig. 16) and with a lead-pencil mark a line (on the ruler) at K (Fig. 17) to correspond with the edge of the big

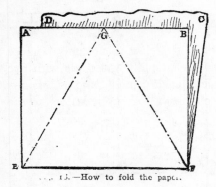

Fig. 18.—How to fold the paper.

piece of paper at E (Fig. 16), and mark another line on the ruler at L (Fig. 17) to correspond with the edge F of Fig. 16; put a pin in the ruler at K and let the point go into the table or drawing-board at E alongside of the piece A B C D (Fig. 16); swing the ruler around until its edge at the mark L just touches the line G M, then holding the ruler there, rule the line G E, next rule the line G F and you will have a triangle of equal sides, that is, E G = E F and E F = G F. This is a simple way to make an equilateral triangle; but do not be alarmed, we are not going to demonstrate a proposition in geometry, but simply cut some triangles out from the paper for material for our Fairy Air-ship. To do this, fold the paper again at E F, as shown by Fig. 18, but it must be so folded that the side edges correspond with each other and folded as tightly as the leaves of a closed book. Then take the scissors and

Cut Out the Two Sides

of the triangle G F and E G, as shown by Figs. 19 and 20, the last being a perspective view of the double triangle sail or set of wings. Make five of these sets of wings and

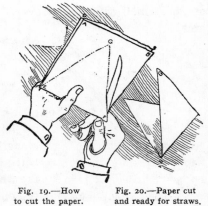

Fig. 19.—How to cut the paper.

Fig. 20.—Paper cut and ready for straws.

see that they are all of them alike in dimensions, that is, supposing E F to be five inches, then E F, E G, and G H of all the triangles will each be five inches. I use five inches only because the air-ship or flying machine which I built was made with five inches, the measure of each side of each triangle, and as this air-ship sailed well, I feel safe in giving the same dimensions to the reader.

It is evident that

Flimsy Writing-Paper

alone will not stand the pressure of even a light breeze, but if we stiffen it along the edges with broom straws, it is astonishing how strong this

Fragile Appearing Air-Ship

will be. We need one or more strong, stiff straws for the keel of the ship, as shown in Fig. 21, and we can put them in place by weaving them in and out of a series of small slits cut for the purpose along the centre folds of the wings or sails; in a like manner we can stiffen the sides of the wings as shown by Fig. 21.

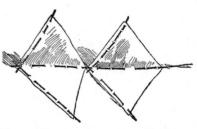

Fig. 21.—Two double triangles on one straw.

To Prevent the Wings from Closing

together when the winds blow against them, it is necessary to have some braces, and these may also be made of broom straws with their ends split B (Figs. 22 and 23), or bent over, as at B (Fig. 24), and made fast to the points of the sail by pasting a small piece of paper

over the split ends, as at B (Fig. 23).   After fastening one end of
the brace straw, as in Figs. 23 or 24, take your paper-ruler (Fig.
17) and placing L of the ruler at the edge of the sail, press the
opposite wing tip (C, Fig. 24) inward until the edge of this wing
corresponds with the mark K on your ruler, then split or bend

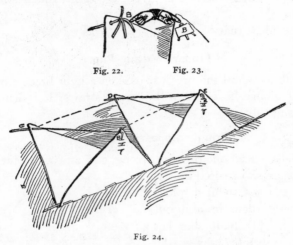

Fig. 22.   Fig. 23.

Fig. 24.

Fig. 22.—Shows how to split the end of a straw.
Fig. 23.—Shows how to paste down the split ends.
Fig. 24.—Shows the straws bent down and woven into the paper.

your brace straw at K and you will have B C (Fig. 24) equal to
each side of the triangle, and B C D E (Fig. 24) will be a perfect
square.   We will need

Another Set of Wings

on the keel to place behind the two (Fig. 24) already in position;
but these wings are stiffened with straws on their after edges and
not on their forward edges, as may be seen by referring to Figs.

25 and 26. A close inspection of this last diagram will also show how the straws are used to connect the two pairs of top wings to those below. Of course a little paste would make this more secure,

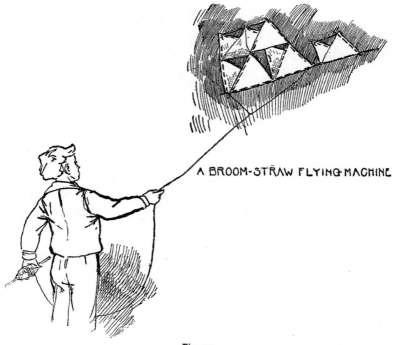

A BROOM-STRAW FLYING-MACHINE

Fig. 25.

especially if the lower ends of the straws, reaching down on the cover sail, were split and spread fan-shape on the paper, then covered with paste and a paper patch, like the patch shown at B in Fig. 23. But the problem which interested me was to build a flying machine of

Nothing but Paper and Broom Straws,

using no tools of any kind but my fingers and a pair of scissors, and **Fig. 26** was the result.

The Belly-Band

was attached as shown in the diagram and, picking up a spool of thread from a basket of sewing material, I carried the fragile toy

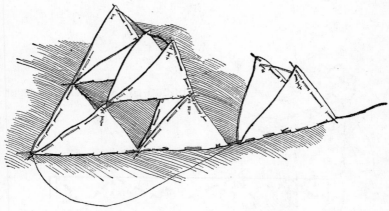

Fig. 26.

up to the roof to test it, and it sailed away on the breeze like a real, full-grown flying machine. The parts held together until it got mixed up with a chimney while I was pulling it in; even then it was not wrecked, and the only damage done was the slipping of some of the brace straws. The kite was flown in a light breeze—a strong wind necessitates a stronger kite. By duplicating the front kite and placing it where the rear wings are, you will have

A Pyramidal Box Kite

Practically speaking, almost any form of kite, aeroplane, or air-ship may be manufactured of broom straws and paper. Fig. 27 shows

A Broom-Straw Hargrave,

or box kite, and also shows the way it may be made of strips of paper and straws. It is possible that your box kite may be so

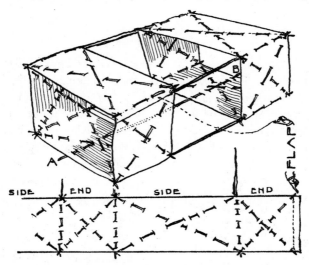

Fig. 27.—How to pin a paper box kite together with straws.

large as to need a stronger spine (A B, Fig. 27) than that afforded by a single straw, in which case use two or even three straws lashed together with thread. The straw sticks may be lengthened, when necessary, by binding the ends of two straws together (Fig. 28); but if the reader wishes to build a really beautiful little air-ship let him take

Different Colored Tissue Paper,

and using some good paste to secure the straws, placing them along near the edges of the paper as in Fig. 29, and after snipping

Fig. 28.—The straws lashed together.

a triangular piece out of the paper at the angles, as shown at A, B, and C (Fig. 29), apply the paste to

The Flap of Paper

outside of the straw, carefully turn it over the straws as is shown on the side A C (Fig. 29), and press it down like B C is in Fig. 29. To make a curved edge, bend the straw to the desired curve, fasten it temporarily with a thread (D E, Fig. 6), place it over the paper as in the diagram and snip out the little wedge-shaped pieces of the outside paper as shown between the H flaps (Fig. 6). Paste one down at a time, as already described, and press the flaps over as shown by F and G (Fig. 6).

Fig. 30 is the

Broom-Straw Frame of a Fish Kite

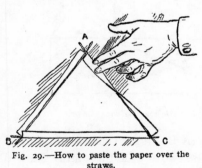

Fig. 29.—How to paste the paper over the straws.

and the paper cut for pasting. You will see that the streamers on the tail at F are not to be pasted over, but allowed to hang loose, and, if you make one of these kites, make the two outside tail streamers at F three or four times as long as the middle ones, and three or four times as long as they are shown in the diagram. The fins E and E (Fig. 31) should be exactly alike so as to balance each other, and may be made of separate pieces of paper and then pasted on the kite proper as they are in Fig. 31. The gill flap H is also made of a

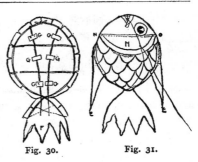

Fig. 30.   Fig. 31.

separate piece of paper pasted only at the edge N O; this is not necessary, but done to give it a realistic appearance. The scales, mouth, and eye are painted on the paper with black paint or ink, and the belly-band attached to the wing straws, through the holes punched in the paper with a pencil-point, and the string is tied to the straws where they cross at their ends.

Experiments have proved that all these small kites fly well when thread is used for kite-string. I have made kites with very fine sticks, of about the thickness of slender matches, and let them up with thread, using three and four large spools of thread in one flight.

The Advantage of Broom Straws

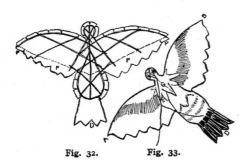

Fig. 32.   Fig. 33.

is that one can stiffen the paper in all directions without materially adding to the weight of the kite, as in Fig. 32, the hawk kite. The lower edges D and D, in Figs. 32 and 33, are unpasted like the tail of the fish, so also is the bottom of the wings at F, except the small flat P at the points P and P (Fig. 32).

To make any form of kite, cut the paper according to the pattern you desire and then brace it with straws, like the example shown, in such a manner that it will keep its shape. When tails are necessary, make them of long strips of colored paper and they will add greatly to the beauty and decorative effect of your toy.

CHAPTER III

HOW TO MAKE A HERBARIUM

A few years ago the writer landed from a small steam launch at a rude log pier on Macdonald Lake in the midst of the Rocky Mountains, and as he "toted" his luggage up to the canvas-ceiled hotel he noticed a young man spreading sheets of paper in the sun to dry and at once made up his mind that in this young man he would find a playfellow, for the sheets of paper were evidently used for botanical specimens, and any one found in such employment is generally a good fellow and interesting companion, and so this young man proved to be.

Mr. Frederick Vreeland, member of the Torry Botanical Club and a long list of scientific societies, expert in wireless telegraphy, author, all around sportsman, good shot, and good woodsman and my boon companion on many a fishing and collecting trip from Montana to Maine, is the young man I first met spreading botanical papers to dry at Macdonald Lake. From him I have received the following information which I now give to the reader, and I know of no better authority than Mr. Vreeland to tell the boys just how to make a herbarium.

The chief thing in collecting material for a herbarium is a good

Collecting Case or Vasculum

(Figs. 34 and 35) to keep the plants fresh until they can be studied and pressed. This is a box of tin, at least 18 inches long, oval or rectangular in cross section, and of a size suitable to the col-

lector's needs.   It should have a cover on one side, opening the
whole length of the box and hinged at the bottom.   Do not be
prevailed upon to buy one of the green German boxes with a

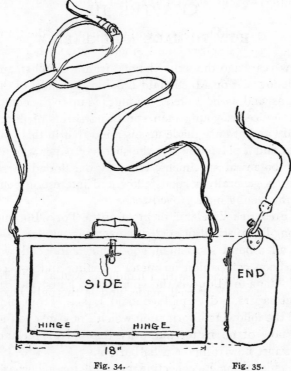

Fig. 34.   Fig. 35.
The proper form of collecting case or vasculum.

little opening about a foot long in the middle.   This will be a
continual annoyance, for it is almost impossible to get the plants
in it without breaking the stems off some of the flowers.   Be sure
to have the cover run the full length of the box, with the hinge

at the lower side, when the box is slung over the shoulder, with a lid which can be opened without spilling the contents. It should be fastened with a secure catch that will not open when you walk through the brush and scatter your treasures along the trail.

A good box is sold by Queen and Company, by the Cambridge Botanical Supply Company and other dealers in botanical sup-

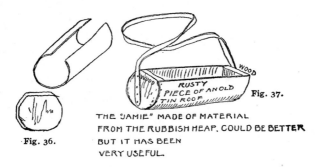

THE "JAMIE" MADE OF MATERIAL FROM THE RUBBISH HEAP. COULD BE BETTER BUT IT HAS BEEN VERY USEFUL.

Fig. 36.   Fig. 37.

Figs. 36 and 37.—A make-shift vasculum.

plies, for a moderate price. It is roughly rectangular in outline (Fig. 34) and is provided with a handle as well as with rings for a shoulder strap. It is well made, and is the only box on the market that I know (and I have at least four others) which possesses all the desirable features mentioned above. Do not get a box too large for your needs. It is astonishing how much squeezing delicate plants will stand without injury. There is

Always Room for One More

in the box and the plants keep fresher when packed tightly than when shaking around loose. It is best not to wet the plants if the box is full, but if you have only a few specimens they may be sprinkled lightly or a piece of clean wet bog or Sphagnum moss may be put in one end of the box to keep them fresh.

Specimens for the Herbarium

should be either in flower or in fruit—properly both. When flowers and fruit cannot be found at the same time it is a good plan to collect two specimens at different seasons, one in flower and the other in fruit. When collected at different times or places they should be mounted on separate sheets.

If possible,

Take the whole Plant,

root and all (Figs. 38 and 39). A large plant may be folded or bent to make it fit the herbarium sheet. In the case of shrubs, trees or large herbs when it is impossible to take the whole plant, be sure to get all the characteristic parts, such as lower leaves, where those differ from the upper ones, pieces of bark, etc.

A Large, Stout, Sheath Knife

with a blade 6 inches long is a great convenience in getting up large roots, and is better than a trowel. Pack the specimens in the box carefully, shaking or washing off dirty roots, which should all be placed at one end of the box so as not to soil or crush delicate flowers

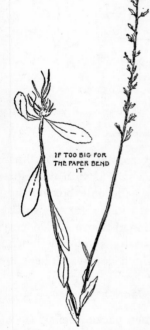

IF TOO BIG FOR THE PAPER BEND IT

Fig. 38.—How to fit a long plant to a short piece of paper.

at the other end. When properly packed, most specimens will keep fresh in the vasculum for several days, but as they are apt to bend and take unnatural shapes it is better to

Press Them as Soon as Possible

after collecting. Some collectors carry a portable hand press in the field in which the specimens are placed as soon as collected, to be transferred later to the regular press. Specimens may be sent successfully by mail if packed with moss in an air-tight tin box of any kind.

How to Press Plants

To properly dry the specimens two things are absolutely essential: first, a good, firm pressure, and second, an

Abundant Supply of Dry Papers

frequently changed so as to dry the plants quickly before they have time to mould or lose their color. Old newspapers answer the purpose very well. Some plants will fade or turn brown in spite

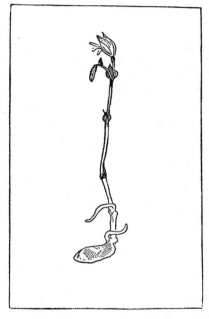

Fig. 39.—A properly mounted specimen.

of all your care, but only a few of the worst of them fail to respond gratefully to good treatment. Many people pick a flower, put it in a book, and leave it to soak in its own moisture for weeks, and then they wonder why it looks more like a dead autumn leaf than the beautiful flower they pressed.

In Pressing Flowers,

as in everything else, care and diligence are necessary to success, but the sight of a well-pressed specimen, looking as if painted on the white herbarium sheet, amply repays the collector for the little trouble it costs.

The Press

One can get along on a pinch by putting the specimens under trunks or by piling stones on them, but a suitable press will save many times its cost in ruined specimens and barked shins. When portability is not an item, nothing is better than a letter copying press, with screw and band wheel, as any desired pressure may be obtained and regulated at will.

A Very Satisfactory Portable Press

may be made in the manner indicated in Fig. 40. I have such a press made just long enough to go in the bottom of a trunk, and it served me well for many summers.

When making a business of collecting and pressing specimens by the hundreds, it is usual to dispense with the press and use straps instead. The specimens with their dryers are piled one on another until a stack two feet high is made with heavy pieces of binder's board on top and bottom and the bundle is then tightly strapped together with trunk straps. This is rather a strenuous task, and the method does not recommend itself except to professional collectors who have several hundred sheets drying at a time.

Avoid the Delicate Little Hand Presses,

having thin wooden slats held together with straps, which are sold at the stores (Fig. 42). They are convenient to carry in the field instead of the vasculum, but are useless for pressing.

How to Make a Portable Press

A very convenient and serviceable press may be made by any one who is a little handy with tools. Take a piece of pine

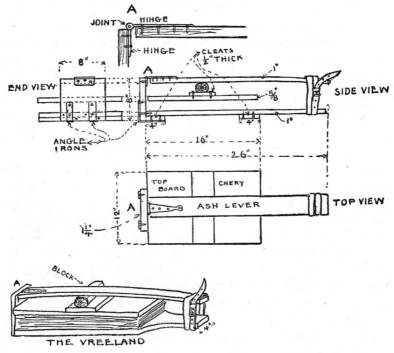

Fig. 40.—Showing all the details for the construction of the Vreeland press.

board 1 inch thick and 1 foot wide by about 2½ feet long. Cut away 4 inches on each side 1 foot from each end, rounding the corners so as to leave a rectangular piece 12 x 18 inches, with a

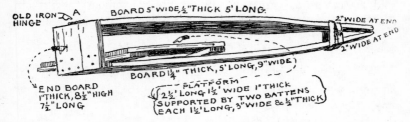

OLD IRON HINGE A
BOARDS 5"WIDE,½"THICK 5'LONG.
2"WIDE AT END
2"WIDE AT END
END BOARD 1"THICK, 8½"HIGH 7½"LONG
BOARD 1¼" THICK, 5'LONG,9"WIDE
PLATFORM 2½' LONG 1½' WIDE 1"THICK SUPPORTED BY TWO BATTENS EACH 1½'LONG, 3"WIDE & ½"THICK

Fig. 41.—A log cabin press used at the author's camp, made of material from the rubbish heap.

tongue or handle 4 inches wide at one end (see the Vreeland Fig. 40). At the opposite end fasten securely with long screws an upright piece of 1¼ or 1½ inches stuff 6 or 8 inches high. This upright should be strongly braced with angle irons on the outside, for this corner is the weak point of the press.

Make a lever of ash or other hard wood 4 inches wide by at least ⅝ inch thick, and attach it to the top of the upright by a strong iron hinge (A, Fig. 40) having a tongue several inches long screwed to the *top* of the lever. Be sure to screw the other half of the hinge to the front of the upright, not to the top, otherwise the screws will soon pull out. If the press is to be carried in a trunk, this

Fig. 42.—The trade press.

hinge may be made with a loose pin so that it can be taken apart for packing. Make a rectangular top board of hard wood, or of pine well stiffened with cleats and keep it flat, and cut it the size of the rectangular part of the bottom board. A rectangular block made like a brick with all its dimensions different, to fill the space between the top board and the lever completes the press.

How to Use the Press

Place the plants enclosed in their wrappers and dryers on the bottom board, put the top board over them, bring the lever down and bind the whole together with a stout strap put around the end of the lever and the handle of the bottom board (Figs. 40 and 41), as this strap is drawn tight the lever bends, and so keeps a constant pressure on the plants even when they shrink in drying.

The Dryers and Wrappers

Having the press, the next thing needed is a supply of pressing papers. These are of two kinds: the "dryers" and the "wrappers." The dryers are sheets or pads of absorbent paper to take up the moisture from the plants and at the same time to yield to the varying thickness of the specimens so as to keep an even pressure all over them. These papers should be about 12 x 17 inches in size, a little longer than the herbarium sheet. The dryers may be bought ready cut to size from a sort of thick absorbent paper, like rough brown blotting paper, which is the material used by the botanists on account of its convenience, portability and durability; but there is nothing better than

Pads of Ordinary Newspaper,

of about eight thicknesses. The average daily when folded once in the middle makes a sheet about the right size. This is elastic and highly absorbent, and is easily dried.

The wrappers are folded sheets of white unglazed paper,

cut to double the size of the dryers and folded in the middle like a sheet of note paper. Their function is to hold the plants and protect them in handling and when carrying them about. These also may be bought from the supply dealer, and cut to order at the local newspaper office. The cheapest kind of unprinted newspaper is the best—indeed printed newspapers may be used on a pinch, but they are not to be recommended, as there is danger of confusing them with the dryers and so throwing away some valuable specimen.

Do not Use a Glazed or Sized Paper;

it is not sufficiently porous. Instead of the folded wrappers, single sheets of half the size may be used in pairs, and the plants placed between them, but the folded wrapper is more convenient, and the plants are less liable to injury by the slipping of the papers.

Preparing the Specimens

Having a box full of specimens, sit down at a large table with a pile of dryers and another pile of wrappers close at hand. Lay down a dryer and upon it put a wrapper, opened out to its full width. Lay your first specimen on the half of the wrapper nearest you, and then carefully fold down the other half to cover it. Press it down gently with the hand and then place a dryer on top. Take another wrapper for the next specimen, and proceed as before, piling up dryers and wrappers alternately, until all are done. Then put them in the press. It is best not to attempt too much in arranging the specimens in the wrappers. Their natural attitude or "habit" is often characteristic, and usually more graceful than any artificial arrangement. Occasionally an unruly leaf or branch may be twisted into shape, but after a little practice the plants may be put in place in such a way that they fall naturally into the best position.

Where a Plant is too Large

to fit the herbarium sheet it may be folded or bent to the proper size (Fig. 38). If very large it may be divided into two parts and dried in separate sheets. Thick roots may be split, if necessary, (Fig. 39) to facilitate drying, but it is surprising how even the thickest parts yield to the uniform pressure of the elastic dryers.

The best pressure varies somewhat according to the nature of the specimens. Where there are thick pods or fleshy parts which are likely to burst they may be put first under light pressure, which is gradually increased as the plant dries; but usually the full pressure may be put on at once, and this can hardly be too great except when a screw press is used. Too little pressure results in wrinkled leaves and shriveled flowers.

Never put a Plant Directly Between the Dryers

A partly dried specimen is very soft and easily injured, and once placed in the folded wrapper it should be left there until dry. This may take from two or three days to as many weeks, according to the nature of the plant and the frequency of changing the dryers.

The Dryers should be Changed

at least every day, and when pressing plants that are likely to fade, twice or three times a day is not too often. After changing the moist dryers should be thoroughly dried by spreading them out in the sun or by placing them in an oven. They should be put back between the wrappers while hot—the dryer and hotter the better. When the specimens are thoroughly dry they should be taken out of the press, still in their wrappers, and tied up in bundles until you are ready to use them.

How to Take Field Notes

Be sure to keep notes of all your specimens. The best way to do this is to write a number in one corner of each wrapper as you put it in the press, and then enter a corresponding number in your note book. Opposite this number put the date, the place of collecting and nature of the soil, and any data of interest, and also the name of the specimen when you have determined it. This practice will prevent much confusion when you come to mount and label the specimens, and it takes very little time when done systematically. Some collectors prefer to write the field notes directly on the wrapper of each specimen, but the note book system is more satisfactory and makes less work in the long run.

How to Poison Specimens

Before the specimens are mounted they should be poisoned, to protect them against the ravages of insects and mildew. In the large herbaria formalin is the preservative quite generally used, but for the amateur corrosive sublimate (bichloride of mercury) is preferable, as it is more convenient, quite as effective, and lacks the disagreeable irritating fumes of the formalin. The corrosive sublimate is dissolved in alcohol, in the proportion of an ounce of the crystals to a quart of alcohol, and kept in a wide-necked bottle having a flat camel's hair brush half an inch wide stuck through a hole in the cork. Be sure to

Mark the Bottle "Poison"

and keep it out of the way of small children and servants, as corrosive sublimate is deadly. Do not use the poison brush for anything else and burn it up when the work is done.

Provide a Piece of Window Glass

the size of the herbarium sheets, to support the plants while they are being poisoned. Lay this flat on a table, and, taking the first specimen from its wrapper, place it, face down, on the glass. Then go over the whole surface of the plant with a soft brush moistened with the poison. Be careful not to get the delicate parts too wet, as they will be likely to curl up, but the thick or fleshy parts should be well saturated, going over both sides if necessary. The specimen may then be replaced in its wrapper while you are poisoning the others. A delicate plant should be allowed to dry a few moments before lifting it from the glass.

How to Mount Specimens

After being poisoned the specimens are ready for mounting. Be sure to begin right by mounting your specimens on separate herbarium sheets of standard size ($11\frac{1}{2}$ x $16\frac{1}{2}$ inches). Do not mount them in a book as that makes it impossible to arrange or classify them, and leaves no room to add to your collection. Each species (and when you have specimens of the same species collected at different times or places, each collection) should be mounted on a separate herbarium sheet, but when the plants are small it is well to put several specimens of the same kind on the same sheet.

Standard Herbarium Sheets,

$11\frac{1}{2}$ x $16\frac{1}{2}$ inches in size, may be bought from the dealers, or you can have them cut to order. They should be of good quality of stiff linen paper with smooth surface (ledger paper is the best) and not too thin. For the large specimens you may, to save money and space, use a sheet not much heavier than thick writing paper; this, however, is hardly stiff enough to protect the fragile specimens, and it is better to use a heavier grade; the thickness of a thin visiting card is none too heavy if you take a pride in your collection and want it to look its best. It pays to buy the best quality of linen paper, as it has a snap and crispness that enables it to bear a great deal of handling without bending or cracking, and it will last longer and preserve your specimens better than a cheap paper of twice the thickness.

For mounting the specimens on the sheets nothing is better than the ordinary liquid glue,

Fish Glue,

but it is usually too thick as it is bought, and should be diluted with from about half to three-quarters of its bulk of water. Lay the poisoned specimen face down on a sheet of paper and brush over its whole surface with the thinned glue, using a camel's hair or other soft brush. The delicate parts should be touched very lightly, lest they tear, but the thicker parts should be well covered. Lift the specimen carefully and turn it over, face up, on the herbarium sheet which you have ready at hand. Be careful to

Place the Specimen Just Where You Want it

to stay, as in Fig. 39, for if you move it you will have the sheet disfigured with unsightly streaks of glue. Press the plant firmly into contact with the sheet with a clean handkerchief, lifting carefully and touching with glue any parts that fail to adhere, then mark the number of the specimen in the corner, cover it with a clean sheet of paper (the wrapper it came from will do), and lay it aside under light pressure until the glue is dry. Any thick or woody parts which do not stick properly may be held down by thin strips of gummed paper (which may be bought by the sheet at the stationers) laid over them and stuck down at the ends. The specimen is then ready to be labelled and filed away in its proper place in the collection.

Labelling and Filing

The form of the label is largely a matter of taste, and tastes differ widely. A good form for a private collection is shown in Fig. 43. The labels should be neatly printed on smooth white paper of a kind that takes ink well, and cut 2 x 3½ inches in size. The botanical name of the specimen is plainly written on the ruled line in the centre of the label,

> Herbarium of
> Jhon J Jhonison
> Cypripedium hirsutum, Mill
> Hab Woods shore of Big Tink
> Pike Co Pa
> June 15th 1906
> no 41144

Fig. 43.—A practical form for a label.

and below it is recorded the locality and character of ground in which the plant grew, the name or initials of the collector, the date of collection and the serial number of the specimen (the same number that appears in the field notes); any other facts of special interest may be noted on the label. This label is pasted in the lower right-hand corner of the herbarium sheet, which is then ready for filing away.

All the sheets belonging to the same genus are gathered together and placed in a

Genus Cover,

a folded sheet of stiff Manila paper, cut 17 x 23 inches and doubled in the middle so as to have a quarter of an inch margin around the mounts that it contains. The name of the genus is written on the outside of the cover in the lower left-hand corner. The various genera belonging to one family may be placed in a portfolio of stiff cardboard and filed away on shelves or in the drawers of a cabinet, or, as the collection grows large enough, a separate pigeon-hole for a family or a group of allied families. In these days of popular short cuts to teach us the names of things without giving real knowledge about them, to classify plants by the color of their flowers as one would divide the families of men according to the color of their clothes, we are too apt to lose sight of the real nature of things. When we find, in the spring, a dainty, yellow adder's tongue, or "dog-tooth violet," we perhaps do not recognize it as a near relative to the splendid Turk's-Cap lily we found last summer, but when we look up the dried specimen in the herbarium the relationship is at once apparent. There is no greater delight to the thoughtful student than to find some "missing link" in his pedigree of plants, and to see how perfectly it fits into the vacant space in his herbarium, and there is pleasant occupation for many a winter evening, sorting and arranging the specimens collected during the summer, and recalling the happy vacation days with which they are associated.

CHAPTER IV

HOW TO PLANT QUAIL

Like Corn in a Field

Quail farming makes a delightful occupation for boys and one that is appreciated by their elders, for all know that many good shots would rather shoot quail over well-trained dogs than engage in any other sort of hunting, and the universal appreciation of the delicate and savory flavor of the bob-white's flesh, has given these birds a popularity which threatens them with extermination. A price is placed upon their heads which encourages an army of trappers, poachers and market hunters to defy the game laws and the laws of common sense in their greedy rush to supply the city market-men and the cold-storage houses with the coveted food. The ranks of the bob-white have been so rapidly thinned that a person is now seized with wonder upon seeing a bob-white or hearing its cheery call in the fields, which, but a few years ago, were thickly populated with these beautiful and useful American game birds.

It is high time that country clubs, owners of large estates and farmers reserved some small portion of their lands for a

Sanctuary,

in which the bob-whites may breed and flourish undisturbed, and it is the boys who should persuade them to do it.

Do not misunderstand this suggestion—it is not intended to

put a stop to quail shooting; on the contrary, the overflow from
the preserves will tend to constantly restock the adjacent lands
with birds for the gunners to slay. The few game preserves already established have proved this. There are English pheasants
in the woods where I am now writing which come from preserves
twelve miles away, and the overflow from one wild turkey preserve supplies about all of these grand game birds which are
known to the writer in the State of Pennsylvania.

The plan proposed is that individual land owners establish
private breeding fields where the bob-whites may be protected
from trespassers and poachers the whole year round.

The great body of the American people, though properly
jealous of their rights, are not unreasonable, and when they
understand the unselfish purpose of these preserves they will not
only respect the rights of the birds, but be quick to punish the
selfish and lawless persons who may seek to violate the sacredness
of the bird's sanctuary.

Strange as it may appear, the sportsman—men whom thought-
less sentimentalists accuse of a bloodthirsty desire to kill all living
creatures—are the very ones who are doing the most systematic
and effectual work for the protection of our brothers in fur and
feathers.

It is hoped that these same big-hearted men will be persuaded
to plant birds upon their own estates and induce others to follow
their example. To those not devoid of sentiment there is an
esthetic value in the very presence of the bob-whites which is
worth more than the little cost of seed birds and their protection.
Because there are thousands of people of esthetic taste, there
is a real money value attached to the sound of the cheery "Bob-
white, bob-bob-white" from the fence post, and the sight of the
plump little birds dusting themselves in the road or promenading

over the close-cut lawns—a money value which even the financial mind of the real estate man is quick to perceive.

If the reader meets with people who are devoid of sentiment and are hard, practical utilitarians, it may interest them to know that bob-white is a useful adjunct to a farm, and that the Agricultural Department at Washington, in its year-book of 1903, says that not only does the bob-white do no injury to fruit or any other crop, but that they destroy great quantities of the seeds of troublesome weeds and also the worst insect pests with which the farmer has to contend.

After examining a wholesale lot of crops and droppings, and after careful experiments with captive birds, Sylvester D. Judd, Ph. D., says the bob-white is probably the most useful wild bird on the farm.

But, after all, this world divorced from sentiment would be a dreary place in which to sojourn, and the association connected with *Colinus virginianur* are very dear to the hearts of many who may never have heard its scientific Latin name. There are few of us, I imagine, who do not feel a thrill at the bursting of the

"Animated Bomb Shell,"

which the bob-whites make as the covey bursts with a startling whirr when disturbed, or who do not appreciate the wholesome charm of the clear honest love-call of the cock to his dapper little mate, or feel the mystic influence of the plaintive assembly call of the covey when it is heard in the gloaming.

Fig. 44 is a map of an imaginary

Breeding Field for Bob-Whites,

but it is not expected that any one will make an exact duplicate of this field; the drawing is only made that the reader may better understand what is meant when it is said that an appropriate field should be selected or prepared for the exclusive use of the birds. It is essential that the birds should have a good cover handy for retreat on the advent of predaceous hawks; for this purpose thickets of thorny vines, blackberry bushes, haws, alders, rose bushes, cat briars and laurels—in fact, a tangled mass of thorny underbrush of any kind will answer the purpose and be

THE ANIMATED BOMBSHELL

appreciated by the birds. Let the thickets be next to the fences and they will also form a more effectual barrier for two-legged marauders than posted signs. I know of one covey of birds in Greater New York surrounded by thickly populated districts where the birds have managed to defy all enemies for the last twenty years, and this they have done by living in a swamp overgrown with the thicket of poison sumac, briars, grape vines, alders, rank weeds, skunk cabbage and cat tails, which with the treacherous bog under foot, has until now formed a safe refuge for the hardy little flock of bob-whites.

Give your birds

Fig. 44.—A breeding field for Bob-Whites.

A Well-Drained Field

interspersed with bushes to protect their nests and plant late a small patch of buckwheat especially for their delectation; see that there is also

A Supply of Good Water

After the field is prepared something on the order of the accompanying map, furnish some artificial

Nest Boxes

of slabs or sections of hollow logs after the manner of Figs. 45, 46, and 47.

Fig. 48 shows a natural nest shelter chosen by a pair of bobwhites, whose nest I discovered in a pasture lot in Ohio. The

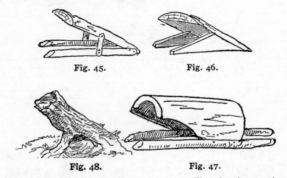

Fig. 45.　　　　　Fig. 46.

Fig. 48.　　　　Fig. 47.

Figs. 45, 46 and 47.—Three designs for nest covers.　Fig. 48.—A natural nest cover.

stump shown in the diagram was concealed by a rank growth of grass or reeds which also arched over and concealed the thirteen pretty white eggs.

Use weather beaten slabs with the bark on them and lichen-covered wood for the nest boxes, and if you cannot obtain that, from old fence boards or some similar source; paint the wood a dull, unobtrusive gray color. Fig. 47 is made part of a sec-

tion of a hollow log, to which two sticks have been fastened to give it a firm surface to rest upon. Place these nests in clumps of bushes, under leaning stumps or similarly appropriate places, and see that they are situated on a gentle incline, as in Fig. 49, where the slope

A CROSS SECTION OF GENTLE INCLINE SHOWING NEST NATURALLY PLACED, BRUSH OMITTED TO SIMPLIFY DIAGRAM.

Fig. 49.—Quail on nest.

of the ground will drain the water from the neighborhood of the nests. Fill the boxes with hay, straw or dry leaves as shown in the diagram.

If the bushes for hiding the nests are not growing on the ground selected, it is a simple matter to plant them there, and make them grow just where you wish—especially is this true if you plant the bush in the spring while the ground is still soft from the melting frosts.

A YOUNG BLACK OR SWEET BIRCH (*Betula Lenta*) PULLED UP BY HAND, SOIL ADHERING TO ROOTS

Fig. 50.—A sketch from a bush as it appeared torn from the soil.

Two years ago, in the dry month of August, I forcibly tore up by the roots a young black or sweet birch, 6½ feet high, of which Fig. 50 is a sketch made at the time, and kicking a hole in the dry earth of a path with the heel of my boot, I planted the birch in the hole and secured it in place with a large stone laid over its dirt-covered roots. This rudely transplanted tree, as yet, shows no

signs of wilting leaves or drooping branches; so it should be a simple matter to transplant brush in the wet soil of early spring wherever you wished to locate a nest-box. When the nests are all arranged and concealed by rose bushes, briars or any sort of thick-growing plants it is time

Fig. 51.—The birds were left to preen themselves.

To Plant the Quail

This simple secret I learned when a very small child, from a Kentucky colonel with an Irish name and the soul of an old-fashioned country gentleman.

The colonel always had an abundant supply of quail upon his plantation, and he said that he planted them the same as corn, and so he did.

Fig. 52.—Planting quail.

On a bright spring morning about the mating season for quail he would start out with his two "boys"—boy being the name for any negro too young to be dignified by the title of uncle —one boy carrying a covered basket full of captive birds and the other a pail of water (Fig. 52). When the planter reached a likely spot, where food had already been placed under his direction, a cock bob-white was produced from the basket and soused into the pail of water until it was too wet to fly. When liberated, as a matter of course, the bird ran for the nearest cover (Fig. 51), which was the very place prepared for its reception. The hen was treated in the same manner with the same result, and thus the birds were left to preen themselves, dry out, discover the food at their feet, make each other's acquaintance and ultimately go to housekeeping right there on the spot where everything seemed so handy for them. What could be more natural? What more simple? This old sportsman knew the habits of his favorite game bird and wisely took advantage of them, and in place of trying to force the birds to conform to theoretical rules of conduct he invented a way by which he could make use of the birds' peculiar habits for his own advantage and entertainment.

It is probably not necessary to souse the birds in the pail of water until they are half drowned, as the colonel's "boys" delighted in doing, for it is only requisite to so thoroughly wet their wings that they are unable to fly.

Choose a bright, sunshiny day when the birds can dry out with no danger of being chilled to death, and you may, like the colonel, plant quail as you would plant corn, and have reason to expect, proportionately, as bountiful a crop for the seed birds planted as you might get from the same amount of seed corn.

Seed Birds

are easily obtained from dealers in wild animals whose advertisements are found in many of our periodicals, but it will be better to write to the secretary of some of our numerous gunning clubs and game preserves who know from personal dealings the most responsible men in the business. In looking over a number of records of quail planting I find that American bob-whites have been successfully planted practically all over the United States, as far north as Buffalo and south of Maine to Texas, and that they have even been sent to New Zealand, where, according to recent reports, they are thriving and multiplying.

Mr. W. J. Coon, Superintendent of Blooming Grove Park Association, Pike County, Pennsylvania, says that "quail are not indigenous to this section," but across the river a few miles from the club there have been native quails as far back as tradition goes.

CHAPTER V

HOUSES FOR USEFUL BIRDS

How to Make Swallow Boards, Robin Shelves, and Phœbe Brackets

In the centre of almost every colonial back yard there used to stand a tree which had been pollard in midsummer, while the branches were full of sap, the result being that decay produced holes where the branches had been, thus making natural homes for yellow hammers, downy, and red-headed woodpeckers, blue-birds, black-capped chickadees, and birds of similar nesting habits. From long poles, dipper gourds were hung for the purple martins, and all the old hats of the household were saved and nailed by their brims under the eaves of the sheds; holes cut in their crowns answered for doorways for the wrens. Our bird-loving ancestors, even collected the skulls of horses, oxen and sheep and erected them in the corners of the fences for bird houses.

In place of the myriads of beautiful native birds we Americans now have

Flocks of Noisy "English" Sparrows,

an ever-increasing number of squeaking starlings and a forlorn remnant of our own native songsters.

But even with that remnant there exists the opportunity to restock our groves and hedges with the birds of our grandsires.

The birds ask only to be allowed to live unmolested. For centuries they have taken care of themselves and we have many curious instances of their capacity to adapt themselves to new environments.

Before the white man came to this country there were no horses, and consequently the chippy sparrow's nest was not then lined with horse hair. The Indians did not erect martin boxes, and hence the martins must have originally built in caves or holes in trees. The red men had no chimneys, and the chimney swifts probably used

Hollow Trees for Nesting Places

until the white man's flues offered them sites more to their liking. The hornets most likely supplied the material which has since been supplanted by bits of newspaper in the greenlets' nests.

Metal is sometimes now used by birds for building material. I recently saw a photograph of a magpie's nest which was constructed of a piece of wire netting and bits of wire. In France some pigeons built their nests entirely from hairpins gathered on the paths of the Luxembourg.

The museum at Soleure, Switzerland, contains a wagtail's nest built of steel watch springs.

I have proved by experiment that

The Baltimore Oriole

will accept the material provided for it, and you may have red, blue, green or yellow nests in your trees by placing colored worsted yarn on the bushes or lawn where the birds can find it. Do not use silk; it entangles and cuts their feet.

Not only will the birds use new and novel material for constructing their nests, but they will select the most unexpected places to build. A human skull, an old dried elk's head, the head of a wooden statue, an ever-moving weather vane, a clock on the mantle, a tin cup on the shelf of a pantry, the machinery of a dredge, the arm of a windmill, the mouth of a cannon, the framework of a drawbridge, and the pocket of an old coat are a few of the recorded sites chosen by these little creatures as desirable places to build their nests.

For many succeeding summers the

Phœbe Birds

have built their nests (Fig. 53) on a projection over the kitchen door in the writer's summer camp.

The Robins

took possession of the window sill and of a shelf which was nailed to a post under the shed. It had been intended as a place to

Fig. 53.—A Phœbe and nest, from nature.

put a cake of soap. Not only did the birds use this place as a nesting place, but they used the tin hand basin for a bath tub, and the ravelings from the towel to work into their nests.

These Phœbe birds and robins suggested the making of the

Bird Shelves

shown by Figs. 54, 55 and 56.   The construction of them is so simple that no other description than the diagrams afford is necessary.   Hang the robin shelves high on the trunks of trees and place the Phœbe shelves in shady, damp places near streams or ponds.

Birds are grateful and trustful creatures; even in the out-skirts of large cities they are willing to live near man and his dwelling, if they are assured of friendship

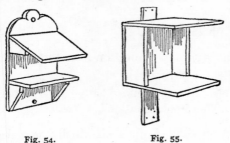 

Fig. 54.   Fig. 55.

Figs. 54 and 55.—Phœbe shelves.   Fig. 56.—A boxed bird shelf.

and protection; build a home for them and you will be sur-prised to find birds whose presence, perhaps, you did not suspect.

While I am writing this in the great city of New York there are six long-eared owls roosting in a spruce tree almost within a bow shot of my desk.   I have known these birds for several years, and because they are not only interesting and a novelty in the family of city birds, but also because they are most useful crea-tures and live exclusively on mice and English sparrows, I keep their roost a secret, as the only safe way to protect my six friends from human vandals.

To Entice Barn Swallows

to build on the swallow boards, here described, set in the ground a shallow box about 3 x 4 feet and fill it with good, clean, yellow or blue clay. If this is not procurable, common mud will answer. Keep the clay moist and leave a little water standing in its depressions. If you can get some last year's swallows' nests, stick a few of them on the cleats of the swallow board, using damp clay for glue.

As with men, birds follow the line of least resistance in their labors, and with clay handy and a sheltered board which seems to have already been used for the purpose, it will be strange if you have no flourishing colony of barn swallows the first season.

A rough surface offers better opportunities for the barn swallows' clay nests than a smooth one. At the Glacier Hotel, near Illecillewaet glacier, Selkirk Mountains, I noticed a barn swallow on its nest just above the dining-room door. I also noticed bits of clay at different points on the smooth boards above the doorway, marking so many failures on the bird's part to make its nest adhere to the wall; but Frank M. Chapman, the New York ornithologist, had happened that way and had kindly nailed a cleat over the door. The swallows had taken advantage of this immediately for a foundation and finished their nest without further trouble. When I saw them the female was sitting on her eggs.

For a

Swallow Board

select a rough plank $\frac{1}{2}$ inch thick by 10 inches wide, and cut it into two pieces, each $1\frac{1}{2}$ x 10 x 60 inches (Fig. 57); place the pieces edge to edge and nail to their ends two braces, then cut four cleats, each ½ inch thick by 2 inches wide, and a trifle over 5 feet long. Rule a line parallel with the top edge and 8 inches below it fit the upper edge of the cleat along the line and nail

Fig. 57.

Fig. 58.

Fig. 57.—Detail of swallow board.
Fig. 58.—A sketch from nature of barn swallow and nest.

it securely in place. In the same manner nail the lower cleat 3 inches from the bottom of the board and saw off the protruding ends flush with the ends of the boards.

Next take the two remaining cleats and saw them off to fit snugly on the opposite side of the swallow board and nail them in place at 8 inches from the top and 3 inches from the bottom respectively. Since the middle of these last cleats must be cut away to allow room for the post, drive no nails in their centre. It is understood that the dimensions and figures here given are not necessarily to be followed exactly, but it simplifies the explanation to give directions and figures. What is absolutely necessary is to put the upper cleat far enough below the roof to allow room for the swallows and their nest and to leave sufficient space between the cleats for the same purpose.

The swallow board proper is now finished, but if erected in this form in the open air there would be no protection for the nests against rain and the birds would refuse to use the board, for centuries of experience has taught these little builders that their adobe homes are soluble and water will destroy them, hence it is that the barn swallows seek the shelter offered by a hayloft or the overhanging eaves, and hence it is we must make

A Roof for the Swallow Board

This is not a difficult undertaking even for the amateur. The swallow board itself forms the ridge board, and it is only necessary to cut out two end plates, two side plates, and four rafters. All of these pieces may be cut from dressed lumber and made as neatly as consistent with the skill of the workman.

Let the first plates be each 5 feet long and 3 inches wide and the second plates about $5\frac{1}{2}$ feet long and 3 inches wide. Find the centre of the first by measuring $2\frac{1}{2}$ feet from the ends and marking the point; measure from each end, and if your 5 feet board happens to be a trifle too long or too short, you will have two points and the centre will be midway between them.

With a single nail fasten the first plate to the swallow board
3 inches from the bottom; now with a carpenter's square see that
it is exactly at right angles with the edge of the swallow board,
and then fasten it there securely with more nails.   Do the same
with the opposite end plate.

From each end of the plates measure, on the top surface,
toward the swallow board, 7 inches and mark the point with a
soft pencil.   Now measure the distance from one of these points
diagonally to the top of the ridge and make your rafters 2 inches
longer than this measurement.   Cutting your material a trifle
longer than called for by measurements is a safe course to pursue; the extra length can be sawed off at the last moment to
make a fit, but if it happens to be too short it must be cast aside
and a new piece used.

Make the rafters about 1½ inches broad, hold one of them
temporarily in place with one end at the pencil mark on the plate
and the other end protruding beyond the ridge, but with its upper
edge even with top of ridge; while the rafter is in this position
trace the outline of the proposed notch with a pencil at mark near
the end of the plate.   Do the same with the four ends at the
pencil marks and saw out these notches to fit the ends of the
rafters, after which it is a simple matter by trial to find the angle
at which to cut the upper end so as to fit.   Now nail the rafters
in place and saw off the square ends of the plates in a line with
the rafters as shown in the diagram.   Bind the ends of the frame
by nailing on the side plates and the roof framework is finished.

Fig. 57 shows a perspective view of the frame erected and
attached to the pole; boards used as shingles, and the cracks between covered by narrow strips.   Before making the board fast to
the pole, cut out of the middle of the cleats pieces large enough
to allow room for the post to fit snugly between.

Fig. 59.—A two-post swallow board on grounds
of a country home.

The Two-Post Swallow Board

differs from the one-post board only
in being longer and having two supports in place of one (Fig. 59).

Bird Elocutionist

When all the birds have learned
to look upon your grounds as a safe
retreat you will be astonished to dis-
cover how tame they will become, and interested in learning
their different calls and songs.

The bluejay is a great elocutionist, as well as a great nest rob-
ber, and gives utterance to many unlooked for remarks, but the
one most often heard in the woods relates to the possession of a
chee-tidley-enk.   Just exactly what sort of a creature or thing
this is no one can tell, but whenever I am in the wood I hear the
jays exclaim "chee-tidley-enk—got him."   To which the meadow
lark in the pasture clearly replies, "Oh-so-cheap," with a most
sarcastic drawl on the "so" and an inflection on the "cheap."   As
a rule the meadow lark says his say while perched on a fence post

Fig. 60.—The robin's nest on the soap shelf at the author's camp; sketched from nature.

and he speaks with his mouth wide open. There are a lot of little people in the thickets who are always in such a hurry and speak so fast that it is difficult to tell what they say. There is that gayly colored little fellow, the red start, crying, "T-wet wee-whee-whe-whisett," and the dainty summer yellow bird who has something to say in the same line and much in the same manner. What he wants is wheat, and although he never eats it his constant cry is, "Wheat, wheat, wheat, T'weat, wheat, wheat, wheat!"

But the really most accomplished elocutionist is the Brown-thrasher. His song is:

> " Quick! quick! quick!
> Look-a-here, look-a-here,
>   There, there,
> Yellow link, yellow link;
> Pretty bird, pretty bird.
>   Wheat oh! wheat oh!
>   Tweet, tweet,
>   Tur-r-r- tur-r-r,
>   Wee-ah! wee-ah!"

Next to the thrasher is the cat bird. Whenever you think you hear a robin singing as if it had a sore throat and you wonder why his voice appears strange, hunt him up and you will discover the songster to be no robin at all, but our most beautiful and brilliant bird, the scarlet tanager. I have a note book filled with the songs of birds, but it will spoil the fun of the reader to give them here. Let him takes his own notes, for in personal investigation is the greatest charm that nature offers us.

CHAPTER VI

HOW TO MAKE FLYING CAGES

When my wife and I were driving through Yellowstone Park, we were delighted beyond measure to find that the wild creatures did not take flight at the sight of the surrey and its occupants.

One of the acquaintances made on this trip was a Mr. Dooley. There is a mistake about the Mister, for it should be Miss Dooley; however, that is another story. Mr. Dooley was at that time a comical, vicious, little grizzly cub bear, which had strenuous objections to being sketched.

On the writer's desk at this moment is a photograph, taken by a young friend, of an unchained, unconfined, big, fat, two-year-old grizzly bear. This dangerous and fearful wild beast was photographed in the act of standing on its hind legs, eating prunes, which its friend and admirer, Mrs. Walker, of the Canyon Hotel, is feeding him, and this is Mr. Dooley! Wherever man has let the wild creatures alone, they have become as tame, almost, as domestic beasts.

Thus you see that the only wild animals in this world are the persecuted ones the two-legged animal, calling himself a man, shoots, traps and murders until the poor creatures learn to dread the sight of a human being more than any other living thing on earth. Why, boys, only think of it, we can have the shade trees in all our villages, towns and cities filled with all varieties of birds and squirrels if we will only allow them the privilege of living there! But when everybody in this world, of course, excepting the reader and writer, is a bloody savage, bent on killing everything he dares to kill, we must build houses for our wild animals, if we wish to enjoy the society of our little brothers in fur and feathers.

These houses are not prisons, but forts made to protect the occupants from their two-legged enemies, who are ever ready with clubs, stones, and guns to carry on their senseless war of extermination against any wild creature caught at large.

To those boys who live in the country the material for the framework of

The Squirrel's Flying Cage

can be cut in the woods or found in the lumber pile, and need cost nothing. To those living in the neighborhood of saw-mills and planing-mills the long strips of waste wood sawed from the edges of boards can be had for a few cents or for nothing; but to the unfortunate lads who live in thickly populated places, everything costs money, and they will probably be compelled to buy a few pine boards and saw them up in strips themselves (Fig. 61).

The Wire Cloth

used to cover the cage comes in rolls of varying widths and mesh. This woven wire is called wire cloth when the mesh is square, and wire netting when the mesh is six-sided, or hexagonal. For our purpose, wire cloth with a No. $2\frac{1}{2}$ mesh and a No. 17 galvanized wire will be the best, but any wire with a mesh small enough to prevent the escape of the proposed occupants will answer the purpose.

Make Your Plans Fit Your Purse

Find out what the different woven wire costs, get its dimensions and then calculate how much you can afford to buy. The larger the house, the more freedom there is for its occupants and the more fun for the boys who run the zoo.

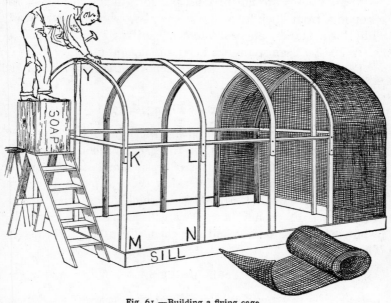

Fig. 61.—Building a flying cage.

To Make the Framework,

cut a number of studs, and make them tall enough to reach to the builder's chest, "breast high." These are to be nailed to the sill board (M, N, Fig. 61) at just sufficient distance apart to allow the edges of the wire cloth to be tacked to the studs, as it is at the far end of Fig. 61. If the wire cloth is of double width, it may be necessary to have a stud in the middle of each breadth for stability's sake. After sawing off the tops of the studs K-M, L-N and the others, so that they are all exactly the same length, nail the side plate K-L on the tops of the studs, being careful to have the angles all square; that is, right angles. In the same manner nail the second set of studs to the second sill, and fasten another side plate on to the tops of these studs, making the two side frames of same dimensions.

The End Sills

are duplicates of each other, and just half the length of the side sills. Set up the side frames the proper distance apart, and fasten them in position by a couple of temporary braces, which run from the right-hand end of one side to the left-hand end of the other side, and cross each other like a letter X. If necessary, fasten both top and bottom in this manner, then nail the end sills in place.

The Ridge Pole

is supported by two tall studs at each end of the frame (Fig. 61). These studs can now be nailed to the middle of the end sills, as shown in the illustration, and the end plate at K and its duplicates made fast in that manner. Nail one end on top of the side plate K-L at K, Fig. 61, and "toe nail" the other end to the long stud Y. To toe nail is to drive a nail slantingly through the side near the end of the plate, so that the point will come out at the end of the plate and there enter the stud. Fasten the other end plates in the same manner, and then nail your ridge pole on top of the long studs, so as to form the ridge of your proposed roof (see Fig. 61). You may now put

The Rafters

in place, first sawing off their ends at such an angle that they will fit on top of the side plates with their other ends against the ridge pole where they can be nailed in place; but if you have strips of wood elastic enough to bend into half hoops to extend from side stud over ridge pole to the opposite side stud (as in Fig. 62), you can give a prettier form to your house and have more room

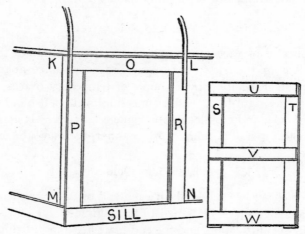

Fig. 62.—Door-jam and door-frame.

inside. The ends of the hoops can be either nailed or bound with wire to the studs and ridge pole.

The Doorway

may be placed wherever it is most convenient, which in this case we will suppose to be between K-M and L-N (Fig. 62). P, O and R are boards to be used as door jambs; they must be made to fit snugly in the positions shown in the illustration. After nailing P and R to the studs, fit O in its place, and nail it securely by driving the nails through the side plate K-L into the top of O. Toe nail P and R, both to the sill board and to O. To give strength as well as to prevent the door from swinging inside, cut a couple of studs to fit on the inside of the door jamb and extend from the side plate K-L to the ground; nail one of these to the inside of R, flush with the edge, next to doorway; nail the other to inside of P, but allow about a half inch of this stud to extend beyond the edge of P next to the doorway for the door to rest against when closed. S U T V W shows the framework of the door, which is to be covered with wire cloth and then hinged to the studs. U V and W will rest against the inside stud and prevent closing the door tightly, unless they are sawed off where the stud interferes. Use staple tacks to fasten wire cloth to frame of door and cage.

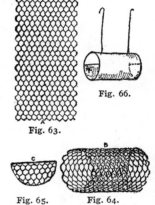

Fig. 66.

Fig. 63.

Fig. 65.   Fig. 64.

Fig. 63.—Piece of wire netting.
Fig. 64.—Same made into a cylinder.
Fig. 65.—End piece of wire netting.
Fig. 66.—Cylinder with ends in place and wires attached for hanging it.

Squirrels have two kinds of nests, one for cold weather and another for warm weather; the former is generally in the hollow of a tree, and the latter is made of leaves and is placed in the top of the tree. While tramping in the Cascade Mountains last summer the writer was much interested in the squirrel-like animals there called "pack rats," and the nest of one of these rats, which was in an old powder can down in a gold mine, is practically the same sort of nest all the rat and squirrel-like animals make. This old powder can suggested the swinging nest for the squirrel house, a simply contrived affair, and one which your pets will appreciate.

To Make a Swinging Nest,

take a small strip of wire netting (A, Fig. 63), and bend the ends together, so as to form a cylinder (B, Fig. 64) about 1 foot in diameter and 2 feet long; fasten the netting into this form by wiring the edges of the net-ting together.   Next cut out two pieces of netting and make them to fit over the ends of the cylinder B in such a manner as to leave a half circular opening at each end, as is shown by the small diagram (Fig. 65).   Fasten two pieces of wire to the top of this cylinder (Fig. 66); hang it to the ridge pole and fill the in-side with dry leaves for a summer nest.

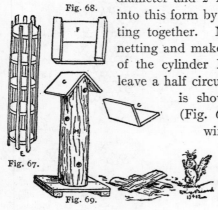

Fig. 68.
Fig. 67.
Fig. 69.

Fig. 67.—Frame of stump.
Fig. 68.—Stand for stump.
Fig. 69.—Finished stump.

The Artificial Stump

for cold-weather quarters is made by first making the framework or skeleton (E, Fig. 67) of the proposed stump and then trimming off the projecting ends of the ribs at the bottom and nailing the bottom disk to the stand (F, Figs. 68 and 69), next trimming off the top ends of the strips to fit the roof G, and last tacking on rough bark, so as to completely cover the frame.

Doorways to the different compartments of this squirrel's flat house are made by boring a hole in one piece of bark before nailing it on to the stump. The squirrels will arrange their own nests inside of it if you will furnish them with wool or any other soft, warm material, and the little scamps will enjoy themselves in the commodious quarters and reward you for all your labor by their appreciation of your work.

If it is birds, in place of squirrels, you wish to keep in the cage, set potted shrubs inside, or plant them in the bottom of the cage, and as the long, high structure gives the little birds an opportunity to use their wings, Mr. Hornaday, director of New York Zoological Park, has named this sort of building a flying cage.

CHAPTER VII

HOW TO MAKE A LAND AND WATER AQUARIUM, AND HOW TO MAKE AND STOCK A VIVARIUM

One of the air-castles of the writer's youth was a land and water aquarium, and many were the attempts and many the failures he made in his efforts to materialize his dream with the aid of the lumber of a dismantled dry-goods box and the glass from a discarded window sash. Our materials and available tools were crude in those days.

But there has been a great change since then, and even poor boys now have more spending money than the so-called "well-to-do" lads formerly possessed; besides this, tools and manufactured material are much more easily obtained, and it is not now necessary for the reader to use a discarded washing machine as a tank for an aquarium as the writer was compelled to do; but good material, well adapted for this purpose, may now be easily obtained.

When about to build the

Land and Water Aquarium

it is well to first decide where the thing is to be placed and upon what it is to rest. For an ordinary aquarium a north light is to be preferred, but this is not so essential for the one in question, because, in this case, the land part is supposed to face the window, where the light and heat will encourage the plants to grow and also give the turtles, frogs, toads or lizards the opportunity of taking the sun bath which they so much enjoy. At the same time this arrangement keeps the fish in the shade and also in a position to be inspected and enjoyed by persons in the room where the land and water aquarium is located. Select some small unused table, and take the measurement of the top, and let that govern the size of the base-board of your aquarium.

The Sides of Your Box,

A B F E, B F C G and D C G H (Fig. 70) will rest an inch or so inside of the outer edges of the base, as in Fig. 73. The proportions of the structure, if made to fit the top of a table, will, in all probability, be somewhere near those in the accompanying diagrams, but the arrangement will be different, the sides becoming the front and back, and the front and back becoming the sides. That is, the aquarium which fits the top of a table will in all probability be broader than it is long, but these diagrams are drawn so as to best show the construction, and not for the purpose of giving any fixed form or dimensions.

Make the sides of any sort of hard wood, wood that can be stained and polished, or of pine that may be painted. For the inside you will need a special sort of paint which will not soften in water. But before describing the paint it will be necessary to tell

How to Make Aquarium Cement,

and for this I quote the "American Boys' Handy Book."

"Take 10 parts, by measure, of litharge; 10 parts of plaster of Paris; 10 parts dry, white sand; 1 part finely powdered resin. Mix them when wanted for use with linseed oil into a pretty stiff putty."

This will stick to stone, wood, metal or glass, resists the action of salt water and hardens under water. Nevertheless,

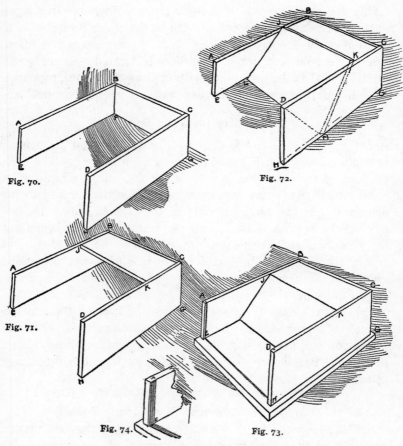

The land and water aquarium.

Fig. 70.—Two sides and one end of box.
Fig. 71.—Shelf in place.
Fig. 72.—Shore in place.
Fig. 73.—All ready for glass front.
Fig. 74.—Detail of corner.

better results are obtained if the aquarium is allowed to stand three or more days before it is used.

Another Aquarium Cement

can be made of 1 pound of asphaltum, ¼ pound of resin, 1 ounce of beeswax. Mash the resin fine and add it to the melted asphaltum, after which add the beeswax; mix well over a slow fire, and apply while hot. The beeswax is to give some elasticity to the otherwise brittle compound.

A Waterproof Paint

may be had by diluting a portion of this last-named cement (after it is taken from the fire) with turpentine. The paint thus secured is not pretty, but, as you wish to use it only on the inside of your tank, the color is not important.

Now that you are supplied with paint, cement and wood, select two pieces of board 1 inch thick, for the sides, and another piece of the same thickness for one end of your tank, and with small nails or screws fasten them together as in Fig. 70. Use great care to see that the boards at the joints are well trimmed and fit against each other snugly. To make doubly sure, paint the parts, where the boards join, with the waterproof paint, immediately before you join them.

Next cut out the shelf J B C K (Fig. 71) so that its smoothed edges will exactly fit between the two sides, A B F E and D C G H, and also against the back board, B F G C (Fig. 70).

After satisfying yourself that the edges are true, give them a light coat of waterproof paint and fasten the shelf in place as it is shown by Fig. 71. This gives you the dry "land" for your miniature landscape, and now the slanting "bank" must be supplied by adding

The Bank-board

shown in Fig. 72, J K L H. The same care must be used here to make the edges of the sides of the bank-board fit snugly against the sides of the tank, but the upper and lower edges of the bank may be allowed to extend above the shelf and below the lower edge of the side boards, so that it may be planed off evenly after the bank is nailed, or screwed, securely in place. But before doing this turn your tank upside down and paint the inside of the back board, F B C G, and the under side of the shelf-board J B C K, with a good coat or two of waterproof paint. The under side of the bank-board L J K M, should also be painted, and after it is in place all the corners again touched up with the asphaltum paint.

If the work has been properly done the shelf-board, bank-board, backs and side boards L J B C K C M (Fig. 72), when the structure is reversed, should form a tank which will hold water without leaking a drop.

When this is found to be true, plane off the edge J K (Fig. 72) until it is exactly level with the top surface of the shore-board J K C B (Fig. 73).

The Base-board

had better be made of $1\frac{1}{2}$ or 2-inch stuff, and after it is smoothed and fitted to the bottom edges of the rest of the tank, it, too, should have a thorough coating of waterproof paint, except where it extends beyond the tank on all sides (Fig. 73). Ordinary paint will do for the outside, and give a good finish.

The Glass Front

may be made to fit in grooves cut for the purpose, as shown at A E H (Fig. 73), and finished by tacking small cleats upon the outside (as shown by Fig. 76), the cracks made tight by carefully pouring the hot aquarium cement in them, or you may make the slots for the glass by neatly tacking cleats side by side, with a

space the thickness of the glass between them, as is shown by the corner of the front of the tank in diagram 74.

If you cut the slots in the wood, as first suggested, slip the glass in place (Fig. 75), and then add the cement before you put the outside cleats in place against the glass.

Paint the Inside of the Tank

thoroughly, using care not to daub it on the glass front; after the paint is set fill it with water to see that there are no leaks; Fig. 76 shows the tank as it appears after the glass has been set and all is ready for the artificial bottom of cement and pebbles made to represent

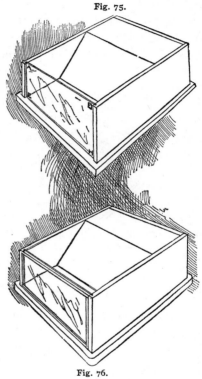

Fig. 75.

Fig. 76.

Fig. 75.—Glass front in place.
Fig. 76.—Cleats in place.

The Natural Bottom

of a brook or lake; shown by Fig. 77, and the cross-section view, Fig. 78.

This false bottom is made of Portland cement, in which a number of white, water-washed pebbles are set, not only for appearance sake, but also to afford a foothold for the land and water creatures which may need them as steps to aid them in scaling the "bank" to reach the "shore" of the miniature lakes. It is evident that without some sort of an enclosure the turtles, crawfish, frogs and other inhabitants of your land and water

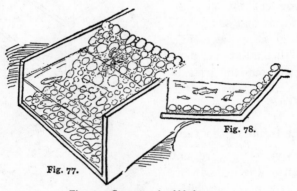

Fig. 77.

Fig. 78.

Fig. 77.—Cement and pebble bottom.
Fig. 78.—Sectional view.

garden, would soon be creeping and hopping all around the room, so

A Glass Top Must be Devised

to prevent such accidents.

If a frog, turtle or even a land-loving toad, be left a comparatively short time to wander around the floor in the dry atmosphere of a modern dwelling house, it will dry up until it is at last so brittle that the legs may be broken like dried twigs. But if by chance any of our valued pets are reduced to this uncomfortably brittle state, do not, on that account, throw them away, for it may be possible to

Bring the Mummies to Life

again by soaking them in tepid water for a few hours.

This fact is not generally known, and will be doubted by most people, but I personally know of two instances in which the dried, mummified and apparently dead creatures were restored to life by this method. In one instance it was a toad

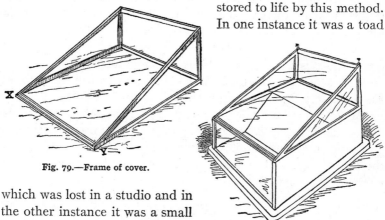

Fig. 79.—Frame of cover.

Fig. 80.—Arranged for free circulation of air.

which was lost in a studio and in the other instance it was a small turtle which escaped from a broken aquarium.

But it is best to prevent the necessity for experiments in re-vivification by using a framework of the form shown by Fig. 79, and fitting the sides with glass. It is not necessary that this frame shall be watertight, and it is not even desirable to have it so, for it would then smother all your pets both in and out of the water. Even fish cannot live without fresh air. So have the glass put in the sides of the frame, and secure a loose piece to fit on the top. Let the lower edge of the glass lid rest against a wooden cleat X¦ Y (Fig. 79), and the top edge on the two buttons Z and T (Fig. 80). This arrangement will imprison the inmates, protect the plants growing on the shelf, and yet allow the free circulation of air through the crevice made by resting the glass on the buttons Z and T.

When you finally put the water in the tank, do not fill it to the top of the bank, but let it be about two-thirds full, as shown in the diagrams 77 and 78. You will notice that the cement extends up higher than the shelf in Fig. 78; this is to make a basin for

Earth and Moss

and to do this it is necessary to use a temporary support for the cement, which may be made of wood and which can be removed as soon as the cement has set enough to hold its form.

Make a similar wall of cement around the other three sides of the shelf, and let it be about 1½ inches high on the outer edge and taper down to nothing on the inside, but before doing this the top of the shelf should have a good coating of waterproof paint. This paint is said to be also

Acid-Proof

and will not only withstand the chemical action of salt water, but it can be used for all sorts of purposes.

An electrician acquaintance told me that he frequently used common cigar boxes painted inside with this stuff to hold, not only water, but various acids which he used in his experiments.

To Prepare the Land

First cover the bottom with coarse gravel mixed with small pieces of broken flower pots. Over this spread some of the coarse moss to be found in marshy places and known as sphagnum.

You can always get this from the florist, who uses it for packing plants. Cover the moss with black mould composed of rotten leaves, to be found in the woods. Over this spread green moss and in it plant your ferns.

A Word of Caution

Do not over-stock your water or land with a mess of swimming and wriggling creatures, which will soon perish from lack of sufficient pure air; neither is it wise to overcrowd your shallow basined shore with plants. Select a few very small fish and aquatic creatures, and only the smallest of turtles, crawfish, frogs and tree toads, otherwise the big ones will soon devour the smaller ones.

For the land, use just sufficient earth to fill the shallow basin made by the cement walls, and in it plant a few diminutive ground vines or small maidenhair ferns, which, with some moss, will make a very pretty appearance.

Let the vegetation begin to grow, and leave the water standing in the tank a few days before you add your stock of live creatures. Then, if you use self-restraint and resist the temptation to over-stock, you need never change the water or lift the glass lid, except for the purpose of cleaning the glass and feeding your pets.

Some Little Neighbors in the Woods. How to Know Them and How to Keep Them in Captivity

It is a mistake to suppose that you are alone in the woods when there are no birds or mammals in sight, for though you may see no living thing the chances are that many little live creatures are all around you. The most casual search along the trail or among the damp leaves in the woods, especially after a shower, will disclose to view numbers of the little red lizard-like creatures known as the red eft or

Vermilion Spotted Newt

which scientists call the *Diemyctylus viridescens*. Don't look with loathing or contempt upon this tiny newt, it is not only perfectly harmless and very pretty but it has a wonderful life history.

When you go down to the lake for water you will probably see a lot of small, yellowish-brown aquatic lizard-like creatures swimming lazily around in the water and occasionally rising to the surface, but it will never occur to you that these are the same as the little red newts which you saw upon your trail. Yet this is the case; the vermilion spotted newt, or as it is commonly known in the country, the red "lizard," deposits its sticky eggs upon stones or upon water plants in the water, the eggs are hatched in the water, the young live in the water as aquatic animals, afterwards leave their nursery and take to the land, and for two or three years are air-breathing, land animals; then the desire to visit their birthplace seizes them and they toddle and creep and squirm their long pilgrimage back to the water, change their color, change their habits and even change their form and again become aquatic animals. Last summer I took a tin pail of the vermilion spotted newts to my home and kept them in some damp moss all winter, during which time more than half of them changed to the yellowish-brown color. My experiment was interrupted by a sudden cold snap in the latter part of February, which killed them all.

How to Ship Salamanders and Newts

Vermilion spotted newts may be sent safely across the continent, in fact they may be sent almost any distance if put in a pail with a perforated lid and plenty of damp sphagnum moss inside.

When digging for angle worms in the bog you may find

A Milk "Lizard,"

a large, dark salamander with two rows of yellow spots down his back like the buttons on a coachman's coat.   It is not as interesting an animal as the one just described, nor as common; it prefers spending most of its time buried in the mud or wet moss, but at night will come out and creep around in moist places.   This is the violet or spotted salamander known to the country lads as the milk "lizard" and to scientists as the *Amblystoma punctotum*.

In the mud along a trout brook or by a spring you may find

Another Salamander

of a brilliant vermilion color, which is also a large and very lively creature.   It is bright vermilion in color, speckled with black and very quick in its movements, but like the spotted salamander, it is of a retiring disposition and prefers to be buried in the cool, wet moss or muck of a spring hole to wandering around in broad daylight, yet at night it will creep out from its hiding place and forage for its food.   One that I secured last summer in Pennsylvania survived the frost which proved fatal to the red efts, and is now snugly buried in a lot of sphagnum moss in an old aquarium in my studio.   Its scientific name is *Speterpes ruber*.   Both the violet and the red salamander will live in confinement.

As you knock off the wet, soggy bark of a log to get at the dry inside, when you are splitting wood for the camp fire on a damp day, you will probably see a number of

Little Brown Salamanders

with a reddish-brown streak down the middle of the back, squirming desperately to escape. These are the red back salamanders. On a damp night the little fellows will travel around in search of food, or each other's society and a careful observer may discover their tiny heads sticking up above the wet leaves, their bright eyes taking in all of the landscape. I have kept them in confinement for a whole season—in fact any of those named may be kept with little trouble in a vivarium.

A Vivarium

can be made of any old, leaky aquarium with a pane of glass put on the top to keep the little inhabitants from escaping. Spread over the bottom a lot of crockery broken into bits about the size of your thumb, and mix with it some coarse gravel devoid of sand, then spread some sphagnum moss on top. This makes the foundation soil for your vivarium and will keep the surface free of a superabundance of water. Over the top of the sphagnum moss you may spread some black earth mould, such as you find under trees in the woods, and which is composed of decaying leaves. In this you can plant ferns and various wild flowers, and then cover the surface with green moss. This will give you a natural soil upon which all of these little creatures can live and thrive, and you may put several handfuls of them into the vivarium with no danger of overcrowding.

There are several

Small Snakes

which will live in a vivarium, but I warn you here that they will also feed upon the newts, frogs and tree-toads which may occupy the same prison cell with themselves. There is a little brown, red-bellied snake which you find under stones and bark, and the beautiful little green snake and the ringed snake. Of these the green snake is the prettiest and the most gentle. The garter snake is not poisonous but has a very disagreeable odor and is so very pugnacious that, while one cannot help but admire its pluck, the green snake is much to be preferred as a pet.

When you put the glass on the top of your vivarium, have four small corks or similar objects at the corners to prevent it fitting too tight, for all the denizens of the vivarium need air.

This miniature bit of forest land in the old aquarium can be kept in your house winter and summer, and afford constant entertainment and amusement, besides which the moss ferns and little wild plants make a most beautiful decoration. To feed your strange pets, put in a lot of angle worms every week or so. Earth worms will live in health in the soil of your vivarium and furnish a food supply for the other inhabitants. There are many butterflies and other insects, especially grasshoppers, which you can keep in confinement and which will live in the glass box as long as the newts and snakes will allow them. I kept and tamed a katydid one season, and it lived in my library until after Christmas. This insect was a source of great amusement to my guests and a great favorite with our maid, who fed it with salads and mourned for it when it met a sudden death by creeping into the hot ashes of the open fire. Make one of these vivariums and keep it in your window, south window in winter and north window in the summer time. The newts and salamanders do not care for the sunshine, which dries them into mummies, but the snakes and toads delight in sunning themselves.

CHAPTER VIII

HOW TO BUILD A FIRE ENGINE

Never does a normal boy see a fire engine go by without the keenest interest and excitement, and whenever an old-fashioned hand engine happens to be used, the chances are that there are more boys than men tugging on the hand lines and responding with a vim to the commands of the fire chief. But parents often object to having their children pull the ropes of the big hose-carts which are still used in many towns; they are very heavy carts, and there is always some danger.

To gratify the boy's natural love of excitement and to encourage him to do mechanical work is a great thing for him, and for his parents, too. I am telling you this so that you can use it as an argument with your parents if you should need some tools or materials with which to work. It does not require a great outlay, however, to build a fire engine for yourself.

For your material, select four boards of smooth wood with straight grain, free from cracks, knots and blemishes. If half an inch thick, the board should be about four inches and a half broad, and a little under three feet in length. Nail the four pieces together to make the box of the pump.

Before joining the edges and nailing them in place put on a coating of white lead paint where they meet, to insure a close fit.

Let the front and rear boards be about three-quarters of an inch longer than the side pieces (Fig. 81), and notch these boards at the bottom as shown by Fig. 82. Make the bottom of the pump (Fig. 81) of one-inch wood, and give the edges of this a coat of white lead, too, before it is fastened in place with screws B (Figs. 81 and 82).

A leather valve must be made, large enough to fit in the pump, and tacked along the edge of the bottom block, the latter being first perforated with holes, as shown by Fig. 85. Another block is necessary, and this also must be of good, sound wood, of the same dimensions as the bottom piece. This additional block is to be used as the plunger of the pump and must be attached to the iron or brass rod of the pump (see P, Figs. 81 and 86). A leather valve is necessary for the top of the plunger; it must be fastened with tacks in the centre of the plunger surrounding the rod hole (Fig. 87). If you can procure a rod with screw threads at the end, this end can be securely fastened to the plunger by first twisting a nut on the rod about an inch and a half from the end, then slipping the plunger with the leather valve (Fig. 87) attached (P, Fig. 81) up against the nut; the bottom of the plunger may be secured with an iron washer and another nut screwed up tightly against it (P, Fig. 81). Fig. 88A explains the position of the nuts.

In case the rod has no threads it may be hammered to a tapering end B (Fig. 88), and after a washer is forced up about an inch and a half the plunger can be put up against it. Another washer is now necessary for the bottom of the plunger, and the end of the iron rod can be carefully beaten to a blunt end to clinch it.

When the plunger is forced down the pressure of the water will lift the valve around the edges, thus allowing the water to flow above the plunger.

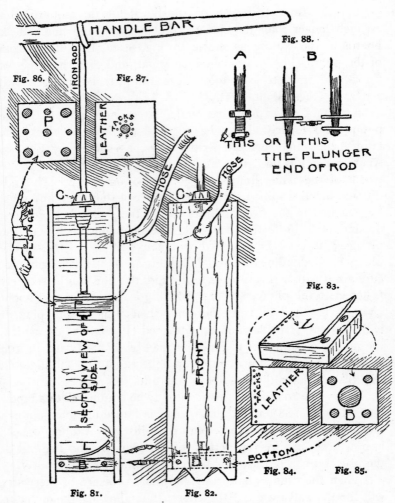

HANDLE BAR

Fig. 86.

Fig. 87.

Fig. 88.

A

B

THIS OR THIS
THE PLUNGER
END OF ROD

IRON ROD

P

LEATHER

TACKS

C

HOSE

C

HOSE

PLUNGER

SECTION VIEW OF SIDE

FRONT

Fig. 83.

L

LEATHER

TACKS

B

B

B

BOTTOM

Fig. 81.

Fig. 82.

Fig. 84.

Fig. 85.

Section and Parts of Pump Box.

Thus the two valves will work of their own accord, so to speak—that is, automatically open and shut just at the right time. But it is necessary that the top of the pump be both water-tight and air-tight, and yet the plunger rod

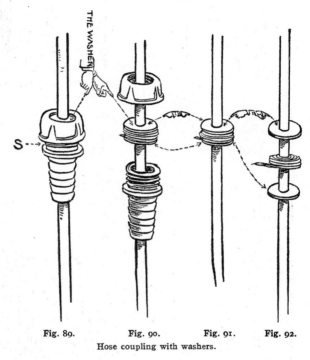

Fig. 89.   Fig. 90.   Fig. 91.   Fig. 92.
Hose coupling with washers.

must pass freely through it. This necessitates a "packing-box," a simple contrivance for a trained mechanic to make, but at first a rather difficult problem for the novice. The best thing to do is to look for some sort of hollow piston-ring which can be packed. Fortunately we have only to go to the garden hose to find just what we want. Figs. 89 and 90 show the brass hose coupling, but to make these water-tight we must pack the inside with greased candle-wick. If that is not obtainable, take ordinary white cotton string and twist two or more pieces together, then wrap the rod between the two

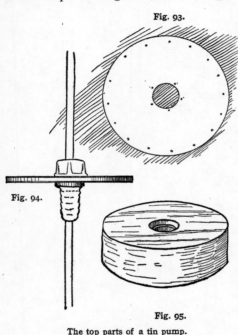

Fig. 93.

Fig. 94.

Fig. 95.

The top parts of a tin pump.

washers, as in Fig. 91, and slip the washers together as in Fig. 92. The hose coupling must be unscrewed, and the lower piece slid on the rod before the washers and packing are put there (Fig. 90); then, when all is ready, the top piece of the hose coupling may be slipped down and the two pieces screwed together (Fig. 99), inclosing the packing with its protecting washers. The latter must be selected to fit in the upper hose coupling, as in the diagram, or brass ones made which will fit; these secure the packing around the plunger-rod between them so that the rod can slide up and down without letting in air or letting out the water. Have the hole in the top of the pump-box of the proper shape and size to fit the coupling. C, Figs. 81 and 82, show the hose coupling in place.

Of course, it is not necessary to have a square, wooden pump-box. If you happen to have a smooth metal tube of the proper dimensions it may be utilized for the purpose, or a tin pump can be made of a tube of tin which will cost very little when made to order by the tinsmith. To make a top for your tin pump cut a thin disk of wood (Fig. 94) and two disks of tin (Fig. 93). After the wooden disk is sandwiched between the two tin ones it should exactly fit between the upper and lower couplings when they are screwed together—that is, the combined thickness of the tin and the wooden disks should be just equal to the space S (Fig. 89) between the couplings. After the tin sheathing is tacked with small brads, or with pins filed off short, to the wooden disk, put in the packing as already described; then, with the disk under the washers, bring the upper and lower couplings together and screw them tightly, inclosing the disk between them, as in Fig. 95. The top block (Fig. 95) can now be slid up over the lower coupling, and when the disk is nailed to it it is ready to be fastened into the top of the tube by small nails or tacks and soldered there.

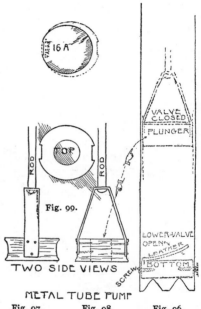

Fig. 99.

TWO SIDE VIEWS

METAL TUBE PUMP
Fig. 97.   Fig. 98.   Fig. 96.
The interior arrangement of a tin pump.

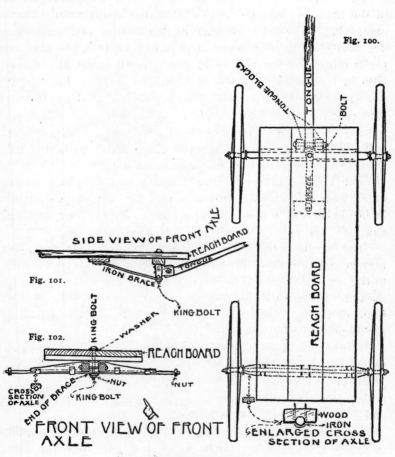

Fig. 100.

TONGUE BLOCKS

TONGUE

BOLT

BRACE

REACH BOARD

WOOD
IRON
ENLARGED CROSS
SECTION OF AXLE

SIDE VIEW OF FRONT AXLE

REACH BOARD

IRON BRACE   TONGUE

Fig. 101.

KING BOLT

KING BOLT   WASHER

Fig. 102.

REACH BOARD

CROSS
SECTION
OF AXLE   END OF BRACE   NUT   NUT

KING BOLT

FRONT VIEW OF FRONT
AXLE

Details of the Truck.

Figs. 96, 96A, 97, 98 and 99 show the interior arrangement of the tin or metal pump. As far as the construction is concerned it is practically the same as that of the wooden one just described, but there are some details which differ. The plunger, for instance, has its valve (Fig. 96 A) tacked to one side rather than in the middle, and the plunger itself has one big hole in the centre (Fig. 96) instead of numerous scattered small ones. The plunger-rod is fastened to a strip of brass or iron (Figs. 97 and 98) which extends down on each side of the plunger, and the latter is cut in or grooved like a spool, so that it will hold a winding or packing of greased candle-wick.

The hose is attached to an ordinary hose coupling, set securely in a hole in the pump-box made for that purpose, a few inches below the head of the pump-box, as in Figs. 91, 103 and 104.

The handle of the pump is the last thing to be attached, and may be made of a pole or cut from a piece of timber and fitted to the hands; it may be attached to the plunger-rod by having the latter run through it and fastened with nuts as in the plunger itself, or the rod may be bent and encircle the pole as shown in the diagrams.

The truck can be made from any old wagon-bed or coasting-wagon, or by connecting two axles with a reach-board composed of two or more planks on which a barrel or box water-tank may rest; in this the pump is fastened, as in Figs. 103 and 104.

Figs. 100, 101 and 102 show detail plans of a truck built to fit bicycle wheels. An iron rod is used to extend the axles through the hubs and the wheels are secured by washers and nuts. Two washers may, perhaps, be necessary, because otherwise the revolution of the wheels would unscrew the ordinary nuts. The iron-rod axle runs in a groove cut in the under side of the wooden axle and is secured there by staples which are clinched through the reach-board (Fig. 100) on the rear axle;

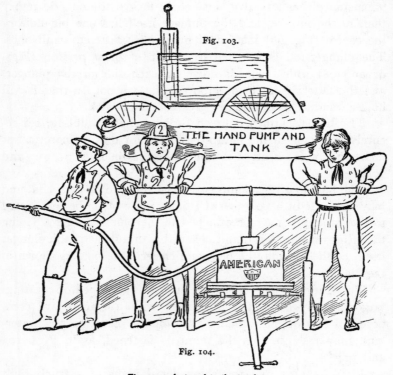

Fig. 103.

THE HAND PUMP AND TANK

AMERICAN

Fig. 104.

The pump fastened to the truck.

on the front axle hoop-iron straps are nailed to hold the axle-rod (Fig. 102).

A tongue may be attached to this truck at the front axle

by fitting it between two tongue-blocks (Figs. 100 and 101) and securing it firmly by a bolt and a nut.

This will make a beautiful truck, but if you want it for a rough-and-ready hand engine, four solid wooden wheels and a reach-board will answer.

It may be stated that, although the pump here described will force the water through the hose, the stream will be an interrupted one, going by jerks. But a continuous stream may be obtained by introducing an air tank, fitted with another valve, at a point just above the place where the water enters the hose, while those who are not sufficiently skilled in mechanical work to do this can use the pump given in this article, or even take a garden force-pump and a pail of water mounted on a four-wheeled wagon of any sort.

SUMMER

CHAPTER IX

HOW TO MAKE A DIVING CART, POLES, SLINGS AND CHUMP'S RAFTS FOR BATHERS

At this season of the year not only the woods, river banks and lake shores are dotted with the camps of jolly people, but the country houses are filled with vacation parties, and it is safe to say that among all the people taking an outing, four-fifths of them spend part or all of the time on the sea coast or the shore of some river or lake. This is because the water, with the boating, bathing and sailing, adds greatly to the enjoyment of one's vacation. But we frequently find among a party some unfortunate individuals who have neglected to learn to swim during their childhood, and after growing older have been deterred from learning this useful art, through fear of the water or fear of the ridicule of their companions. Such an individual is a constant source of anxiety and real danger to the others in any party, for should the canoe upset, the sail-boat capsize, or the row-boat meet a similar accident, or should this person chance to be precipitated into the water, some one of his companions must necessarily jump in to his rescue, thereby endangering two lives. Wherever there is known to be a man or boy in an outing party who is unable to swim, the rest of the party should insist upon his learning then and there. It is safe to say that every normal human being, if he or she will, can learn to swim. Personally, I have had great success in teaching grown men to swim by use of

The Chump's Pole and Sling

This is a simple contrivance consisting of a stout sapling from which the branches have been trimmed and to the end of which a short line is attached, as in Fig. 114. From the end of the line the novice is suspended in a rope sling, as shown in Fig. 109; or one made of a bath towel, as shown in Fig. 113. To make a rope sling, tie ends of rope together securely in a square or reefing knot, sling the rope over the branch of a tree or some similar projection, and test the knot with your weight to see

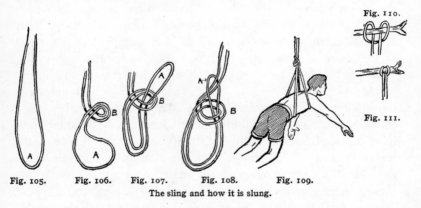

Fig. 110.

Fig. 111.

Fig. 105.   Fig. 106.   Fig. 107.   Fig. 108.   Fig. 109.
The sling and how it is slung.

if it is perfectly secure. When you have found that it will satisfactorily support your weight in the air, you need have no fear but that it will support any man's weight in the water. To make

The Sling

lay the loop of the rope down on the ground, as in Fig. 105, bring the end of the loop A up and bend it down over itself (B, in Fig. 106), next bring the end of the loop up again, and pull it through the bend B, first made, as in Fig. 107; then take the opposite loop (the top loop is not shown in the diagram), and bring it through the first loop, as in Fig. 108. Adjust this to suit the person, draw it tight, as in Fig. 109. You will then have the chump's sling, and it is now only necessary to fasten the other end to the chump's pole. To do this take the top loop and bring it up over the end of the rod, then pull the sling down through the loop as in Fig. 110, and draw it tight, as in Fig. 111. If you have done this as directed it will be impossible for the beginner to break the line or loosen the hitches.

The Towel Loop

is made by knotting together the ends of a long bath towel, as in Fig. 112, and then fastening the line to the towel, as in Fig. 113. The towel loop possesses the advantage of being more comfortable on the naked body of the novice than the rope sling, but there is more danger of it being insecure. However, this danger may be avoided by thoroughly testing the sling with your weight, as you did the rope in the first instance. The illustration in Fig. 114 shows

How to Use the Chump's Rod and Sling,

but it may be well to give the details. Let the tutor or swimming master grasp the rod firmly, as he would a fish-pole, and allow the beginner to adjust the sling on his body until it fits comfortably. He may then wade out to deep water, feeling perfectly safe with the knowledge that the swimming master can easily keep a bather's head above water by aid of the chump's pole. If convenient the beginner may let himself down into the deep water along the edge of a float or pier.

It is the Swimming Master's Duty

to inspire perfect confidence on the part of his pupil, and to
do this he must prove to him that there is not the slightest danger
of the bather's head going under water. This is a serious
undertaking, and no one should trifle with the beginner, for a

Fig. 114.   Fig. 113.   Fig. 112.

The towel sling and how to use it

ducking may strike the novice with a panic which will cause
him to try to climb the rope or get out of the sling and, if no
more serious consequences occur, it will give the novice such a
fright that he will be afraid to again put himself in the hands
of the swimming master. After the pupil shows confidence in
the water let the swimming master move him gently forward

and instruct him how to paddle and to kick, and while the pupil's whole attention is fixed upon his hands and feet the rope may be gently slackened so that the man in the water receives no support. It will be frequently discovered that the beginner is unconsciously swimming unsupported by aught save the movement of his own hands and feet; but if he discovers that the rope is slack he will cease his swimming strokes and allow himself to sink from lack of confidence in his own ability. I have taught a full-grown man to swim in one lesson by this method, and at the Nereus Boat Club, at Flushing Creek, I introduced the chump's pole for teaching new club members,

Fig. 115.—Side view of chump's log raft.

whose early education had been neglected, to swim, and in no one case were we unsuccessful. But let me again impress upon the reader the importance of treating the beginner's fears seriously; all old swimmers know that it is only lack of confidence that prevents any one from learning to swim within a few minute's time.

Some years ago I published in one of my books for boys an invention of mine called

The Chump's Raft,

a very simple contrivance, consisting of four smooth planks nailed together in the form of a square, with the ends of each plank projecting a foot or more beyond the lines of the square. The raft, which I built as a model, is still in use at my summer camp, where scores of young people have used it with a success proved by their present skill as swimmers. But many camps are located in a section of the country where boards are as scarce as boarding-houses, but where timber, in its rough state, exists in abundance. The campers in such locations can make

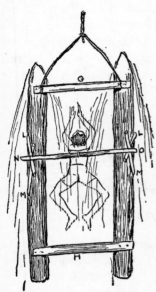

Fig. 116.—Looking down on a chump's raft in motion.

A Chump's Raft of Logs

Such a float consists of two dried logs fastened together at each end by cross slabs, so as to form a rude catamaran. These rafts can be towed through deep water by a canoe or row-boat, with the tenderfoot securely swung in a sling between the logs, where he may practice the hand and foot movement with a sense of security which only the certainty that he is surrounded by a wooden life-preserver will give him. Fig. 116 shows a top view of the new chump's raft. In Fig. 115 the two logs are connected fore and aft by cross slabs; two more upright slabs are nailed securely to the side of the logs; notches having been cut in the top ends of these slabs, a stout cross piece is securely nailed to them and the towel or rope sling suspended from the middle of the cross piece. In regard to the dimensions of the raft it is only necessary to say that it should be wide and long enough to allow free movement of the arms and legs of the pupil who is suspended between the logs. In almost every wilderness stream there can be found piles of driftwood on the shore

Fig. 117.—Learning to swim by aid of a chump sling.

where one may select good, dried, well-seasoned pine or spruce logs from which to make rafts. If such heaps of driftwood are not within reach, look for some standing dead timber, and select that which is of sufficient dimensions to support a swimmer, and be careful that it is not hollow or rotten in the core. Rotten wood will soon become water-logged and heavy. Fig. 117 shows the position of the swimmer supported by the chump's sling. If your raft has a tendency to work so that one log pulls ahead of the other, it may be braced by cross pieces, such as are shown at J and K in Fig. 119. This figure also shows supports for a suspension pole made

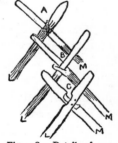

Fig. 118.—Details of saw-buck supports.

by nailing two sticks to each side and allowing the ends to cross so as to form a crotch in which the supporting rod rests and to which it is securely fastened by nails, or by

being bound there by a piece of rope, as in A, Fig. 118. B,
Fig. 118, shows the crotch made by resting L in a fork on the
M stick and then nailing or binding it in place. C, Fig. 118,
shows the two sticks, L and M, joined by notches cut log-cabin
fashion before they are nailed in place.

Although many summers have rolled around since the
author first made his advent on this beautiful earth, he still
feels the call of the bathing pool, the charm of the spring-board,
almost as keenly as he did when he was wont to swim in Blue
Hole at Yellow Springs, Ohio, or dive from the log rafts into

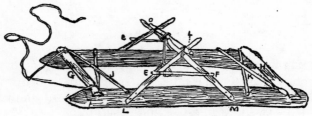

Fig. 119.—Another way to rig a chump.

the Ohio River, or slide down the "slippery" made in the steep
muddy banks of the Licking River, Kentucky, and now that

Swimming Time is Here,

in imagination he can see dear old "Monkey" Bowles and
freckled-faced Lon Lashler peeking over the back fence, each
lad holding his right hand aloft with the first two fingers up,
in the same manner as does the Pope at Rome when giving his
blessing.

The boys of my time found this signal a much more desirable
method of communicating their plans than shouting "Let's
go a-swimming." It meant the same thing and did not at-

tract too much attention. In those days we wore no heavy bathing clothes and never went *bathing;* that expression was interpreted as meaning a washing and scouring of the body and a disagreeable digging at one's ears with the end of a towel wound around one's little finger, an operation which made a fellow's ears sore and could only be endured because it was thought to be necessary torture, a ceremony which we underwent to appease our parents and teachers.

In the Eastern States bathing consists in holding tightly to a rope and bobbing up and down as the breakers come cours-

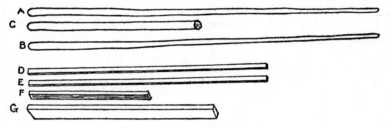

Fig. 120.—Frame pieces for diving-cart.

ing in shore. This is an exhilarating and good sport; but for real fun it cannot approach a little swimming-hole in the creek with the grass and flower-covered banks, the overhanging green branches of the trees and

The Spring-board

A swim is only a dip unless there is a spring-board on which to do stunts and from which one may dive.

Any pine board from a lumber pile will answer for a spring-board, but on account of the shelving shores of most rivers, lakes and sand bars, there is seldom a good place to put the board, unless we have either

A Diving Cart or a Diving Sleigh

It may be well to explain right here that both these machines are intended not as divers themselves, but as movable platforms from which a boy may dive, and it is expected that they will fulfill a long-felt want among that class of readers whose home or vacation grounds are in the inland country on the shores of small streams and lakes devoid of piers and floats from which one may dive and swim. The advantages of the diving cart are that it can be let down at low water, pulled up at high water, and stowed away under a shed during the winter months. It is not a spring-board or a pier, but it is a foundation upon which either may be erected in a few moments, and it may be used as a platform from which to swim or a pier from which to fish.

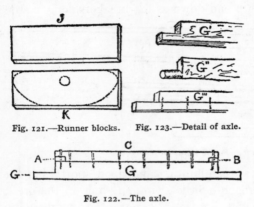

Fig. 121.—Runner blocks. Fig. 123.—Detail of axle.

Fig. 122.—The axle.

Procure, if you can,

An Old Pair of Wheels

from among those discarded on the farm or by the wagon shop; if the wheels are unobtainable, do not be discouraged, but change your plans and build a diving sleigh. The only real difference between these two vehicles is that one has wheels and the other sled-runners, and the only objection to the latter is that the sleigh is moved with more difficulty on sand and dirt than is a cart. But when the banks are muddy the sled-runners move with less friction than the wheels.

In building these machines use the tools and material at hand. The best of lumber is none too good, but the green wood cut in the forest will answer the purpose. A saw, hatchet, auger, and chisel will answer for your tools, and even this list may be c u r t a i l e d ; nevertheless do not despise a chest full of tools if they are handy; when at work supply all deficiences in tools or material with your Yankee resourcefulness and what your grandfather will call gumption.

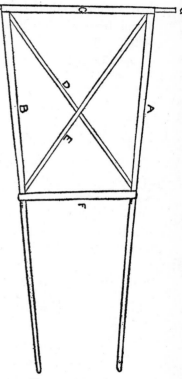

Fig. 124.—Body of cart.

The Vehicle

can be made small and light enough for one boy to manage or so big and heavy that it will take a crowd to move it from place to place.

Of hickory, ash, or some other strong, elastic wood cut two straight shafts, A and B (Fig. 120), and let them be of sufficient diameter at their butts (thick ends) to form a substantial foundation for the proposed framework; then cut another piece C (Fig. 120), and make it about $6\frac{1}{2}$ feet long. D and F (Fig. 120) are only stays and as such can be made of much lighter material than the main part of the frame. F needs to be no more than $1\frac{1}{2}$ inches thick and $4\frac{1}{2}$ feet long. G is a piece of 2 x 4 inch stuff 7 feet long.

Fig. 125.—Rustic joints.

These dimensions are for

A Very Large Frame

and can be proportionally reduced for smaller machines. J (Fig. 121) shows a piece of two-inch plank about $3\frac{1}{2}$ feet long and between 1 and 2 feet broad; the dotted lines on K show

The Pattern of the Runners

Of course it is not necessary to follow a curved line with your saw; the corners may be cut off in straight lines and the angles rounded afterward with a knife, chisel, or plane, to correspond with the dotted lines on K (Fig. 121); after which a hole can be bored, the top rim of which is at least two inches below the

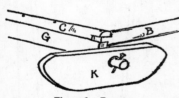

Fig. 126.—Runner.

upper edge of the runner. Make J an exact duplicate of K. Although

The Runners

are intended to slide over the sand or mud, they need not be shod with iron bands; but as the bottom of the creek swimming-hole or river may be obstructed with stones and like obstacles, these runners are made

To Play Freely on Their Axles

This arrangement allows of movement sufficient for the runners to adjust themselves to the uneven bottom.

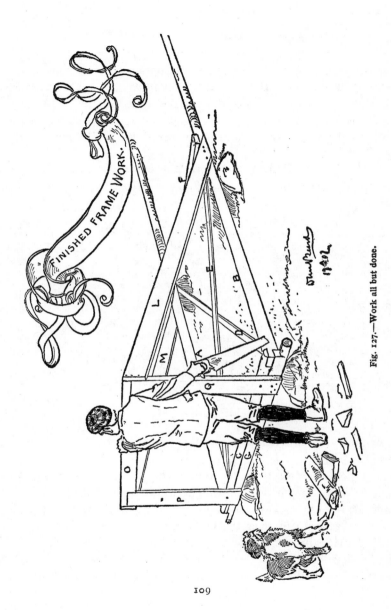

Fig. 127.—Work all but done.

In the diagrams here given G is supposed to be a piece of 2 x 4 inch stuff, and the axle is made by sawing out a block as shown by G′ (Fig. 123) and then rounding off the projecting axle end as shown by G″ (Fig. 124), but if the piece G is of soft wood and the wheels or runners are large and heavy, there will be

Danger of the Axle Breaking,

in which case an ash or hickory pole of proper dimensions or

Fig. 128.—The diving cart in use.

a strip of some other hard wood may be nailed to G, as is shown by G‴ (Fig. 123).

At points 7 feet from the butt ends of the shafts A and B nail F, so as to join the two shafts as shown in Fig. 124. Let there be but one nail used at each end of F so that you may spread the butt ends to fit over the ends of G; mark the slant on A and B made by the inside edge of G, and notch the big ends of the shafts at this line as shown on A at H′ (Fig. 125). Rest the notched ends of A and B on G, and trim the stick C by flattening one side, so that it will fit on top of G.   Notching the ends as shown by H' (Fig. 125).   Spike C securely to G with long wire nails, and

To Prevent Danger of Splitting

at the ends, bore holes through C, A, and G and B, A, and G, at the joints on the ends, and then drive the nail through the holes bored as in Fig. 122.   Now nail F securely to A and B.

The stays D and E (Fig. 120) may next be nailed across the bottom of the frame as shown by Fig. 124.

L M O P Q (Fig. 127) explain themselves in the diagram. O is notched so as to fit over the ends of P and Q.   The latter are then nailed securely to C and G of the bottom frame and the diagonal braces L and M nailed in place.   If it is necessary, put in diagonal braces on P O Q G as D and E are placed on the bottom frame and you have a diving cart of strength sufficient to hold your spring-board and afford you plenty of fun for many coming seasons.

CHAPTER X

HOW TO BUILD A CHEAP BOAT

The old-time raftsmen formerly built their "Yankee Pines" of the rough, unplaned boards fresh from the saw-mills on the river banks, and these raw, wooden skiffs were staunch, light and tight boats, but to-day smooth lumber is as cheap as the rough boards, so select enough planed pine lumber for a $12\frac{1}{2}$-foot boat, and you may calculate the exact amount by reference to the accompanying diagrams which are all drawn as near as may be to a regular scale.

By reference to Fig. 129 you will see that A A represent the two

Side-boards

These should be of sufficient dimensions to produce two side-pieces each 13 feet long, 17 inches wide and $\frac{7}{8}$ inch thick (A, Fig. 130). You will also need a piece for a

Spreader

54 inches long, 18 inches wide and about $1\frac{1}{2}$ inches thick, but as this is a temporary affair almost any old piece of proper dimensions will answer (B, Fig. 130), and another piece of good $1\frac{1}{2}$-inch plank (C, Fig. 130) 36 inches long by 15 inches wide, for a stern-piece. Besides the above there must be enough 1-inch lumber to make seats and to cover the bottom. At a point on one end, $6\frac{1}{2}$ inches from the edge of the A plank, mark the point c (Fig. 130); then measure 37 inches back along the

edge of the plank and mark the point *b* (Fig. 130). Rule a pencil line (*b c*) between these two points and starting at *c* saw off the triangle *bcd*. Make the second side-board an exact duplicate of the one just described and prepare the spreader by sawing off the triangle with 9-inch bases at each end of B (Fig. 130). This will leave you a board (*h k o n*) that will be 36 inches long on its lower edge and 54 inches long on its top edge.

Next saw off the corners of the stern-piece C (Fig. 130) along the lines *j g*, the *g* points being each 6½ inches from the corners; and a board (*ff gg*) 18 inches wide and 36 inches top measurement, with 23 inches at the bottom. Now fit the edge of the stern-piece along the line *e d* (Fig. 130), or at a slant to please your fancy. In Fig. 131, upper C, the slant makes the base of the triangle about 4½ inches, which is sufficient. Be careful that both side-boards are fitted exactly alike,

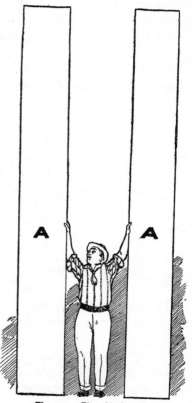

Fig. 129.—The side-boards.

and to do this nail the port side with nails driven only partly in, as shown at D (Fig. 131); then nail the starboard side and, if they are both seen to be even and of the right slant, drive the nails home; if not correct, the nails may be pulled out by using a small block under the hammer (D, Fig. 131), without bending the nails or injuring the wood. Leave the stern ends of the side-boards protruding, as in the upper C, until you have the spreader and stem in place.

We are now ready for the spreader (*h k o n*) amidships, or, more accurately speaking, 6 feet 9 inches from the bow (B, Fig. 131). Nail this as shown by D (Fig. 131), so that the nails may be removed at pleasure. Bring the bow ends of the

Fig. 130.—A, the side. B, the spreader. C, the stern-piece.

A boards together and secure them by a strip nailed temporarily across, as shown in the diagram E (Fig. 131).

The Stem-piece

may be made of two pieces, as is shown at G and F (Fig. 131), or if you are more skilful than the ordinary non-professional, the stem may be made of one piece, as shown by the lower diagram at F (Fig. 131). It is desirable to have oak for the stem, but any hard wood will answer the purpose, and even pine may be used when no better is to be had. Take a piece of cardboard or an old shingle on which to draw a pattern for the end of the stem and make the outline with a lead pencil by placing the shingle over the apex *c* of diagram E (Fig. 131); from the inside trace the line of the sides thus, **V**. Trim your stem down to correspond to these lines and let the stick be somewhat longer than the width of the sides A A.

When this is done to your satisfaction, fit the stem in place and nail the side-boards to the stem.

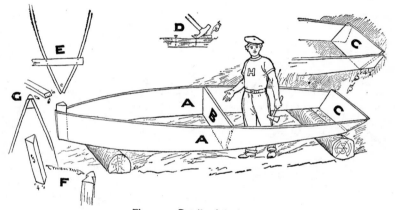

Fig. 131.—Details of the boat.

Turn the boat over and nail on a bottom of 1-inch boards as shown by Fig. 132.

Don't

use tongue and grooved, or any sort of fancy cabinet or floor joining when wet—such matched lumber warps up in waves—but use boards with smooth, flat edges; if these are true and fitted snugly together in workmanlike manner the first wetting will swell them in a very short time, until not a drop of water will leak through the cracks, for the reason that there will be none. Fit the bottom boards on regardless of their protruding ends, as these may be sawed off after the boards are nailed in place.

The Seats

consist of a triangular one at the bow (J), the oarsman's seat (L), and the stern seat (K, Fig. 133). The bow seat is made of 1-inch boards nailed to two cleats shown at M (Fig. 133). N shows the bench for the stern seat and O explains the arrange-

Fig. 132.—Put on a bottom of 1-inch boards.

ment of the oarsman's seat a little forward amidships. As may be seen, it rests upon the cleats *x* (Diagram O, Fig. 133), which are fitted between two upright cleats on each side of the boat; this makes a seat which will not slip out of place, and the cleats serve to strengthen the sides of the otherwise ribless boat. Make the cleats of 1 by 2-inch lumber and let the seat be about 12 inches wide. The stern seat may be wider, 1½ feet at K and 4 or 5 inches more at the long sides of the two boards each side of K (Fig. 133). Of course, it is not necessary to fit a board in against the stern-piece, for a cleat will answer the purpose, but a good, heavy stern-piece is often desirable and the board shown in diagram N (Fig. 133) will serve to add strength to the stern as well as to furnish a firm rest for the stern seat, but it will also add weight.

The Keel Board

is an advisable addition to the boat, but may also be omitted without serious results (H, Fig. 133).

The keel board should be 4½ inches wide, 1 inch thick,

Fig. 133.—Details of bow, stern, seats, and finished boat.

and should be cut pointed, to fit snugly in the bow, and nailed in place along the centre of the floor, before the seats are put in the boat. A similar board along the bottom, joining the two cleats each side of the skeg at *y* (Fig. 135) and extending to the bow will prevent the danger of loosening the bottom planks when bumping over rifts, shallow places, or when the boat needs to be hauled on a stony shore; this bottom board may also be omitted to save time and lumber, and is not shown in the diagram.

The Skeg

is a triangular board (Figs. 134 and 135), roughly speaking, of the same dimensions as the pieces sawed from the side-board *b c d* (Fig. 130). The stern end will be about 7 inches wide and it will taper off to nothing at *y* (Fig. 134). The skeg is held in place by cleats of 1-inch lumber, 2 inches wide, nailed to the bottom on each side of the skeg. To get the proper dimensions experiment with the pieces sawed from the A boards and cut

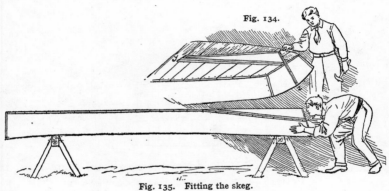

Fig. 134.

Fig. 135. Fitting the skeg.

your skeg board so that its bottom edge will be level with the bottom at *y* (Fig. 134); the diagonal line, to correspond with the slant of the stern, can be accurately drawn if the skeg is left untrimmed until it is fastened in place.

To Fasten on the Skeg

rule a line from the centre of the stern to the centre of the bow and toe-nail the skeg on along this line. This must be accurately done, or you will make a boat which will have an uncomfortable tendency to move in circles. After toe-nailing the skeg to the bottom, nail the two cleats, one on each side of the skeg, and let them fit as closely as may be to the keel. Now saw off the stern ends of the cleats and lay a rule along the stern, as the stick is placed in Fig. 134, where the boy has his finger; rule a pencil line across the protruding end of the keel and saw off the end along the diagonal line, so that the stern cleat z (Fig. 134) may be nailed in place to finish the work.

You can buy row-locks of galvanized iron for about a quarter of a dollar a pair, the brass ones are not expensive,

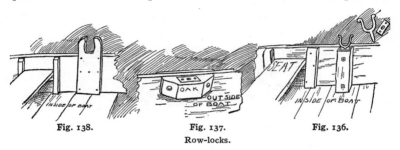

Fig. 138.   Fig. 137.   Fig. 136.
Row-locks.

but even when the store furnishes the hardware there must be a firm support of some sort to hold the row-lock.

If you use the manufactured article, to be found at any hardware store, the merchant will supply you with the screws, plates and row-locks, but he will not furnish you with the blocks for the holes in which the spindles of the row-locks fit. Fig. 136 shows a rude, but serviceable, support for the lock made of short oaken posts much in vogue in Pennsylvania, but Fig. 137 is much better, and if it is made of oak and bolted to the sides of the boat it will last as long as the boat. Fig. 137 may be put upon either the outside or inside of the boat, according to the width amidships.

A Guard Rail

or fender, of 1 by 2-inch lumber, alongside of and even with
the top of the side-boards, from bow to stern, gives finish and
strength to the craft; but in a cheap boat, or a hastily constructed one, this may be omitted, as it is in these diagrams.

If you are building your boat out of the convenient reach
of the hardware shop, you must make your own row-locks.
Fig. 138 shows the crude ones formerly used by the raftsmen
for the Yankee pines, and Figs. 139 and 140 show row-locks
made with the oaken, or hardwood thole-pins fitting in holes

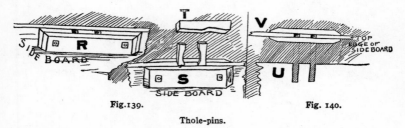

Fig. 139.   Fig. 140.

Thole-pins.

cut for that purpose in the form of notches (U, Fig. 140) in the
side of the boat, or as spaces left between the blocks, as shown
by R (Fig. 139). When the side-boards A A of the boat are
notched a cleat of hardwood 5 or 6 inches wide, and extending
some distance each side of the side-boards, must be used, as is
shown by diagram V (Fig. 140) and (Fig. 139). The diagram
R (Fig. 139) explains itself; there is a centre block nailed to the
side-board and two more each side, leaving spaces for the thole-
pins T (Fig. 139) to fit and guarded by another piece (R) bolted
through to the sides.

If bolts are out of your reach, nails and screws may act as

substitutes, and Fig. 140 will then be the best form of row-lock to adopt.

To fix the place for the row-locks, seat yourself on the oarsman's seat, grasp the oars as in rowing, and mark the place which best fits the reach of your arms and oars; it will probably be about 13 inches aft from the centre of the seat.

CHAPTER XI

HOW TO CROSS A STREAM ON A LOG

How to Build a Logomaran—How to Make a Blow-Bed Ferry— How to Ford Swift Streams

There is a widespread notion that all wood will float on water, and this idea often leads to laughable errors. I know a lot of young backwoods farmers who launched a raft of green oak logs, and were as much astonished to see their craft settle quietly to the bottom of the lake, as they would have been to see the leaden sinkers of their fish-lines dance lightly on the surface of the waves. The young fellows used up a whole day's time to discover what they could have learned by watching the chips as they flew from the skilful blows of their axes sink when they struck the water.

The stream which cuts your trail is not always provided with bridges of fallen trees. It may be a river too deep to ford and too wide to be bridged by a chance log. Of course it is a simple matter to swim, but the weather may be cold and the water still colder; besides this you will probably be encumbered with a lot of camp equipage—your gun, rod, and camera, none of which will be improved by a plunge in the water. Or it may so happen that you are on the shores of a lake unsupplied with boats, and you have good reasons for supposing that big fish lurk in some particular spot out of reach from the shore. A thousand and one emergencies may arise when a craft of some

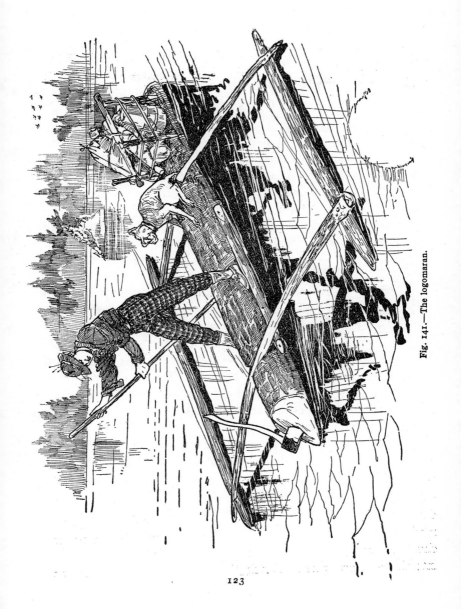

Fig. 141.—The logomaran.

kind will be not only a great convenience, but almost a necessity; under these circumstances

A Logomaran

may be constructed in a very short time which can bear you and your pack safely to the desired goal (Fig. 141).

In the Rocky, Cascade and Selkirk mountains, the lakes and streams have their shores plentifully supplied with "whim sticks," logs of fine dry timber, which the freshets have brought down from the mountain sides, and which the rocks and surging torrents have denuded of bark. These whim sticks are of all sizes, and as sound and perfect as kiln-dried logs. Even in

Fig. 142.—The notch.

the mountains of Pennsylvania, where the lumberman's axe years ago laid waste the primeval forest, where the saw-mills have devoured the second growth, the tie hunter the third growth, the excelsior mills and birch beer factories the saplings, I still find good sound white pine log whim sticks strewn along the shores of the lakes and streams, timber which is suitable for temporary rafts and logomarans.

In the north woods where, in many localities, the original forest is untouched by the devouring pulp mills, suitable timber is not difficult to find; so let the green wood stand and select a log of dry wood from the shore where the floods or ice have deposited it. Cut it into a convenient length, and with a lever made of a good stout sapling, and a fulcrum of a stone or chunk of wood, pry the log from its resting place and roll it into the shallow water. Notch the log on the upper side, as shown by Fig. 142, making a notch near each end for the cross pieces.

The two side floats may be made of pieces split, by the aid of wooden wedges, from a large log, or composed of small whim sticks, as shown by Fig. 143.

The floats, as may be seen by reference to Figs. 141 and 143, are shorter than the middle log.

It is impracticable to give dimensions, for the reason that they are relative; the length of the middle log depends, to some extent, upon its diameter, it being evident that a thick log will support more than a thin one of the same length, consequently if your log is of small diameter, it must be longer, in order to support your weight, than will be necessary for a thicker piece of timber. The point to remember is to select a log which will support you and your pack, and then attach two side floats to balance your craft and prevent it from rolling over and dumping its load in the water.

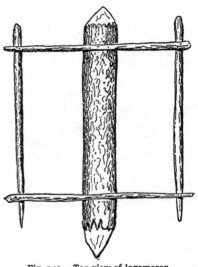

Fig. 143.—Top view of logomaran.

An ordinary single shell boat without a passenger will upset, but when the oarsman takes his seat and grasps his long spoon oars, the sweeps, resting on the water, balance the cranky craft. and it cannot upset as long as the oars are kept there. This is the principle of the logomaran, as well as that of the common catamaran. The cross pieces should be only thick enough to be secure and long enough to prevent the log from wabbling and wetting your feet more than is necessary.

If You Have an Auger and No Nails

the craft may be fastened together with wooden pegs cut somewhat larger than the holes bored to receive them, and driven in with blows from your axe.

If you have long nails or spikes the problem is a simple one; but if you have neither auger, nails nor spikes you must bind the joints with rope or hempen twine.

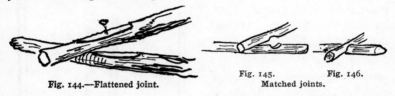

Fig. 144.—Flattened joint.

Fig. 145. Fig. 146.
Matched joints.

If you have neither nails, auger nor rope, a good substitute for the latter can be made from the long,

Fibrous Inner Bark

of a dead or partly burned tree. For experiment I took some of the inner bark of a chestnut tree which had been killed by fire, and twisted it into a rope the size of a clothes-line, then I allowed two strong men to have a tug-of-war with it, and the improvised rope was stronger than the men.

How to Make a Fibre Rope

Take one end of a long, loose strand of fibres, give the other end to another person, and let both twine the ends between the fingers until the material is well twisted throughout its entire length, then bring the two ends together, and two sides of the loop thus made will twist themselves into a cord or rope half the length of the original strand.

If you nail or peg the parts, use your axe to flatten the joints by striking off a chip, as in Fig. 144.

If you must lash the joints together, cut them with log-cabin notches, as in Figs. 145 and 146.

If you have baggage to transport, make

Fig. 147.—The saw-buck crib.   Fig. 148.—The staked crib.

A Dunnage Crib

by driving four stakes in cuts made near the end of the centre log and binding them with rope or fibre (Figs. 147 and 148), or by working green twigs basket fashion around them, or make the rack saw-buck fashion, as shown by Fig. 147, and this will keep your things above water.

A couple of cleats nailed on **each** side of the log will be of great assistance and lessen the danger and insecurity of the footing.

A skilfully made logomaran will enable you to cross any stream with a moderate current and any small lake in moderate weather. It is not an especially dry craft, but it won't sink or upset, and will take one but a short time to knock it together.

Fig. 149.—The blow-bed raft.

A Blow-Bed Raft

But if you are bunking in a sleeping bag and on a "blow-bed," as the cowboys term a pneumatic mattress, you can have a raft ready by pumping up your mattress and lashing it to a blow-bed frame of small pieces of dry wood (Fig. 149).

The frame will prevent your raft from doubling and dumping you. A pneumatic mattress is a fine thing to sleep upon when it is covered with a sleeping bag, but a naked, wet "blow-bed" is a different proposition, and it is almost as difficult to stick on to it as it would be to hold on to the smooth surface of a soap bubble.

Nevertheless, if you are of reasonable weight, and use a wooden frame to stiffen the mattress, the thing will be buoyant enough to serve as a ferry for you to cross the stream that cannot be forded.

Better than a kit of carpenter's tools with which to work is the old-fashioned article called "gumption." With a plentiful supply of this you will find no difficulty in building a blow-bed frame. It is possible for a man to lose his gun, knife, compass, ammunition and clothes, and still exist in a howling wilderness, and if the man is plentifully supplied with gumption he will soon supply himself with some sort of tools and weapons which will be good enough to furnish clothes and food for the naked man.

However, if the man is totally lacking in gumption he will undoubtedly perish.

But when one "hits the trail," it is with no intention of losing clothes, arms and ammunition, and even when plentifully supplied with these useful articles, there will be found abundant opportunities for the exercise of one's gumption: streams to ford, swim or ferry, mountains to climb, swamps to traverse and all that goes to make progress difficult, dangerous, and delightful. For, after all, there is no physical pleasure equal to the wild joy one feels while wresting a living from the wilderness. Such a hold-up of Mother Nature is exhilarating in the extreme, and gives the highwayman bright eyes, firm-set mouth, self-confidence and buoyant health.

In America it is the Huck Finns and Tom Sawyers who mature into healthy, wholesome men, and not the degenerate little Lord Fauntleroys; the latter abnormal characters need the artificialities of the Old World to develop their hot-house peculiarities. They have no place in camp or on the trail where dangerous trout lurk in the streams and wild-eyed woodchucks rove at large.

Without his wilderness training, there can be little doubt that George Washington would have been but a country gentleman, and that Abraham Lincoln, brought up under the watchful eye of a French nurse, would never have been known to fame. History shows that our greatest and most resourceful men are found among those whose physical and mental faculties are

Fig. 150.

strengthened and sharpened by the strenuous exertions necessary to overcome the obstacles and solve the problems which constantly face the man on the trail.

Hence all true and patriotic Americans should rejoice in the fact that each year finds a steady increase in the number of nature lovers, and vacation time fills the woods with enthusiastic campers eagerly studying the rudiments of the gentle art of woodcraft.

When a tenderfoot first attempts to cross a stream on the

bridge formed by a fallen tree, he will try to balance himself by facing up or down stream with his toes at right angles to the log (Fig. 150A), but after he once loses his balance and falls in the cold water below (Fig. 150B), this same tenderfoot will possibly make a careful study of the manner by which the old-timers safely walk a small log which bridges a stream or even some frightful chasm.

If the novice observes carefully he will see that the experienced woodman keeps his eyes fixed upon the opposite shore, points his toes in the same direction (Fig. 150C), and seems to have little fear of losing his balance. Even should a man, walking in this manner, stumble and fall, it would be *on the log* (Fig. 150D), and not in the stream. His arms and legs would encircle the bridge, and he would be safe from serious harm.

Fording Swift Streams

As a general rule the widest place in a swift stream is also the most shallow and the force of the current less; being spread over a wide space it lacks the power and swiftness of the same water where it is pent up between narrow banks.

Not only in a real wilderness but often in the wilder parts of the country near our homes, we meet with swift streams which the camper, hunter, fisherman, photographer or collector must cross by fording unless he prefers to walk many miles in search of a bridge; often the stream is shallow and offers no great difficulties, but again it may be shallow and at the same time run so swiftly as to make it impossible for an unaided man to keep his feet in the powerful current; this is particularly true of glacier streams in the mountains which are both difficult and dangerous for

A One-man Ford

In an emergency of this kind the lone traveller can often make a successful ford by "packing" a load on his shoulders sufficient to steady him in the swift water (Fig. 151).

Before attempting to ford, it is often advisable to remove your clothes with the exception of your shoes or moccasins; keep these on to protect your feet from the sharp stones and your ankles from the round water-worn bowlders.

Fig. 151.—A load on one's back makes one's feet steady.

Adjust your pack so that in an emergency it may be instantly cast off, otherwise a fall will probably mean that it will be your last ford unless you try it next on the River Styx.

If the camp duffel you have with you is not of sufficient weight add stones or chunks of green wood sufficient to steady you, then with a staff in your hands you can ford a stream which would sweep a man without a heavy pack off his feet. (Fig. 151).

Pole Fording

is a good way to cross a stream when there is more than one man. Cut a pole and let it be about 10 or 12 feet long and just thick enough to avoid the danger of it breaking. Put the lightest man, with little or no pack at the small end of the pole and the heaviest man with the weightiest pack at the butt end of the pole; when all are lined up and arranged according to weight, wade in the current with the lightest man up stream and the heaviest man

Fig. 152.—Put the heaviest man down stream.

down stream. Keep the point of the pole pointing up stream and the pole parallel with the current, and work your way diagonally across (Fig. 152). It may happen now and then that the up-stream man is swept off his feet, but if he and all the other keep their hold on the pole, the slack current or eddy caused by the partly submerged traveller makes travel easy for the ones below him. You will find deeper water below big stones, but there will also be less force to the current there than on the up-stream side of the obstruction.

This method of fording was taught me by Andrew J. Stone, the Arctic-American traveller, and he learned it from the Northern Indians.

The young artist and Arctic explorer, Mr. Belmore Browne,

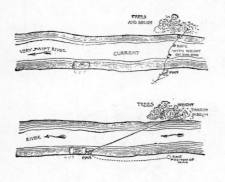

recently described the same method of fording in *Recreation* magazine, and he also learned it in the Northern wilderness.

Where the shores are covered with bushes or heaps of drift wood, swift streams may be crossed by rafts attached to ropes; it is necessary to first fasten the end of the rope to the opposite side of the stream, and this may be done by casting the weighted end of a rope over the water and so working it as to entangle the weight in the bushes or

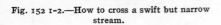

Fig. 152 1-2.—How to cross a swift but narrow stream.

drift wood and then attaching the free end to the raft as is shown in diagram Fig. 152½. The current will swing your raft across the stream.

CHAPTER XII

HOW TO MAKE A BRIDGE FOR SWIFT WATERS

Dams for Swimming Holes, Trout or Wild Duck Ponds

A small, sluggish stream or brook is a comparatively simple thing to dam, but as the incline of the bed becomes steeper and the water rapid, the difficulties for the amateur are greatly increased, and indeed the professional engineer is often put to his wit's end by the same problem when he faces it in the woods, and finds himself unarmed with books of reference and scientific implements.

But the forest folk are not bothered much by such small affairs, and they have a practical method of handling them which is refreshing to witness.

Beaver will successfully dam a swiftly flowing trout brook, and it was some backwoodsmen from Missouri who built a brush bridge at the siege of Vicksburg, over which they crossed with their regiment before the engineers had decided on a plan for a bridge. To the credit of the army engineers, be it said, they immediately abandoned their incomplete plans and devoted their attention to finishing the work of the axemen of the Thirtieth Missouri United States Volunteers, and in a few hours the whole of that command, with their heavy, lumbering artillery, crossed safely over the brush bridge built by ignorant (?) pioneers.

How to Make a Brush Bridge

In the above instance the water was deep but sluggish, and the bridge was built by cutting two trees on opposite sides of the bayou, so that they fell in the water with their branches interlacing. On this foundation of branches was heaped piles of brush, and all weighted down with earth, until a regular road-bed extended from side to side, through the open bottom of which the sluggish stream flowed with little or no interruption.

But few of the readers will find it necessary to build bridges

Fig. 153.   Fig. 154.   Fig. 155.
Constructing straddle-bugs.

upon such an extensive scale. They may, however, use the same principle for very much smaller structures. Attention has already been called to the fact that the difficulties of the amateur increase with the velocity of the current of water; however, even a swiftly flowing river can be quickly bridged by the use of a sort of two-legged wooden horse, which for lack of a better name we will call

The Straddle-Bug

It is a rustic device, and a thing which, with little labor, any one can build who can wield an axe and twist an auger, and with a number of these simple but strictly scientific contrivances even a wide river may be successfully bridged.

Figs. 153, 154, 155, show how the straddle-bug is built. The bug stick consists of a rough post or pole L (Fig. 155), with two diagonal holes H H (Fig. 153) bored near the larger or butt end. The diagram in Fig. 153 shows the butt end of a bug stick sawed off so as to display the H holes.

Into the H holes the leg sticks S S (Figs. 153, 154, 155) are driven. These leg sticks are made from stout saplings or hoop poles, each with one end whittled down like a half-sharpened lead pencil (Fig. 153), and when the two legs are securely driven into the auger holes the bug is finished.

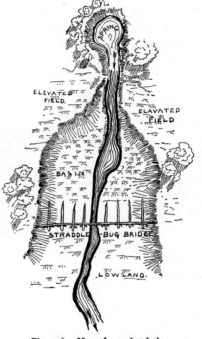

Fig. 156.—Map of a spring hole.

A Straddle-Bug Bridge

The number of bugs necessary for the proposed bridge depends upon the width of the stream and the length of the connecting planks for the walk.

Fig. 156 shows a rough topographical map of an imaginary spring hole which is to be dammed and converted into a trout pond. The skeleton dam is already in place, and in reality consists of a straddle-bug bridge. Upon one of these impromptu affairs I have more than once crossed a wide and swiftly flowing river, too deep to ford afoot and too boisterous for horses and wagons.

Fig. 157 is a diagram of a longitudinal section of a stream by which it is hoped to explain how the very force which might sweep away some bridges is ingeniously made to anchor the straddle-bug and hold it firmly in place. As the water rushes

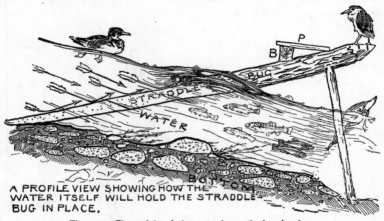

A PROFILE VIEW SHOWING HOW THE WATER ITSELF WILL HOLD THE STRADDLE BUG IN PLACE.

Fig. 157.—The weight of the water keeps the bug in place.

down stream it strikes the bug, slides up the incline, bearing down upon it with all its weight and the added push of the current. A well-made straddle-bug will last until it is swamped by a freshet or wrecked by an ice jam or battered by floating driftwood.

To make the bridge it is only necessary to nail the B (Fig. 157) leveling blocks in place and then nail on the foot plank L (Fig. 157).

By using two poles or logs, a thick one for the lower one and more slender ones for the top ones, a level bridge may be made without the use of planks (Fig. 158).

Bridges require less work and fewer bugs than do

Dams

If you are so situated that lumber from the saw-mill is easily

Fig. 158.—They are useful even on large streams.

obtained, then you can build your dam of that material, as is shown by A B (Fig. 159), but this savors too much of the ordinary mill dam to appeal to a real woodsman's heart; however, for rural districts it is probably the best material to use in making

A Swimming Hole

in the meadow brook. Whether it be a brush dam in the woods or a sawed lumber dam in the pasture, if it is expected to hold a sufficient volume of water to make a deep pool, the dam must be supported underneath by a wall of stones and brush, as is shown by the cross section of a brush dam in Fig. 160. A dam properly built of lumber should not require the thick mattress of leaves, brush, and clay which is necessary to keep a brush dam from leaking.

An observer who claims to have watched some beaver start and finish a dam, states that it only took the mother and three young two or three nights to build a dam 35 feet long across a

Fig. 159.

swiftly flowing but shallow trout brook. The dam increased the depth of the water from a few inches to an average of 3 feet. What one old beaver and her youngsters can do, in such limited time, should not be considered a very strenuous task for healthy boys or grown men.

There is much we can learn from the beaver, and it is well to study the little four-footed engineer's method of work, but do not think that I expect the reader to gnaw down trees with his teeth, an axe will be far more practical and save a dentist bill ; but we can, nevertheless, take some useful hints from our persecuted little brother, and still be allowed to use such artificial tools as an axe, auger, or even a saw.

Labor must follow the line of least resistance, so hunt for an available spot which presents the least difficulties to the dam builder, and after selecting your site set to work manufacturing straddle-bugs. If there is not much current, or you are building the dam principally on land, as in Fig. 156, the bug sticks may be shorter than when they are to rest in swiftly moving water.

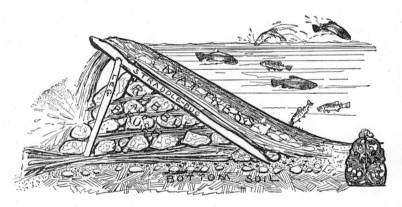

Fig. 160.—Cross-section of a dam.

Place the bugs in line and keep their tops as near level as practical by using long legs for them where a depression occurs and short legs for an elevation. An exact level can be obtained by properly adjusting the top cross bar (Fig. 159) on the bug stick, moving it up or down the bug stick as the case demands, and nailing it in place when level.

The beavers mostly use cottonwood logs and willow brush, but we may use what wood comes handy.

When the straddle-bugs are all in place, nail a top rail from one to the other and also a bottom rail, as is shown in Fig. 159, if that part is not under water; but if the bottom of the dam is submerged, cut some green wood which will sink, or get some water-logged wood and place it along the bottom of the bugs for a bottom rail. If it so happens that you can find no wood which will sink, peg down some green wood by using forked sticks and forcing them in the bottom with the crotch of the fork over the proposed bottom rail. Next rest a number of green wood sticks against the two rails, as in Fig. 159, forcing their lower ends into the bottom far enough to keep them from floating up and out of position, or, if the water does not yet cover the bottom rail, simply rest the sticks against the two rails and nail them in place. Now collect a great quantity of small, green brush with the leaves still attached to the stems, or cut grass or weeds and spread this material over the sticks, weighting it down with stones of the proper size. Lay the first layer of brush in the same direction as the poles; in other words, thatch the frame with brush, pushing the big ends of the branches into the bottom and allowing the tops to lay against the top of the dam. Make a layer of brush and stones, then a layer of gravel and mud, in much the same manner as the beavers build their dams, and at last plaster it all over with a layer of clay or mud (Fig. 156, C D).

In stopping a leak or in building a rather large dam, it may facilitate matters if you make a number of

Beaver Mats

such as are shown by the two sketches in Fig. 161. Fasten four small sticks or the wands, G H, E F, M K and N L, together at their ends, forming a rectangular figure; stiffen this with two diagonals, A C and B D. This makes a frame for one side of the mat, and a duplicate can now be made for the opposite side, after which cover one frame with a layer of fine brush, then a layer of leaves, grass or hay, then a layer of mud, then another layer of leaves, grass or hay, or all three mixed, and on top of them still another layer of fine brush.   Place the second frame over the top layer of brush, and bind the two frames securely together, as is shown by the sectional view in Fig. 161.

There should be enough mud or clay in the mattress to make the frame sink, and these mats can then be placed over the first layer of brush and mud on the dam like paving stones, the spaces between the mats calked up with leaves and mud, and then the whole surface treated to a solid coating of clay.

To make the dam safe, the brush and mud mattress should extend some distance beyond the bottom rail into the mill pond, as is suggested by the cross-section of dam, Fig. 160.

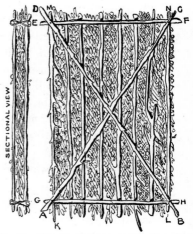

Fig. 161.—**How the beaver mat is made. End and top views.**

Recollect that when the dam is full of water a leak at the bottom is difficult to find and more difficult to remedy, and that much trouble and vexation can be spared by using care before the dam begins to fill.

I have given directions here by which ambitious people can make large dams to hold considerable bodies of water, but the straddle-bug will answer just as well in miniature for little streams which the boy readers may desire to dam to furnish power for their

Jack-knife Water Wheels

or for pools in which to keep their pollywogs and other aquatic pets.

When the structure is nearing completion, the rubble, consisting of sticks, brush, and large stones, may be built underneath the shed of the dam to give additional support to the framework to better withstand the heavy pressure of water. But a low dam, supporting water to the depth of three feet or less, needs no other support than well-made straddle-bugs.

If the stream is small, like the one shown by Fig. 156, allow a little opening to remain unthatched for the escape of the water while you carefully build the dam on dry land, and, when all is in readiness, fill up the opening with sticks and a brush mat or a wad of moss, clay and leaves, or brush weighted with stones and then covered with sods and clay.

On some occasions a hollow log may be used as a spout or escape pipe for the water until the dam is finished. Since no two places are alike in topography or water and wood supply, so no two dams will be alike in detail, and each and every one will present its own problems to be solved; but we must remember that the humble, flat-tailed rodent has solved all these problems, and for thousands of years has been a successful dam builder, also that we are *human beings*. We are the superior animals which have all but exterminated the beaver.

It must not be understood that the brush dam is intended for great rivers or mountain torrents. Such streams can wash away even the most ambitious and costly work of our best engineers, but a brush dam will answer for a trout pond at your summer home, a place for domesticated wild fowl, or a swimming hole in inland country distant from any natural bathing place.

If we follow the example of the beaver and make a succession of dams, one below the other, we will lessen the liability to accidents during the spring freshets, and these dams can gradually be worked over and repaired, until they each in time form a solid embankment.

Small dams built with straddle-bugs will serve to interest the boys and furnish them a place to wade, sail their toy boats, and pasture their sunfish, catfish, and minnows.

Fig. 162.—A simple and effective bridge for dead water.

How to Build a Bridge Over Still Water

Perhaps there is a shallow muck pond near your permanent camp over which a bridge would be most convenient, and one may be built of logs lashed together end to end or held in position by stakes driven alongside the logs into the mud of the bottom, as shown by Fig. 162. The bridge can have a railing made of poles fastened to long stakes upon one side of the logs (Fig. 162), and such a bridge can be safely crossed by almost any one who can walk. The railing does away with all danger of losing one's balance and falling overboard. If you have nails, the stakes may be nailed to the logs, thus making them perfectly steady.

CHAPTER XIII

HOW TO BUILD SUBSTANTIAL PIERS AND BRIDGES AT YOUR CAMP OR SUMMER HOME

Recently there has come to pass a great and wholesome change in public sentiment regarding outdoor life, a change which is as encouraging as it is far-reaching in its effects. People are at last beginning to really admire nature, and to appreciate the subtle charm which lends a gamy flavor to all phases of wild life. One of the consequences of this general awakening of the love for the unfenced world is the sudden appearance in the midst of waste places of shacks, camps, log-houses—yes, and palaces of Oriental splendor.

The last mentioned innovation, it must be confessed, lends no charm to the wild woods, and would not be missed by real nature-lovers, not excepting those examples where a vain effort to disguise the effete luxury inside has caused the proprietors to encase their palaces with an outer shell encrusted with logs and to call the thing a camp.

But we must not judge the poor people who are guilty of perpetrating these paradoxes too harshly; for although the homely quality of the logs extends only to the outside walls, the presence of the bark-covered timber is itself meant as an apology to Mother Nature for the intrusion of artificialities in her domain.

A life in the woods even under the disadvantage of being in a palatial, so-called, camp, is educational, and is already teaching some of the wealthy idlers the value of personal contact with the rough side of nature.   Many of these people are beginning to understand and appreciate the fact that the fascinating pleasure of achievement cannot be bought with money, and that the joy of the creator of things *comes only with the sweat of labor.*

That being the case, if you need a pier on the pond or lake in front of your wild woods home, build it yourself, and you will enjoy it more than twenty structures built by hired hands.

It is, of course, understood that to erect one 35 feet long and

Fig. 163.—The balance logs prevent the crib from upsetting.

10 feet wide with the crib resting in $7\frac{1}{2}$ feet of water, requires more than one man's work, as the writer recently discovered when he built such a one on Big Tink Pond in Pike County, Pennsylvania.

But there is a vast difference between having volunteer, or even hired, help in such an undertaking and letting out the work by contract, leaving all the interesting problems to be solved by others.

In the construction of the framework of

The Crib

select the timber growing near the water's edge and much labor will be saved. A green red oak log, which sinks in the water, can be handled by one man while it is immersed, although the same log on shore would be a heavy burden for a dozen men to transport. Use chestnut, oak, pine, ash or spruce, but leave the water birch alone, for it will not last in an open-air structure. Select logs about 4 or 5 inches in diameter at their small ends for the uprights (Fig. 163), and with an axe sharpen the butt ends to a rough point that may be driven into the bottom of the lake or pond. Build the crib at the water's edge, and make it 10 feet long by 3 feet wide, with diagonal braces on the side to keep it from twisting out of shape, then tow it out to its resting-place. Make two lines fast to the projecting tops of the outside corner sticks, and have some one on shore take in the slack on these lines as the crib is righted. When it assumes an upright position make the shore ends of the lines fast to trees or other objects.

Unless this is done the crib will upset again and again, dumping the workmen and their tools into the water. One of my axes lay two weeks at the bottom of Big Tink before we found it by diving.

Now cut two long logs like those in the diagram, and float them to their places in the water with their butts resting in the shallow water near the shore; raise their tips until they rest on the horizontal bar of the crib (Fig. 163). Spike these balance logs temporarily to the crib, and the ropes may be removed, for the crib cannot now upset.

The Maul

Saw off a small section from an oak or some other hardwood tree, and be careful to saw at right angles to the outside of the trunk; bore a large auger hole through the middle of the piece, and drive in a handle of convenient length.

With this maul you can now gain muscle and experience by driving the four corners of the crib into the bottom of the pond, and if you accomplish the task without making a miss and taking an involuntary bath, you will have better luck than did the writer.

When the crib is firmly set in the bottom and leveled by a rap on this corner and then on that, drive piles a few inches apart inside the side bars and diagonal and close to them, as is shown by Fig. 164. Go through the same process upon the opposite side, and the crib is ready to be loaded up with stones and thus transformed into an abutment for your

Bridge,

as is shown by Figs. 165 and 168.

The problem of the pier now becomes that of a bridge, for the fewer piles you have the less danger there will be of the ice of winter destroying the summer's labor by freezing around the piles and pulling them from the bottom as the ice rises with the water in the spring, thus dismantling your pier; a crib loaded with a heavy inside filling of stones is comparatively safe from such accidents. Fig. 166 shows a simple and strong bridge, the floor being laid upon two horizontal logs, each of which is supported by a

King Post

suspended from two diagonal struts. The foot of the king post is fastened to the horizontal logs by an iron bolt, stirrup or suitable joint spiked in place, or, wanting a spike, held in place by a wooden peg driven through an auger hole.

Fig. 167 shows the same principle with two posts, which in this case are known as

Fig. 164.—Driving the piles for side of crib. Where the winters are severe the front piles should be omitted.

Queen Posts

and are used for longer spans.

Care should be taken to make the notches in the king post and the supported log fit the ends of the struts neatly. A small spike nail will then hold them in place, for the strain is not lateral but is a push against the point where the ends of the struts rest, and it is consequently only necessary to prevent accident from knocking the struts sideways out of place.

Floor your pier with small logs, selected on account of their straight, even sides, and spike them to the horizontal logs. If you now possess any planks, floor the end of your pier with them, as in Fig. 168; this will give you a smooth surface from which to dive while bathing or upon which to sit while fishing.

If desired, a tall pole can be erected at the end of the pier and rigged with a pulley and halyards, by which a flag may be hauled to the peak and lowered at pleasure.

Before you build your crib for the proposed pier, soundings should be made at the place where the crib is to be set. Make the sounding with a long pole, and mark the water line on the pole with a notch cut with your knife. You will then have four notches on the measuring rod corresponding to the depth of water at the four corners of the crib. Make the first notch for the right-hand inshore post, the second for the left-hand one, etc., cutting each notch horizontally. Make an I under the first, an inverted Λ under the second, a V under the third, and nothing under the fourth. The reason for this will be evident when you discover that your soundings vary, so that the marks on the rod become confusing unless each has a special sign to identify it.

Unless the transparency of the water is remarkable, you will be unable to see the bottom at a depth of 7 or 8 feet, and hence

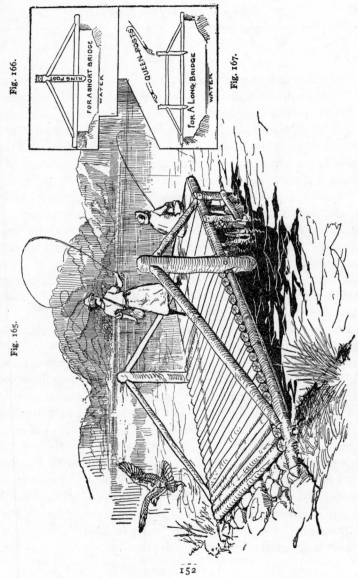

Fig. 165.

Fig. 166.

Fig. 167.

FOR A SHORT BRIDGE

KING POST

WATER

QUEEN POSTS

FOR A LONG BRIDGE

WATER

Showing the finished bridge and the use of king and queen posts.

it will be necessary to mark the spots for the two inshore crib posts by erecting two temporary poles at those points. The two outside posts need not be marked, for the reason that if the crib is built properly when the inshore posts are placed, the outside posts will occupy the places designed for them.

The object of all this is to have the crib set upright, and not list to port or starboard, as the case may be. An uneven bottom means uneven length for the corner posts of the crib, the longest leg for the deepest water, and the shortest leg for the least depth.

Care should also be taken to make the first rung of the ladder-like ends of the crib sufficient distance from the bottom points of the corner post to avoid all danger of the rung being forced against the bottom when the corner posts are driven into the bottom of the pond; otherwise the rung will hold the corner posts back, and prevent you from driving it deep enough to be secure. When building the crib make the two end ladders first, and nail the rungs on, as shown in the diagram (Fig. 169), then connect the two ladders by the horizontal bars and add the diagonals to give the crib stability. This work must be done in the shallow water, or as near the edge of the water as possible, because a crib built of green wood is a very heavy affair and difficult to handle even with the aid of the water.

A very large crib might be entirely too heavy for men to handle unaided by machinery.

Nevertheless two or three strong youths can build one by simply using four small cribs to form the sides of the big one. You must not forget, however, that a crib measuring 10 x 10 feet will hold enough stones inside its walls to keep you busy all the season "toting rock" to fill the inclosure.

If the bottom is rocky it will be necessary to slat the bottom of the crib, and to so cut the end posts that the bottom of the crib will conform to the bottom of the lake. The crib can then be anchored in place by loading it with stones.

If left unsupported in this condition a narrow crib would be liable to be upset by the first object which bumped against it during a gale, but after the bridge connects the crib with the shore, it will hold the framework firm enough to stand all the knocks to which it is liable to be subjected.

PROFILE VIEW OF BIG-TINK PIER.

Fig. 168.—The pier is just the thing for a morning plunge.

Your pier will be found to be a delightful lounging place, a convenient boat landing, and will soon become the favorite meeting spot with your own company and chance callers. You will never regret the labor expended in building a Big Tink pier for your camp, for if you have worked with the axe and maul, cut your own timber, slopped around in the water and made a good job of your undertaking, you have also added to your muscle, your health, your self-respect, and, consequently, to your happiness.

It is, of course, understood by the reader that these piers may be made of various dimensions; but if it is great or small you will never tire of telling your friends how you learned to roll your logs with a "prier" thrust in a rope looped around the log, how the crib upset and threw you into the water, what a splendid place the end of the pier is from which to dive, how convenient it is for a boat landing, and what a big fish you hooked from the end of the pier—but it got away!

Since writing the above we have had a severe winter and the ice in the lake froze so hard that the push on the crib drove it back under the bridge; but the few spiles driven along-side the bridge and nailed to it were unharmed, and my pier still stands in good order and I have learned something of the action of ice in ponds and small lakes. When the water in a pitcher freezes, we all know that it swells and breaks the crockery, so when the water in a pond or small lake freezes it also swells and exerts a tremendous push against the shores or any solid object near them. This push, however, will leave a slender rod unharmed, the ice moving on each side, so that a pier supported by a row of piles will stand when a strong rock crib may be upset, as was mine; however, the crib stood unharmed for three winters, and the pier itself is standing now in good condition, supported by the side piles.

CHAPTER XIV

GATEWAYS FOR PERMANENT CAMPS OR COUNTRY HOUSES

While the work of making the large gateways is too arduous for small boys it is none too strenuous for larger lads, and even the smaller boys can direct the workmen on their father's farm or country house in the erection of the more ambitious structures, and can themselves make small ones for their play houses and camps.

The Daniel Boone Gateway,

shown in the first illustration, is a simple and effective one for a foot-path or bridle-path entrance. It is made of a number of logs of graduated lengths, set upright like the palisaded forts built by our pioneers.

The tops of the logs should be so trimmed as to form a regular incline, which may be roofed over by two slabs of equal length, meeting in an apex over the middle of the path. A better backwoods effect can be obtained by using, for the inside posts, two trees so trimmed as to leave but one branch on each log.

Set these logs so that their branches form a continuation of the roof line and cross over the centre of the path as they do in the illustrations.

Select six or eight logs of equal diameter and roughly point their lower ends; when they are peeled and properly trimmed they may be rolled upon a couple of other logs, called "skids." Place them on the skids with their lower or pointed ends all in line, and see that the logs themselves rest at right angles to this

Fig. 169.—The Daniel Boone gateway for bridle or foot-paths.

line. Leave a space between the two sets of logs corresponding with that to be occupied by the gate.

In other words, place the logs on the skids in the exact order and position you intend that they shall occupy when set upright.

Allow about $3\frac{1}{2}$ feet to go underground, and mark off a point on each of the outside logs which will be about 6 feet above the ground when the logs are set. Place a straight-edged board with the edge of one end at the six-foot mark, and lay it at the angle decided upon for your intended roof. Rule a line over the logs along the edge of this board from the outside to the inside posts of each set of logs.

If there is no straight-edged board handy, take a piece of thoroughly chalked cord and stretch it from point to point. When the cord is pulled up in the middle and allowed to smartly snap back in place, it will mark your logs for you as they are to be cut. The tops of the logs may now be sawed off with a cross-cut saw, as marked, or can be chopped away by an expert axe-man.

Where the Gate is to be Located

dig a trench upon each side of the pathway; make it about $3\frac{1}{2}$ feet deep, and long and wide enough to admit the lower ends of the logs. Erect the two short outside logs first, and secure them in position with temporary props. When these are exactly plumb, nail a narrow board horizontally from a point near the top of one post to a point similarly located upon the opposite post. Or you may stretch a strong cord from point to point across the intervening space; this serves as a guide by which you can keep the other posts in line.

Prop up all the posts with temporary props, and when they are seen to be plumb and in line fill in broken stones and dirt and trample or hammer it down hard and firm.

All that now remains to be done is to roof the exposed ends of the logs with slabs rounded on one side, and the gateway is ready for the hanging of the gate.

A Small Loophole

cut between the logs adds to the effect, and is suggested by the palisade appearance of the structure. Remember to peel the bark from the logs, otherwise big black ants and wood-boring beetles will infest your gateway. Sunshine and rain will tone down the too light appearance of the peeled logs, and they will assume the pleasing neutral tint so admired by artists in old post and rail fences.

I am now writing inside a log house which I built nineteen years ago of peeled logs, and it is as sound as the day it was built. Not many miles away, there are some expensive and extensive log houses, recently built of logs, with the bark being left on them for the sake of the rustic effect it gives to the edifices. As a consequence these houses are already in a lamentably worm-eaten condition, while mine is good for a hundred years to come.

The Davy Crockett Gateway,

shown in the next illustration (Fig. 170), is extremely simple in design and construction, but it nevertheless makes quite an imposing and decidedly unique entrance for a driveway. Its form suggests a Japanese origin, but this is purely accidental, as the design was evolved from actual experiments with some logs.

As the illustration shows, the Crockett gateway consists of a belfry made of the reversed crotch of a tree, supported by a short horizontal log, which rests upon four short uprights pegged or spiked to a long horizontal log supported by two log posts, one on either side of the driveway. The tops of the two post logs are cut wedge-shape and fit into suitable notches upon the under side of the horizontal cross log, and are further secured by long,

Fig. 170.—The Davy Crockett is most appropriate for a camp or preserve.

wooden pegs driven into auger holes bored through the top of the horizontal log into the top ends of the uprights. The auger holes should be a trifle smaller than the pegs, so that it requires some force to drive the pegs home; but not sufficiently so to split the logs.

The first horizontal log may be elevated a sufficient height to admit a load of hay or a top coach. Fasten the four half logs in place, which support the shorter horizontal piece, with wooden pegs or iron spikes, and peg the ends of the forks of the belfry in a similar manner.

Wherever directions are given for the use of wooden pegs, suitable iron bars and bolts or iron spikes may be substituted by the builder, but he will then sacrifice a degree of the sentiment and charm only present when one creates a thing from the crude natural material.

It may be thought that the bell itself is open to the same objection as iron spikes, but it must be remembered that the belfry is built to hold the bell, and that the latter is no more a part of the structure than the contents of a box are part of the box itself. The bell cord can be arranged to suit the ideas of the individual builder. In the illustration it hangs to one side in easy reach of any visitor who wishes to announce his arrival. Built with reduced proportions, the Davy Crockett gateway is just as appropriate for a bridle-path or foot-path.

If the next illustration (Fig. 171) is Oriental in form, this is also the result of accident, for the Simon Kenton portal is as purely American as the man for whom it is named, and was developed by sundry experiments with the materials found in our native forests. Even the grotesque heads terminating the ridge plank were not suggested by Oriental dragons, but by the prow of a Northwestern American Indian's dug-out canoe.

Fig. 171.—The Simon Kenton gateway makes a really imposing and dignified entrance.

Build stone foundations for your log piers, starting them below the frost line in trenches dug for that purpose. If laid upon the top of the ground, it is possible that the upheaval caused by frost and sun may make leaning towers of your piers or even upset the entire gateway.

Make the base wall about 6 by 6 feet and lay the stones "dry" —that is, without the use of mud, mortar or cement. First lay a lot of broken stone in the bottom of the trenches, upon which lay the foundation. If your foundation rocks tilt or rock at the touch, use splinters or thin fragments of stone to bolster up the movable ends until the stones are firm in their beds. The flat, thin fragments used for this purpose are called "levelers" by country dry-wall builders. Lay the next layer of stones over the first, being careful that they break joints—that is, that the spaces between the top layer of stones nowhere correspond with similar spaces below. Continue in this way until your walls are 8 or 12 inches above ground. By the use of "levelers" make the stones firm enough to walk over without displacing them.

To guide you in building, and to insure straight inside lines to your gateway, erect a temporary structure, with two by four timbers for the four uprights, marking the four inside corners of your gateway. Hold these guide-posts in position by nailing diagonal boards from the tops of one set to the bottoms of the other set of two by fours, crossing in the middle of the driveway like an X. Connect the end posts together in the same manner, so as to form a sort of box with X sides and two by fours at the corners.

The outside corners of the log tiers may be marked by lines stretched from pegs in the ground to cross poles fastened to your temporary structure. Cut four logs to fit the foundations on each side of the driveway; lay two logs on opposite sides of one foundation and two logs on top of these, crossing them at right angles, and mark the places where they are to be notched with the axe. Make a U-shaped notch in the bottom log and a re-

Fig. 172.—The plank and the pattern.

versed U-shaped notch in the top log to fit over it. When the top of the piers is reached, use skids to roll the big logs in place.

Fig. 172 is a diagram of the ridge plank for the roof; the full lines show the form of the plank, the dash and dot lines the places to saw, and the small dots the outlines to cut or engrave with a gouge. Saw from A to B, from

Fig. 173.—Set a post this way and it will not decay.

C to D, from K to L, and from M to N, then saw slits from O to E, from P to F, from R to G and from S to H. It will be now comparatively simple, using a rip saw, to saw from T to E F G H and J, and your ridge plank only needs the artistic touch of the gouge to fit it to be put in place as is shown by Fig. 174.

You can now make your purlins, rafters, end and side plates, and nail them together, as in Fig. 174; nail the roof frame fast to the top of your gateway and shingle it with large hand-split shingles, if obtainable; if not, use the machine-made shingles of commerce. You understand that, in shingling, the bottom layer is first nailed in place, and the second layer overlaps and breaks joints with the first, the third with the second, and so on to the top.

There are numerous methods in use to preserve timber which is to be embedded in the ground, and burning the ends until they are protected by a coating of charcoal is one;* but locust posts take years to rot, and chestnut lasts a long time without the use of artificial preservatives.

For those interested in building a gateway to last forever and a day, it may be stated that timber well drained and well aired is

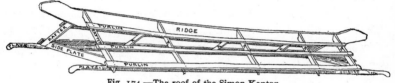

Fig. 174.—The roof of the Simon Kenton.

in a condition to last an indefinite time. Fig. 173 shows a log pier and gate posts embedded in a "dry" stone wall, so arranged that the air reaches all parts and yet there is no place to hold moisture.

By this arrangement your grandchildren can play under the gateway erected while you yourself were but a youth.

* This method is only to be used on well-seasoned timber; on green timber this will close the pores and augment fermentation, inducing rapid decay.

CHAPTER XV

HOW TO BUILD INDOOR PLAY HOUSES, SECRET CASTLES AND HOW TO MAKE MYSTERIOUS TREASURE CHESTS

Making a Play House Out of Packing-Cases

One of the most delightful memories of my boyhood days is that of a certain three-story house, built in a back yard in Cincinnati. Each story was composed of dry goods boxes or, as they are called, east of the Alleghany Mountains, packing cases. There were no stairways and no doors or windows to this wonderful structure, for the house was made of open front boxes piled one on top of the other, and the top stories were only reached by means of a chair from which the tenants could clamber into the open fronts. Upstairs the fronts were protected by brilliant red curtains made from the discarded tester of an antique four-poster bedstead; but in those days there were no grown-up boys to write and make diagrams for us little chaps, telling us how to build more ambitious houses. Nevertheless we managed to worry along in our own primitive way and had lots of fun in our box houses with barrel chimneys.

The great three-story house was not supplied with fireplaces nor stoves and the chimney was only added for artistic effect.

The lower box was our drug store and filled with bottles of wonderful lotions and liquids; some made of poke berry juice was put in transparent bottles, placed on a board which answered for the window sill. The bright red fluid, in our minds, corresponded to the red stuff always to be seen in drug store windows.

On the rude shelves inside were bottles containing licorice water, made by shaking up some Ohio River water with a bit of licorice candy. This was two pins a swallow. Then there was rose water, made of fresh rose leaves well shaken up with sugar and water, five pins per swallow, and there were decoctions of a like character which well developed imagination made desirable drinks, but the ingredients of which are lost, buried under other rubbish in the store room of my memory and are probably best forgotten, as none of these things agree with our modern sanitary ideas. But the contents of the bottles were too precious for us to take more than a sip or two at a time, and this fact may have had something to do with our robust health. Or it may be that our business instincts prevented us from consuming our own wares; at any rate, we had a great time in our little shop, and business was so brisk that our coats fairly bristled with their wealth of glistening pins which we received in exchange for sips of the various concoctions. The poke berry juice was not used for drink, as every youngster knew that these berries were not fitted to human digestion and might produce serious results; but they also knew that the brilliant red juice made a very ornamental and pretty liquid and when mixed with water and placed in transparent glass bottles presented a very imposing appearance in our drug store window.

Our open-front house was left undisturbed in the back yard until the cook ran short of kindling wood, when it was demolished and split up into small pieces to start the kitchen fire.

Very few of the boys to-day would be pleased with such a primitive edifice, and to satisfy their more advanced ideas in architecture there are here given a number of devices and plans for indoor club houses, play houses or secret castles, with hidden rooms, mysterious chests, moving panels and other mysteries in which all boys delight, a boyish fancy which has been shared by many full-grown men and supplied quaint romances to enliven the pages of history.

An Alcove Play House

If there is a recess or an alcove in your attic, barn or stable, your work as builder of a play house is much simplified, as Fig.

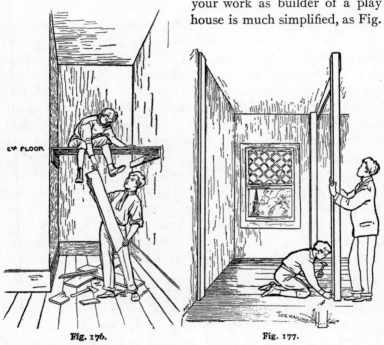

Fig. 176.   Fig. 177.

176 shows; but if the available room for your play house is square and without offsets, odd corners and recesses, you can build a house by erecting a corner post as in Fig. 177, and nailing the bottom to the floor by driving the nails in the sides of the

post near the bottom at such an angle that they will go down diagonally and enter the floor so as to hold the bottom of the post in place. If the walls are plastered find the studs by tapping with your hammer and nail your boards to the solid timber.

The Sidings

will keep the top in place, and even the bottom, too, but if the floor is a rough one which nails will not injure, the post had better be secured by nails. It should be understood that the better the material you have the better the house will be; but nevertheless it is not really necessary to go to the lumber-yard for boards, for I have noticed that on election nights the city boys all seem to be possessed of a wealth of barrels to be used for bonfires, and this they acquire by foresight and economy in saving such material for the occasion.

In Fig. 176 there are two side-cleats nailed to the walls to support the flooring of the second story.

If you build

Fig. 178.

A Two-Story House

you will want something to support the floor so that the weight of the boys upon it will not endanger the structure. If your lumber is mainly short boards from packing-boxes the upright

supports may be made of numerous pieces fitted one on top of
the other and nailed to the wall as shown in Fig. 178; but you
will need a long piece for an upright to support the joist shown
under the boy's foot in Fig. 179.   An opening is necessary for the stairs to reach
the second story.

Fig. 180 shows how to
break the box to pieces

Without Splitting the Boards

which compose it.   This is
done by putting a small board

Fig. 180.

2ⁿᵈ FLOOR

HATCH

WINDOW

DOOR WAY

A

THIS IS THE WAY
TO KNOCK A BOARD
OFF WITHOUT SPLITTING IT

B

Fig. 179.   Fig. 181.

edgewise at the joint of the boards on box and hammering on this
board rather than directly in the box.   When you have loosened
the board at one end turn the box over and loosen the other end,

and in this manner you can not only remove the planks without injuring the wood but you can also save the nails.

One of the most interesting parts about building a concealed castle for a play house will be

Captain Kidd's Treasure-Chest

For this may be used any sort of box which is large enough to hold a boy or two without interfering with the closing of the lid. One like that shown in Fig. 181 will do for the treasure-chest, but one end of it must be removed and supplied with a moving panel in place of the original end of the box. If you are making a play house a space must be left for a window (see Fig. 179), and the doorway should be made a little higher than in the diagram.

The second story can have two windows. A few cleats nailed to the wall under the hatchway will answer for stairs by which to ascend to the second story. Strips of wood nailed along the sides of the lower floor-supports up to the ceiling will be needed to hold the nails of the fronts of the boards.

So far I have described a very simple sort of house, yet if it is well done it will be a very pretty little two-story building in which you may have lots of fun. If you are so fortunate as to possess good lumber and tools this miniature house may be made as perfect as your own home.

The Concealed Castle

is essentially a boy's house, but it is also a most useful contrivance for a permanent camp or country cottage, which is left closed during the winter, for experience has proved that for some unoccupied houses secret closets are safer than locks and bars. To build the castle we proceed as I have already described.

You will notice in Figs. 176 and 179 that in the case of the uprights nailed against the wall, the distance they are placed back, just corresponds with the thickness of the front planks; this is done so that when the front is put on the building it will be flush with the wall where 2d floor is marked on the diagram. In the castle we need but a small doorway, as shown in Fig. 184—only high enough for boys to creep through on their hands and knees.

How to Make a Chest

Fig. 182.—The mysterious treasure chest.

If you have no ready-made chest, one may be built as shown in Fig. 182, to which, of course, it is necessary to attach a lid with hinges of some kind. In this case the bigger the iron hinges you use, the more appropriate they will be, but short sections of trunk-straps, or pieces of leather cut from old shoes, will make good enough hinges. You will see by referring to Fig. 182, that the open end of the chest corresponds with the door to the castle.

This doorway must be closed by

A Swinging Door,

which is the secret panel we read so much about in old romances. The panel is composed simply of a few boards neatly nailed together so that they will correspond with the end of the chest, and the battens which hold the boards together (Fig.183) are upon the inside of the castle, which leaves the smooth surface for the inside of the chest.   This door is hung to the top of the doorway by leather hinges nailed over from the inside of the castle so that they will not be visible from the inside of the treasure-chest.

The Drop

for the hatchway is hinged either to the wall, as shown in Fig. 184, or to the floor.   This is arranged so that, if by chance an outsider should be able to penetrate the secret of the treasure-box, he would not know when he got inside the lower room of the castle that there was a second story to the building.   To make the concealment perfect it is necessary that the fronts of the castle correspond with the adjoining wall, and if this wall is of plaster it must be covered with wall-paper, building-paper, or manila paper, which must extend over on to the wall of the building, thus giving no hint that there is a concealed alcove there.   To do this properly it may be necessary to stretch muslin over the board front of the castle and paste your wall-paper upon it, but if the walls of the building are of boards the front of the castle may be made of boards to correspond with those in the wall, or, if it is in a barn where the walls are rough and will not be damaged, the strips of manila paper or old newspaper may be tacked over, running across from the solid wall over the secret rooms.

How to Play Pirate

Suppose a party of friends come to your house and you tell them that in your loft or attic you have discovered a treasure-chest which once belonged to the famous Captain Kidd. Take the boys up and show them the chest.   Lift the lid and display the treasures, which consist of a number of shot-bags, salt-bags or other small bags, which may be secured from the cook or from the grocery store, filled with sand, and tied at the top with a string. Some large amounts in dollars are marked upon the outside in ink. You tell the others that these represent bags of gold-dust, but they must not be allowed to examine the treasure, for it is watched over by

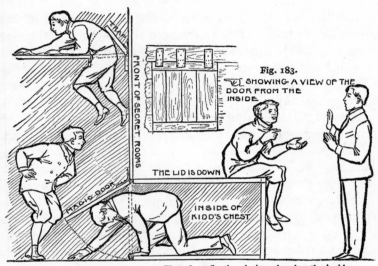

Fig. 183.—The secret door.   Fig. 184.—Sectional view showing the inside.

Captain Kidd's Men

While talking you close down the lid of the chest and seat yourself upon it.

Previous to the coming of the guests to the loft some of the boys in the secret have concealed themselves in the castle, and in red woolen caps, false whiskers and hair, are ready to do the pirate act; so while you sit upon the lid of the box as many as the chest will hold creep in from the castle and crouch there all unknown to the assembled guests. At a signal given by the boys inside you get up from the chest and open the lid again; to the amazement of the rest, up pop the heads of some fierce-looking pirates. At this you yourself must pretend to be very much astonished, and, grasping the lid of the box, force the pirates down into their place, and again seat yourself upon the lid and explain to the company that this thing happened because some one of the company coveted the gold in that chest; otherwise the pirates would not have made their appearance. After you have given the boys time to crawl into the castle again you may show the empty chest. Pirates and treasure have all disappeared.

CHAPTER XVI

HOW TO CAMP OUT IN YOUR BACK YARD

As we cannot all live in the country I am going to tell you how to camp out in your own back yard.

The first thing necessary for

A Real Camp

is the camp fire. But our fire is not to be a fiercely-blazing bon-fire, endangering the lives of the children; no, only a safe little fire

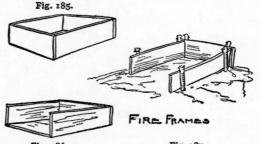

Fig. 185.

Fig. 186.   Fig. 187.
Boards or box; either will answer the purpose.

used for cooking our camp food. To make it doubly safe for the back yard and to prevent all danger of the fire spreading in the dry grass I have invented for your use the Tecumseh camp stove.

Take any old box (Fig. 185) and knock out one end of it (Fig. 186). Then fill it with earth, leaving a pit or fire hole, like the V-shaped hole shown in Fig. 188, and your camp stove is ready for use. Or take three pieces of board (Fig. 187), set them up on edge and hold them in place with some stakes driven into the ground; fill in with dirt or mud and mould it as shown by the plan (Fig. 188) and the elevation (Fig. 189), then build your fire in the pit.

Fig. 188.—Notice that the pit or fire hole is bigger at one end than the other.

You will notice that the pit or fire hole is bigger at one end than at the other. This is in order that the small vessels, such as the coffee-pot or tea-kettle, may rest over the fire at the narrow end, and the larger ones, like the frying-pan, may be set at the broad end. Both the big and the little cooking pots and pans may rest over the fire, bridging it so to speak, with no danger of falling into the fire hole.

The Gypsy Crane

is made by driving two forked sticks on each side of the fireplace and resting a stick horizontally in the forks of the uprights from which to hang the pot-hooks.

Fig. 189.—The fireplace in use.

To Make a Pot-Hook

take an old stick with branches on it (Fig. 190). Trim off all but one branch (Fig. 191), drive a nail in the other end, as in Fig. 192, then hang it on the gypsy crane in the manner shown by Fig. 193.

Or take two sticks like the one shown in Fig. 191, cut them

off diagonally, as in the upper diagram (Fig. 194), and then nail them together after the manner shown by the lower diagram (Fig. 194), and you will have a real rustic pot-hook.

Of course, rustic sticks are not always obtainable in a large city, but in that case any stick will do with two nails, one at each end, in place of the branches.

Now that you have

A Camp Fire,

all that you need in the way of utensils is a few old tin pie-plates, some kitchen knives, forks and spoons, one or two lard-cans for pots, and a fry-ing-pan—and you are ready to bake beans, fry flapjacks, roast potatoes, and live on real camper's fare.

If the kitchen knives and forks which I have suggested are too civilized for you—

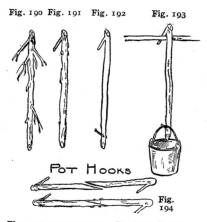

Fig. 190 Fig. 191   Fig. 192   Fig. 193

Pот Hooкs

Fig. 194

Figs. 190, 191; 192, 193.—Pot-hook in process of making.

Fig. 194.—Pot-hook made of two sticks.

that is, if they are not suggestive enough of Robinson Crusoe or the Swiss Family Robinson—you can use your ingenuity in carving some wooden forks from soft pine, cedar, or apple-wood. Hanging on my studio wall is a most beautifully-made wooden knife, and a fork to match it, manufactured by some boys away in the mountains of Kentucky. There is also a large hickory fork for mashing potatoes, made by an ancestor of some of the Long Island people, and I have several wooden spoons and ladles which were made by Americans a hundred years or more ago, whittled out of wood with jack-knives.

Now, what the boys in the mountains of Kentucky can do without the aid of modern tools, and what our great-grandfathers did with their jack-knives, should be a simple task for the up-to-date twentieth-century lad. Take a kitchen fork for a pattern and your pocket-knife and see what you can do.

To Build Your Fire

do not use any paper; there is no paper in the forests, and your camp in the back yard is, we are playing, in the wilderness. In

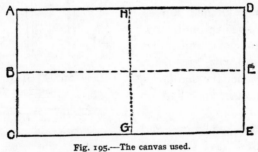

Fig. 195.—The canvas used.

place of paper whittle some shavings from a dry stick and bunch them together in the fire hole; then split some small sticks, make them about eight inches long, and as thick as your finger, cut their edges as if you were going to make some more shavings, but leave the shavings adhering to the sticks. Place these sticks together in the fire hole over the shavings and place them so that they will form a wigwam—so that their bottom ends will spread in a rough circle and their top ends meet. Now light a match and ignite the shavings, and when the fire is blazing, carefully add small, dry pieces of wood until all is burning merrily.

A Good Cooking Fire

should have more hot coals than flame, so you must feed the fire constantly until the fire hole is filled with glowing embers, and then you may put on the frying-pan or kettle, or both. With this fire you can cook almost anything that can be cooked in the kitchen range; it is splendid for popcorn, better than any stove or range for baking beans, and when

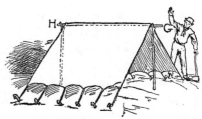

Fig. 196.—A simple form of tent.

green corn makes its appearance the hot coals will roast the corn to perfection.

By having

A Hot Fire,

then scooping out the hot coals, saving them hot, and lining the fire hole with green corn husks, you can make an oven for parching corn as the Indians did. These coals will cook almost anything if you place it on the green corn husks and then cover it with more

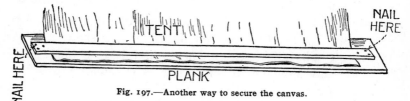

Fig. 197.—Another way to secure the canvas.

green husks, and on the top of these put the hot coals which you scooped from the fireplace before lining it; break and spread them, cover the top with fine ashes, and leave them to do the cooking.

It takes time to cook in this way, but the beauty of it is that your stove needs no care, and after the coals are heaped in place you may go to bed, if you want to, and in the morning find a hot breakfast awaiting you.

A Tent

will be a great addition to the comfort of your camp, but, lacking one, you can make a shelter of poles nailed together in the form of a tent and shingled with barrel-staves. Barrel-staves have very much the appearance of the rived shingles which the wood-men rive or split from logs. They call them "shakes," "clap-boards" or "splits," according to the locality. But if you have a piece of awning, canvas, old sail or similar material you may

Fig. 198.—A shelter tent from the same canvas.

improvise a tent. Suppose the piece is of the form of Fig. 195; it can be thrown over the clothes-line, or a clothes-line prop may be used, supported at each end by forked sticks, and the canvas pegged down at sides, as is shown in Fig. 196. In case there are no eyelets to which to attach tent-ropes and you do not wish to injure the material, the sides may be secured by allowing them to rest upon a plank and fastening them there with a strip of wood nailed over the canvas, as shown in Fig. 197. You will notice that the nails in this case are driven in at the ends of the strip only, and they cannot injure the piece of awning.

Fig. 198 shows another manner of building a shelter tent of this same piece of cloth. Now, if you will cut a piece of writing-paper in the form of Fig. 195, fold it in the middle horizontally along the line B E and crease it, then smooth it out again and fold in the same manner and crease it at G H, the creases will, of course, correspond with the dotted lines B E and G H. Next

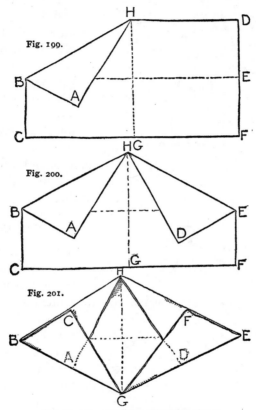

Fig. 199.

Fig. 200.

Fig. 201.

The steps in making the third kind of tent.

fold the corner A over so that the folded edge makes a straight line from B to H (Fig. 199). Do the same with the corner D so that the folded edge makes a straight line fiom E to H; then

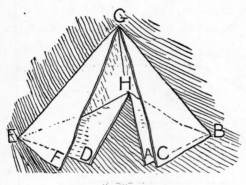

Fig. 202.—The paper tent.

fold up the lower corners C and F, as in Fig. 201, and you will find that you have a little paper tent with a carpeted floor; that is, you will have one after you have taken up the diamond-shaped Fig. 201 and loosened the folds as they are in Fig. 202, after which bring A and D together, and F and C will meet and form the front of the tent, the slit between C G and F G forming the doorway.

What can be done with paper can be done

With Canvas,

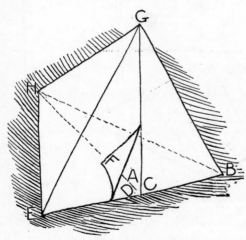

Fig. 203.—You may make a tent of canvas like the one of paper.

but, of course, the latter will not hold its form as paper does unless it has a frame of some sort to support it; so, after you have folded your piece of canvas (Fig. 195) in the form of Fig. 201, measure the line, B G or E G, and cut two sticks about 1 foot longer than these lines (see B G and E G, Fig.

204), join the sticks with a wire nail so as to form a crotch at G (Fig. 204) and drive the ends E and B into the earth until the part left above will correspond with the length of E G and G B (Fig. 203). The distance between these sticks where they enter

Fig. 204.—The tent frame of three poles.

the ground must not be greater than the distance E B of Fig. 203. Indeed, all these distances on the framework should be an inch or two less than on the cover, so as to insure a fit.

Now rest your clothes-line prop in the notch at G and you will have the frame complete. The advantage of this tent is that no nails or holes are necessary in the cover, and when the camping season is over the cover may be removed uninjured.

CHAPTER XVII

HOW TO MAKE A REAL HUNTER'S CLOTHES AND MOCCASINS

If the President of the United States can go camping with the boys, why should not all American men who can get a week off follow his example? Many boys are so young that their parents may object to their camping alone, but there can be no objections if the father of some one of the boys goes with them to teach them woodcraft and keep them under his eyes, and it is safe to say that the man who volunteers to take a bunch of boys camping will have the time of his life, and the boys will help him enjoy himself.

A Uniform

Boys are dead in earnest about appropriate uniforms. Although the author has written personal letters to dozens of lads, every mail is still loaded with requests for patterns by which to make Boone hunting shirts. So the writer has taken his own buckskin shirt and made patterns from it which are here given, with notes telling how to put the shirt together.

When buckskin can be obtained it is more like the real thing; nevertheless the hunters in Boone's days often wore homespun shirts of blue or butternut color, and some even wore plaids.

Select the color you wish and have your mothers, aunts, grand-mothers or big sisters cut two pieces for

The Front

like Fig. 185. Take care that the edge A is the selvedge

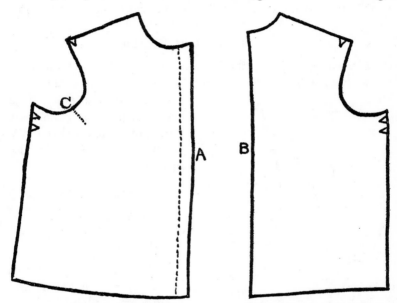

Fig. 185.—Pattern of the front of the shirt.

Fig. 186.—Pattern for the back of the hunting shirt.

of the goods, and allow for the seam, as shown by the dotted line along the edge A. Make

The Back

of the shirt by folding a piece lengthwise of the goods at B (Fig. 186), and then cutting it the form of that pattern.

The Sleeves

are each made of two pieces, Figs. 187 and 188, cut lengthwise of the goods.

The Cape

should be folded on the dotted line and cut as per pattern (Fig. 189).

To Put the Shirt Together

First baste together the front piece (Fig. 185) and the back piece (Fig. 186) in such a manner that the points on the shoulders (marked with a notch or a V) fit together, and the seam under the arms marked VV on Fig. 185 and Fig. 186, also fit together.

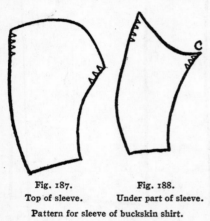

Fig. 187.
Top of sleeve.

Fig. 188.
Under part of sleeve.

Pattern for sleeve of buckskin shirt.

To Sew the Sleeves

Fit the back of the sleeves marked VVVV of Fig. 187 and Fig. 188 together and the front of the sleeve pieces marked VVV together and baste them in place.

To Fit the Sleeves to the Shirt

place the point marked C on Fig. 188 exactly over C on Fig. 185 on the front piece of the shirt and baste it in place. Do the same with the other sleeve, which is of course a duplicate of the one shown in the diagram and is basted to the other front half, which is also a duplicate of Fig. 185.

The Cape

can now be stitched around the neck of the shirt and the garment
tried on to see how it fits.

The Material

may be of outing cloth,
either dark blue or buck-
skin color. Of course it
is understood that

The Fringe

(Fig. 190) must be sewed
in the back seam of the
sleeves, and in the side
seams of the shirt; it is
inserted as shown by Figs.

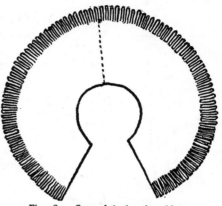

Fig. 189.—Cape of the hunting shirt.

191, 192, 193, 194. Fig. 191 shows the inside of one piece of cloth;
Fig. 192 the outside of the other piece; Fig. 193 a bit of fringe,
and Fig. 194 shows the bit of fringe in the seam between the two
pieces of cloth. F and G on Figs. 191 and 192 are the same as
F and G on Fig. 194, and H, the top of the fringe on Fig. 193,
is the same in Fig. 194. In
these last diagrams the cloth
is not shown stitched, but
loose, so as to more plainly
indicate just how the fringe is
inserted in the seams. Your

Fig. 190.—The fringe is a characteristic
part of a hunter's costume.

mother will know how to sew it. The sewing may be done on
the sewing machine, and after it is finished according to directions the bottom of the shirt may be neatly hemmed and fringe

sewed on the under side, or the bottom may be cut into a fringe or left with only the hem, to suit the taste, but all of the same club must be alike. A leather strap belt with buckle or a sash may be worn about the waist. As for leggings, they may be purchased at the store and the fringe added by your mother.

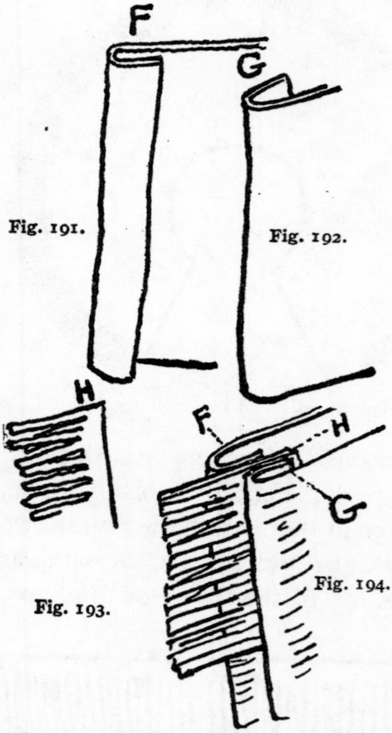

If you choose blue shirts let the fringe be yellow, because that was always the color of the fringe on the old backwoodsmen's shirts.

The shirt may have ordinary cuffs, with buttons, and button up in front like a coat.

How to Make Buckskin Leggings

Take your pattern from a pair of close-fitting drawers and sew the fringe inside the outer seams (Fig. 195), as shown in the diagrams of the buckskin shirt (Fig. 194). Leave the bottom of the leggings slit up for 5 or 6 inches (Figs 195 and 197). This is to allow you to slip your foot through when putting them on.

Fig. 191.

Fig. 192.

Fig. 193.

Fig. 194.

This is the way to insert the fringe in a seam.

Have each leg separate, as shown in Fig. 197, and sew two stout loops at the top for the belt which supports them to run through. They will fit on over your other trousers, if necessary, or may be worn as shown by Fig. 196, and the waist part covered up by the hunting shirt as shown in the full dress figure (Fig. 195). These leggings being tight and cut to the shape of the limbs will support themselves in a measure and a belt is all that is necessary to keep them in proper position.

Fig. 195. Fig. 196. Fig. 197.
Fig. 195.—In full pioneer's costume. Fig. 196.—How the leggings are put on.
Fig. 197.—The leggings are cut like a cowboy's leather chaps.

How to Make Your Own Moccasins

The different Indian tribes all have their own tribal way of building or making a moccasin. Some have the soles cut the shape of the foot, with others the toes are as pointed as were the toes of a society man's shoes a few years ago, and in still others the toe is rounded, and there are just as many varieties of styles to the tops of the moccasin.

The ordinary moccasins known to the general public is the

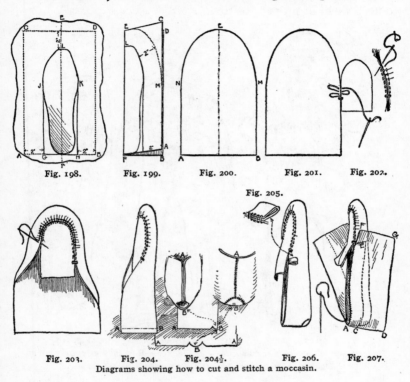

Fig. 198.   Fig. 199.   Fig. 200.   Fig. 201.   Fig. 202.

Fig. 205.

Fig. 203.   Fig. 204.   Fig. 204½.   Fig. 206.   Fig. 207.
Diagrams showing how to cut and stitch a moccasin.

style worn by the Canadian Indians and these are not difficult even for a boy to make.

First put your foot down on a piece of paper and make a pattern of it by drawing a line around it with a pencil, as shown by Fig. 198. Then draw a line E F through the centre and parallel to the centre line draw two lines, J G and K H. Next measure 2 inches from each side and draw the lines A C and A B respectively 2 inches from J K and K H. Two inches above the toe draw the line C D connecting J G and K H; you will now have a parallelogram A C, D B. Fold this along the centre line E F as in Fig. 199. Then with the scissors cut a curve around the toe, keeping about 2 inches from the pattern of the foot, as shown by the curved line from M to E. When the paper is unfolded you will have the pattern E N A B M (Fig. 200).

For the top of the moccasin you need a smaller piece of material of the same shape as E N A B M. This piece forms the tongue of the moccasin as well as its top. Roughly speaking, it will be about half the length of the foot. If you place your stockinged foot on the pattern that you have made and carefully fold the paper up and around and over the foot you will see that the space across the foot between the edge of the paper on each side will be that which the small piece of paper is to fill. But to get the width of the small piece it is better to take a piece of tape and measure around the ball of the foot and up over the top, then measure the width of the piece from M to N and the difference between the two measurements is the width of the small piece. You need a small awl, a darning needle and some waxed shoemaker's thread with which to do your work.

Put the small piece edge to edge with the large piece in such a manner that the point where each begins to curve coincide with each other, as shown in Fig. 201, and punch three holes close together with the awl through the edges of both pieces. Through these run the thread under and over as in Fig. 201, then punch three or more holes, as shown in Fig. 202, and sew it, running the needle in and out. This will bring you to the curves of the two pieces of leather, after which the toe of the moccasin is crimped. This

you can do by taking a stitch in the sole piece E N A B M twice
as long as the one in the small piece, as shown by Figs. 202 and
203.   If this is done carefully there will, of course, be exactly
the same number of crimps on each side of the foot and you will
end just opposite where you took the three stitches in the first
place and where you will take three more stitches and end with
the overlapping tie as shown in Fig. 202.

Now you have the front part of the foot of the moccasin complete and it is necessary to sew up the heel.

Fig. 208.

SUMMER

WINTER
Fig. 209.
The two best known styles of
moccasin.

After the front of the moccasin is
sewed up slip your foot in it and
catch it up at the heel to fit your foot;
say A B (Fig. 204) is the line, then
cut away the surplus along this line.
To make the heel of the moccasin,
round off to fit the heel of the foot,
notch the material on each side of B
as in the diagram Fig. 204½, after which
sew up the line A B by an over and
over stitch.   This leaves an opening
at the heel, but when you have turned
up the rounded part B, and stitched
it in place (Fig. 204½), you will have a good house slipper (Fig.
206).   To this the flap A D G F can now be sewed with an
overhand stitch, if the moccasin is for winter wear (Fig. 207).
But if for summer use a smaller flap like the one shown by the
dotted line C E (Fig. 207).   The diagrams Figs. 208 and 209
show the summer and winter moccasins when finished.

The right and left foot moccasin do not differ from each other
and are in fact duplicates; the material being soft they take the
form of the foot.   Some of the western Indians make their moc-

casins as we make our shoes, rights and lefts, but it is not necessary for the amateur to try that; the style here described has been proved by centuries of trial to be a good one. All the seams should be pounded or hammered flat.

To half-sole a moccasin cut a piece of leather the shape of the foot but considerably larger (Fig. 210). Punch the holes at A B C D with an awl and run a thong through these holes and the sole of the moccasin to hold them temporarily in place, then

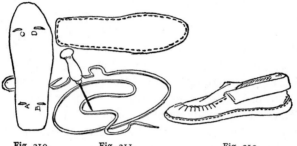

Fig. 210.   Fig. 211.   Fig. 212.
An extra sole on a moccasin will make it wear better.

take another long thong, point one end of it and using the awl to make the holes and the pointed end of the thong for a needle stitch on the soles, as shown by Fig. 211. Beginning at the toe sew both ways so that the stitches will meet at the heel, then bring the ends up above the stitching through holes punched in the moccasin and tie them in a square or reefing knot. When it is done and the moccasin put on the foot the stitching will come up on the side as in Fig. 212. Moccasins will last a long time if supported with extra soles.

CHAPTER XVIII

HOW TO BUILD BEAVER-MAT HUTS, CAMPS AND COTS, FAGOT HOUSES, ROADS AND FENCES

Ever since our arboreal ancestors with prehensile toes scampered among the branches of the pre-glacial forest, men have built brush shelters for camps or temporary refuge, and I make no claim to inventing this time-honored style of forest home. The truth is that no contrivance of any description is ever invented at once in its entirety, but everything is evolved from something else, everything grows. Not only is this true of plants, animals, and men, but it also holds good with men's clothes, tools, and houses; all are products of evolution.

Our birds never invented their wonderful nests, they have but modified and improved the cruder nests of their more undeveloped ancestors.

So the brush huts here given, while new themselves, are evolved from the shacks and camps familiar to every one who visits our north woods, and the application of the beaver-mat and the mat itself is new; so, also, is the use of the bundles of fagots to make the core of the walls of the adobe house here described.

Figs. 198, 199 and 200 show the simple frame work of the well-known open Adirondack camp; Fig. 198, shows one where two standing trees have been made to do duty as corner posts for the lean-to. Fig. 199, shows the same form of shelter with two forked sticks planted in the ground in place of the growing trees of the first diagram, and Fig. 200, is simply a profile view of same.

These camps are shingled with birch bark, spruce bark, or covered with brush. Even a novice can cut birch bark, but might fail to get the same results from the spruce tree. Let the beginner hunt through the woods for a comparatively smooth spruce tree, and when a suitable one is found, cut a ring around the bottom and another about 5 feet above the first; then cut a perpendicular slit connecting the two rings; it is now a simple matter to peel off the section of bark by the careful use of the

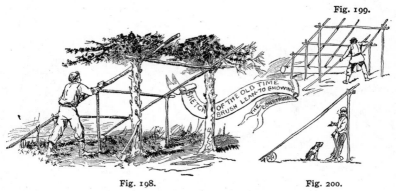

Fig. 199.

Fig. 198.   Fig. 200.
Loose brush is used in the old time camp.

hatchet and the help of a comrade to hold on to the edge of the bark.

In this way enough pieces can soon be secured to roof the shack, but it is to be supposed that you know all this and also how to lay the bark, beginning at the bottom and working up, so that each layer overlaps the lower one and breaks joints with the ones below it; also, it is to be supposed that you know how to weigh down the bark with poles laid from the ground at intervals so that their top ends protrude over the open front of the camp. Loose brush is used in the old-time camp to set up against and inclose the two ends of the shack, leaving the broad front open.   This is the well-known Adirondack camp of former days, now generally superseded by structures of similar form built of logs, but unless logs are used, a much neater, more durable and a better protection from the rain and weather can be obtained by building

A Camp of Beaver Mats

similar in form to the one shown by Figs. 198, 199 and 200.   The roof, by the way, should be much steeper than Fig. 199 and more

Fig. 201.

Showing how to make a BEAVER-MAT for side of brush lean-to

Fig. 202.

Fig. 203.

The manner of putting the end piece together.

like that shown in the profile view of Fig. 200.   After you have erected the framework or skeleton of the camp, shown in the above diagrams, make four triangles to correspond with A B C (Fig. 201); do this by fastening the ends of three poles together (Fig. 201).

Next nail some branches from side to side of the triangle, as shown by Fig. 202, then, with the triangle flat on the ground, cover the frame with selected brush, being careful that it is placed in an orderly manner, with the tips pointing down and overhanging the stick A C, as is shown at D, Fig. 203.   Over this lay another layer of brush in the same manner (E, Fig. 203), and over the second layer put a third (F, Fig. 203), as one would shingle a house. Continue in this manner until you have a triangular mat a foot or more thick.

Next make a duplicate frame (Fig. 202), but with the cross sticks placed up and down in place of horizontal, as in Fig. 202. Fit the second triangle over the first (Fig. 204) and lash the cor-

Fig. 204.—This makes a triangular mattress.

Fig. 205.—After the mats are in place the whole thing should be thatched.

ners together, using sufficient pressure to make the mattings between the two frames hard and compact. One side of your camp is now ready to set in place, but another beaver mat must be made for the opposite side, and then both can be set up against the ends of the camp, where they were intended to fit. The roof may be made of a beaver mat of rectangular form constructed with diagonal braces, like those shown by G H F E, L M K J, or D C B A of Fig. 207.

After the mats are in place the

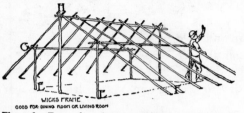

WICKS FRAME
GOOD FOR DINING ROOM OR LIVING ROOM
Fig. 206.—Frame for a large assembly room of any sort.

Whole Thing Should be Thatched

by inserting the end of a layer of small flat brush near the bottom of the mat, then one above overlapping the first and so on until the top is reached. A carefully built beaver mat lean-to, with thatch of palm leaves, if in the South; or pine, spruce, hemlock, or sweet-smelling balsam thatch, if in the North, can shield you from a hard shower of rain, and in cold weather offer a wind shield which will be appreciated by the tired hunter.

Fig. 207.—You will notice in this that the small mats leave space for a window.

It does not take long to make beaver mats, but it does require care to make good ones. However, one who loves woodcraft will love to work with the twigs of evergreen, and one who loves his task may be trusted to do good work. If the reader is indolent he had better keep out of the woods altogether, or travel with a valet and a bunch of guides, being careful to sleep only in the palatial houses paradoxically called camps. But this sort of a person will probably not read this sort of a book, and I can as-

sume that the reader loves the woods for their own sake, loves the hardships and exertion of travel and making camp, loves the glow of the camp-fire and the nights under a birch-bark roof, or even with no shelter but the trees overhead, where he can watch through the interlacing branches the twinkling of the distant camp-fires of heaven.

But even the true-hearted woodman and seasoned camper may wish to make a more artistic abode than that offered by a brush lean-to. He may expect to receive ladies at camp, his mother and sisters, for instance, possibly accompanied by some

Fig. 208.   Fig. 209.   Fig. 210.
This is a pretty window suitable for an ornamental cot.

other fellow's sister, in which case he can exercise his artistic ability by constructing

A Beaver Mat Cottage

for the ladies, which will be certain to find favor and win the feminine approval of the woods for a vacation. Fig. 205 shows a very plain and simple beaver mat hut, but one which can be embellished with quaint little hooded windows, a comfortable veranda, and as many other improvements as the time and inclination of the builder will allow.

The Wicks Frame shown by Fig. 206 is suitable for a detached open dining-room, a general camp assembly-room, or it may be made of smaller dimensions and used as a camp cottage.

The rafters (F) may be cut off just below the eaves (G), and the frame covered with beaver mats, or the sides may be used for the front and rear ends of a hut, in which case the two uprights on one side may be made tall, for the front, and the two rear ones cut short for the rear, which will give the colonial type of roof (Fig. 205), such as the old Dutchmen of New York used on their quaint dwellings, and such as may still be found on ancient houses both in New England and on Long Island.

To make the beaver mats very large is not a very practicable idea. Rather make them smaller and build your house as a

Fig. 211.—A fagot hut.

Fig. 212.—Lay up the brush as you would a stone wall.

child builds a house of blocks. Fig. 207 shows a wall of four mats with a window opening. Fig. 208 shows a bow stick, pointed at both ends, to be used for a window hood. Fig. 209 shows the framework of the hood, and Fig. 210 the hooded window when finished.

The window hood sticks are held in place simply by forcing their ends into the compact mass of the beaver mats, the hood is then thatched by forcing the ends of branches in above the window, so that the twigs rest on the hoops as the plain sticks do in Fig. 209. Over this first row of branches a shorter lot is laid with their ends thrust into the beaver mats like the first, and over these a still shorter lot until the hood is covered with a thick, green thatch.

The Fagot Hut

is built of bundles of sticks, as shown by Fig. 211, laid like a stone wall, so as to "break joints"; that is, so that the joints are never in a continuous line. The green fagots are laid between stakes, as shown in the diagram (Fig. 212), but the leaves and small branches are left adhering to the individual sticks in the bundle, although for convenience in drawing they are omitted in the diagram.

In place of mortar or cement, leaves and small branches are strewn over each layer of fagots, before the next course is laid. Fig. 213, a window opening, shows how rods are laid for a window sill; in the same manner rods are used to rest the fagots upon over the window and doorway openings. Fig. 211 shows a fagot shack finished with a beaver mat roof; when such a building is well thatched it makes a very serviceable house.

Fig. 213.—Rods are used for window sills.

One great advantage which recommends the beaver mat and fagot camps to nature lovers and students of forestry, lies in the fact that it is unnecessary to cut down or destroy a single large tree to procure the material necessary to make the camp; as a rule the lower limbs of the forest trees about you will offer sufficient material for building purposes, and these may be cut off close to the trunk without injury to the trees themselves.

Fagot Roads, Paths and Fills

offer the proprietors of permanent camps a use for the brush which accumulates when a clearing is made in the woods. By experiment I have found this to be excellent material for levelling a path or even a "tote" road.

The lower side of the hillside driveway in front of my log house in Pennsylvania I made level by adding bundles of brush weighted with stones, covered with fine loose brush, a layer of leaves and dirt. This driveway has now been in use each season for twenty years, and is still firm, hard and level.

But when one is out for a short vacation, building roads is not an occupation generally sought, especially when one may never again have occasion to use them; but it may be very necessary to fill up some dangerous crevice between rocks or some bog hole in the path near the camp, and it is well to know that this

Fig. 214.—**Water can run through the brush without spoiling the road.**

can be done in a few minutes' time, as already described with bundles of brush (Fig. 214) covered with dirt. The fagot bundles may be made of the small branches of any sort of brush, which can be trimmed into reasonably straight sticks, and bound together with bits of rope, twine, withes, the twisted inner part of chestnut or cedar, pliable roots or vines.

In making a clearing for any purpose there is always left a great accumulation of brush, which is generally disposed of by placing it in long wind rows and setting fire to it. This practice is a fruitful cause of forest fires, which do incalculable damage; but if this brush is cut into suitable lengths and bound into bundles it will be found to be useful in many ways. A most picturesque

Fagot Fence

may be built of long bundles set on end, or of short ones laid like a stone wall (Fig. 212), and such a fence offers protection against stray cattle, sheep, goats, pigs, and even dogs; besides which it can be made highly ornamental and affords the best possible support for wild or cultivated climbing vines of all kinds.

An Adobe House

may be made by daubing wet clay plentifully over the surface of an old dry beaver mat or fagot hut, which will also do away with the inflammable nature of the original structure.

AUTUMN

CHAPTER XIX

EVERY-DAY WOODCRAFT FOR EVERY-DAY PEOPLE

There is but one way to learn to do a thing and that is *to do it*. When a city-bred lad finds that he must use an axe he soon learns how to chop fire-wood without cutting off his own toes; nevertheless it is an excellent plan to keep one's feet away from the wood which is to be cut, and thus do away with the possibility of losing a toe or two and slicing up a good boot or shoe with no accommodating surgeons and shoemakers handy to sew up the cuts. But we take it for granted that the reader can swing an axe without endangering his body or his apparel, and even under these circumstances there are many other problems which must be solved by the axeman.

Suppose you need a puncheon, are building a dug-out canoe, or for any one of the many good reasons it is desirable to have a log with a flat surface in place of the original cylindrical one. To shape such a log accurately it is necessary for the novice to have a chalk line and snap it along A and B, Fig. 215; old woodmen use no chalk line but work by "sensation," that is by sight, but if you have no chalk, you may procure a substitute. If one end of a string wet with mud is held at A and the other at B, and the middle pulled up and allowed to snap back on the log it makes a mud line from A to B. The black ashes from the camp-fire may also be used to cover the string as a substitute for chalk.

To Make a Puncheon

Snap the chalk line from A to B, Fig. 215, then with the axe cut the notches C, D, E, F, G, H, J, as in Fig. 216, after which it is a simple task to split off the pieces A-C, D-E, E-F, etc., until all the blocks are cut away and you have the log as shown in Fig. 217.

If you find it necessary

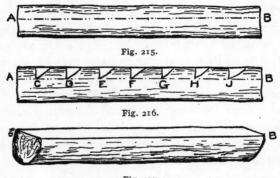

Fig. 215.

Fig. 216.

Fig. 217.

Fig. 215.—The log.   A, B the chalk line.
Fig. 216.—C, D, E, etc., the notches.
Fig. 217.—The log flattened into a puncheon.

To Chop Down a Tree

first clear away the underbrush all around within reach of the swing of your axe, otherwise it may turn your axe and you may be seriously hurt.   Also cut any vines or branches within reach overhead which might catch your axe or deflect the falling tree from its course.   But before doing this look over the ground well and in selecting the place where the tree is to fall, avoid as far as possible places where the tree is liable to lodge in the big branches of another tree as it falls, for this is always accompanied with more or less danger to the woodman and no end of trouble. Don't try to fell a tree against the wind if there is even a moderate breeze blowing at the time.

Suppose that we want the tree to fall to the right-hand side of this page; in this case the chopper cuts a notch on the right-hand side of the tree more than half way through the trunk (A, Fig. 218). Make your notch large enough to do away with the danger of wedging your axe. But if you find that the cut is going to be too small and that it is necessary

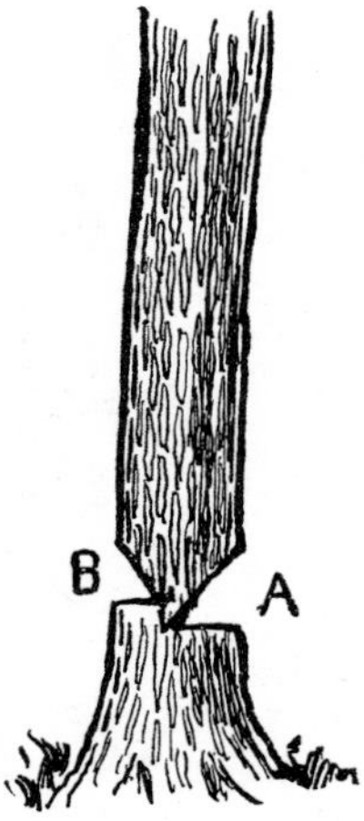

To Enlarge the Notch on a Tree

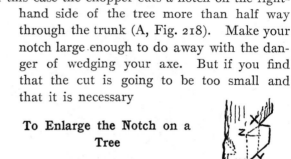

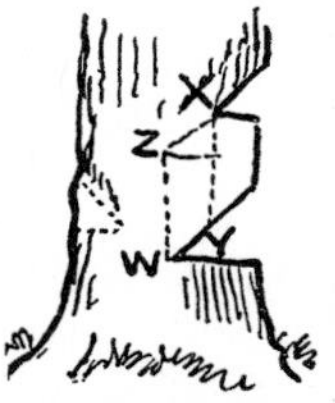

Fig. 219.—Shows how to enlarge the kerf.

Fig. 218.—Showing how to fell a tree. Tree will fall towards A.

which you are felling, use the method just described in making a puncheon. For instance, suppose that you have cut the notch Y in Fig. 219 and find it too small for your convenience; cut another notch at X (Fig. 219), and chop away the block of intervening wood by splitting it down X, Y; then cut another notch at Z and split off the block Z, X, Y, W, and you will have room to continue your cutting.

When the right-hand notch (A, Fig. 218) is finished, more than half the hard work is done and you may begin to cut the left-hand notch (B, Fig. 118) several inches higher than the first, as shown in the diagram. When the support between the right and left notch becomes too small to sustain the weight of the tree the latter will begin to waver at the top and crack at the bottom. This is the signal for you to step to one side of the tree.

By No Means Stand Behind

it as it falls, for if the bushy top lodges in another tree, the butt

Fig. 220.—The danger of standing behind the tree.

of the falling one is liable to shoot backward. This is called kicking, and many a man has lost his life from the kick of a tree (Fig. 220).

How to Make Clapboards, Splits or Shakes

Every one who has traveled in the mountain districts of the South, in the Maine woods, or in the wilderness of the Northwest, has noticed the long, rough shingles used by campers, trappers and settlers with which to roof, or even cover the sides, of their shacks. In the South these shingles are called clap-

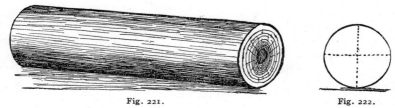

Fig. 221.

Fig. 222.

Fig. 221.—Billet for shakes.
Fig. 222.—End of billet. Dotted lines show how to split it.

boards, in Maine splits, and in the West shakes, and very handy they are for many purposes.

The best wood, when it can be had, is the white cedar, but any wood that is straight of grain and splits easily will serve the purpose. The cypress is an admirable wood, also the bass-wood, while on the Pacific coast the Murray or black pine makes a good shake. The Western cedar, the Sitkan spruce and the Douglas fir are used successfully.

Fig. 223.—Woodmen's axes.

Fig. 224.—One form of the froe.

Often the pioneer has nothing but his axe with which to work, but even then he soon becomes an expert in making splits. Select a

Good Straight-Rifted Tree

as free from knots as may be, chop it down, and cut the butt as high as the first limb into billets, 4 to 6 feet in length (Fig. 221). The small end must in each case be cut off squarely, although the larger end may be left "sniped" or pointed. Next the bark must be hewn off by short, half-arm blows with the axe, grasping the handle nearer the axe-head than one does when chopping. To make a really first-class shake, the sap-wood should be taken off, but for temporary buildings it is usually left on, and not infrequently the bark as well.

One inch is sufficient thickness for a wide shake, and half that thickness may suffice for a narrow one.

A Complete Outfit

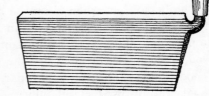

Fig. 225.—Another form of the froe.

is made up of an axe (Fig. 223), a froe, (Figs. 224 and 225) and a cross-cut saw. With the axe the tree is felled and the bark and sapwood hewn off; with the cross-cut saw (Fig. 226) the ends of the log are squared, and with the froe the shakes are peeled off one by one.

Fig. 226.—The saw.

In the case of some large logs it is often found expedient to quarter them (Figs. 222 and 229) and then cut out the heart or what corresponds to the pith, as in Fig. 230.

When camping in a rough country, it is most necessary to have a safe place for the canoe, some arrangement by which labor is saved and the danger of damage to the frail craft from

Fig. 227.

Fig. 228.

Fig. 229.

Fig. 230.

Figs. 227, 228, 229 and 230.—Various stages in the process of making shakes.

snags or stones is removed. This desirable end is obtained by the simple arrangement of two logs shown in Fig. 231 known as

Canoe Skids

which are made by resting the butt ends (M N, Fig. 231) of two small peeled logs on the bottom of the water and the upper ends

(K L) on the bank. It then is an easy matter to run the canoe over the submerged ends of the skids, turn the light craft over and push it up out of harm's way.

The skids may be made more secure by joining them on the under side by cross pieces. A boat pulled upon the bank is almost invariably scratched and more or less damaged by the process, and if it is tied to the shore a high wind may put it entirely

Fig. 231.

out of commission in one night, as the writer can vouch from actual experience; but when slid up on the canoe skids your craft is safe from anything but a sudden flood or a wind of sufficient force to lift it bodily from its bearings and blow it away.

The ordinary way

To Split a Log

is by using a wedge. You start to split with an axe at one end, and then drive the wedge into the crack, as at D, Fig. 232. The next stroke of the axe is at the end of the crack on the top of the log and this splits it open to about where E is when the wedge is driven through, as shown by the dotted line. If the log is a very large one they drive wedges in the end of the log also, so that it will split straight through and not shear off at an angle. Some sort of hard wood should be used in making the wedges, but

Fig. 232.

wedges are not absolutely necessary, for the log may be split by the use of two axes. For instance, we drive the axe in at A (Fig. 232) and leave it sunk in the crack, then drive another axe in at B; this will open A so wide that the first axe may be easily removed and driven in at C, and so on until the ends of the log are reached. In the splitting of the shakes they are sometimes split off of the quartered log, as shown by Figs. 228 and 229. This gives a long clapboard, thicker at one edge than the other, as may be seen by the diagram (Fig. 228), or they are split off "square," as shown by Fig. 227. The other figures show the log, the halved log (Fig. 227), and the quartered log (Fig. 229), with a section of the end to one side.

It sometimes happens that a vise is needed in the woods, either to hold a piece of wood to be worked or a saw which needs sharpening, and the forest furnishes the material for a

A VISE

Fig. 233.

Rustic Vise

with every tree stump. Saw the slit C A B (Fig. 233) down the stump, using a lumberman's two-handled saw for the purpose; then bind the bottom of the stump slightly with a rope and your vise is ready for use. To open the vise take a wedge D and drive it in the crack until it widens enough for your purpose, insert the saw or other object, knock out the wedge, and the wood will spring back and tightly hold whatever object you may have inserted in the opening A C.

Reckless Waste in the Woods

should not be encouraged or countenanced by any boy or man who loves nature. Our forests are as necessary to our land as hair to an animal, and a bald, treeless land is as pitiful a sight as a hairless cat.

It is unnecessary to say that the preservation of our streams is necessary to the preservation of our fish, but many of the readers may not yet have considered how intimately the preservation of our forests is connected with the preservation of our streams, and hence the very existence of many fish, especially brook trout, depends upon the preservation of the forests.

To illustrate this relationship between forests and water, make a couple of troughs, Figs. 234 and 235, line one with clay (Fig. 234) to represent the country denuded of trees, the opposite trough line with sods of grass or moss (Fig. 235) to represent the forest-clad mountain side, set them on an incline and connect their upper ends with a rough reservoir. Pour a pail of water into this reservoir and there will be a wild rush of water down

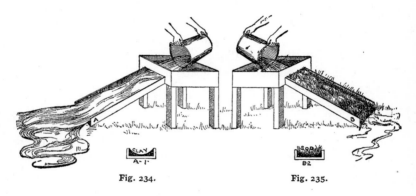

Fig. 234.   Fig. 235.

the clay-lined trough, while the moss and grass-lined one will drip for hours.

It only needs a little imagination to convert this machine into a forest-clad mountain and one denuded of timber.

The cloudburst, represented by the contents of the bucket of water suddenly poured into the top reservoir, is only a dangerous cloudburst on the barren slope. By the use of this simple device you can explain to a child the absolute necessity of preserving the forests upon the water-sheds, if we would have continuous running water, and not the certainty of flood and drought which are caused by the water-sheds being recklessly denuded of timber.

To Make a Withe

put your foot on one end of a green hickory, white oak, ash, or some similar tough sapling, and grasping the other end of the stick in your two hands twist it until the fibres of the wood or bark separate into strands and are twisted like a rope. When this is done the withe will be pliable and can be used for many purposes around camp. I had the big gate to my Pike County camp swing with hinges made of withe loops, and the hinges outlasted the gate. Young white oaks, hickory, ash, all make good withes, and in Maine the yellow birch was formerly in great demand for use in making withes, and all sorts of packages, from bales of hay, bundles of furs and household goods to the very coffins in which the people were buried, were fastened together with yellow birch withes.

A Maine correspondent to the *Sun* says that:

"It seems as if those old chaps who cleared up farms for us were associated pretty intimately with withes from the time they came into the world until they quit it for good. The hood of the cradle was made from yellow birch limbs woven in basket-work.

"The first time and every time the child went wrong he received an application of yellow birch in the place where yellow birch did most good. From early manhood to old age withes were the most useful and the most needful articles about the farm, and when death stepped in and wound up the business a sheaf of birch withes enwrapped the coffin and held it in shape until all inside had turned to dust."

Fibre Rope and Twine

Chestnut, osage, orange, buckeye, red cedar, yellow locust, slippery elm, mulberry, basswood, thistles, some kinds of milk-weeds and Indian hemp bark can be used for making twine or rope. Properly prepared these woods all furnish fibre which can be twisted into twine and braided into larger cordage. To prepare the tree bark you must remove the rough, brittle outside bark and then boil the inner bark in a solution made of fine wood ashes and water. This will make the wood fibres pliable, and when this material is dried and pounded it will separate into small, thread-like particles of considerable length.

The Indians Make Vegetable String

by twisting these fibres together. They do this by rolling them with the palm of their hand on their thigh, but it is not necessary to go into the details of twine-making here. It is sufficient to know that twine can be made of the inner bark of many trees, weeds and wild plants. I have pulled up the young tamarack trees from where they grew in a cranberry "mash" and used the long, cord-like roots for twine with which to tie up bundles. So pliable are these water-soaked roots that you can tie them in a knot with almost the same facility that you can your shoe-string. It is the small, cord-like roots of the white spruce that the Indians still use to sew the seams of their birch-bark canoes. They select roots about the size of a slate pencil, split them and soak them in water. The same roots are used for stitching together the barks which compose their wigwams and for sewing up small birch-bark utensils used for holding liquids. The Concow Indians make most excellent thread, twine or rope from the inner bark of the dried stalks of the tall bo-coak weed which grows in profusion 7,000 feet above the sea at the foot of Black Butte; but we must not expect to find this white flowering weed in Maine, Canada or down in Florida. Every section has plants of its own, the fibrous bark or roots of which can be used for cordage.

The reader must not suppose that the inside bark of the trees and plants here named is the only material which can be used to manufacture cordage at camp. There are hundreds of trees, weeds and plants which may furnish the fibres for camp rope or twine. Each section of the country has its own peculiar vegetable fibre which was known to the ancient redmen and used by them for the purposes named. Even if the writer was well enough posted to give a printed list of the names of these plants, it would occupy more space than is allotted for this story. Look for trees with long, stringy inner bark, test it and see if it can be twisted into cordage stout enough for your purpose. Dig up the trailing roots of young firs or other saplings suitable for your purpose; coil the green roots and bury them under a heap of hot ashes from your camp-fire, and there allow them to steam in their own sap for an hour, then take them out, split them into halves and quarters, and soak them in water until they are pliable enough to braid into twine or twist into withes. Don't gather roots over one and one-half inches thick for this purpose.

All experiments in this line made during idle hours in camp will be interesting and entertaining, and the results may be of vital worth to you in times of emergency.

Thongs Cut from the Skins

of wild animals have been used for cordage since our ancestors lived in caves and carried stone axes.

In the writer's boyhood days every cobbler and all the farmers were experts at making shoe-strings from calfskin, which they did by first making a "wheel" or disk of leather about 4 inches in diameter, and after sticking the point of a sharp knife blade through a slit at the edge of the leather disk down into a board and placing the thumb the thickness of a slate pencil from it, they quickly drew out the string cut by the knife blade as the hide was pulled through the opening, the leather disk of course revolving; the outside, or perimeter, was constantly reduced by the thickness of a slate pencil at every measure of the circumference. The string when finished was rolled between the sole of the shoe and the floor, then greased with tallow. Such shoe strings will outlast any modern machine-made laces.

Fig. 236.—Dip the water up by using the top of the brim.

Have a Drinking Cup

It is an excellent idea to take a flexible rubber drinking cup to the woods with you, but none of us are ever supplied with all the useful little articles now manufactured for campers, and if we were it would make a load too great for a pack horse; hence it is sometimes a problem how to drink when the water is at our feet. Nature's old way wherein one lies prone on the ground and sinks his mouth in the cool spring is not always convenient, and in such a case

Your Felt Hat Makes a Good Drinking Cup

But do not fill the inside of your hat with water; simply dent in the top as in Fig. 236, and dip up the water, using the top of the brim and the outside of the crown to hold the fluid.

A felt hat has a woolly surface which holds the dust so that it does not mix with the water, and the outside of such a hat makes a very much more sanitary drinking cup than would be supposed by one who never tried it.

It sometimes happens that the spring, water hole or stream where one must quench his thirst is roiled or that there is a suspicion of pollution from one source or another, and it may be practicable to scoop a hollow in the sand alongside the water and by this means procure

Filtered Water,

as is shown by the sectional view in Fig. 237. Water will find its level, and a hole dug next to a stream or pool of standing water will fill up to the level of the adjoining supply with the water which seeps through the intervening bank, the latter furnishing a natural filter, which, however imperfect it may be, will yet furnish more palatable water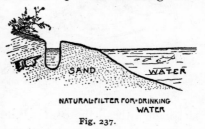

NATURAL FILTER FOR DRINKING WATER

Fig. 237.

than can be obtained from the muddy stream, spring or pool.

In an emergency where good water is unobtainable a filter may be made by wrapping a bunch of sphagnum moss on the end of a hollow reed and burying the moss-covered end in the moist earth, then gently sucking up the water as it accumulates in the hole; but such emergencies seldom happen to pleasure camping parties if they use ordinary caution and care in selecting a spot to pitch their tent. Remember that it is much better to stop at a good place early in the afternoon than to have darkness overtake you on the trail.

Blazed Trails

are the common highways of woodmen through the forests and are made in several ways: a spot trail is one where a large blaze is cut with the axe or camp hatchet on the trees, the spot facing the person following the trail and so arranged (O P Q R, Fig. 238) that one spot is always visible from tree to tree. Of course it is understood that the "spot" trees in the diagram are much closer together than they would be on the trail; they were drawn in this manner to show their arrangement to better advantage and to meet the requirements of a diagram.

A SPOT TRAIL   A SURVEYORS TRAIL

Fig. 238.

Fig. 239.

Two notches like those shown at X and Y in the small figure of a tree trunk in the southwest corner of

Fig. 238.—Right hand side is a spot trail; left hand side is a surveyor's line.

Fig. 239.—Is a line tree sometimes used to indicate location of camp.

Fig. 239 are sometimes made upon the opposite side of the spot trees to indicate the back trail; but the surveyor's blazes upon the side of the trees, as shown by T U V W in the west side of Fig. 238, are all that are necessary to direct persons who possess ordinary knowledge of the woods Personally I make a habit of bending small bushes, as shown by Fig. 240, whenever I travel away from camp in a strange country where there is plenty of underbrush. Where the land has been burned over by forest fires and the new growth is just high enough to cover one's head, it is most difficult to keep one's direction and it is not difficult to get lost. One travelling in such places should always take the precaution to break the stems of small bushes and bend them back to indicate the direction taken, and also to show the traveller himself how to retrace his own steps. The white under sides of the leaves are very easily seen on the return trail.

MARKING THE TRAIL

BACK TRAIL — WENT THIS WAY

Fig. 240.

The Panic of the Lost

I know of no more distressing sound in the forest than when the hush of the night is broken by the distant cry of "help!" If you are really lost sit down where you are and make camp, and then mark or blaze your trail to and from the camp whenever you make little journeys of exploration. Always return to your camp to sleep at night, and sooner or later you will be found. Many people lose their head as soon as they lose themselves, and rush madly through the woods until exhausted or driven mad by their fright, thus making it almost impossible for searching parties to discover their whereabouts, and rendering themselves incapable of finding their own way out of the woods. A very sad example of the effects of this sort of a panic has just occurred. I left this manuscript on the floor of my studio yesterday to go out and see a balloon which was poised in mid-air near my house. The talented young sculptor and painter who alone occupied the basket returned my salute by a gallant wave of his hand, then leaning on the edge of the basket he surveyed the people with apparent amusement before he threw out ballast and ascended to where there was a greater current of air. Taking my field glasses with me I followed him for quite a distance without difficulty as the big bag of gas floated slowly through the air. I never saw a man more at home with a balloon, and yet this same young man a few hours later, after he had made a skillful and perfect landing on a sand-bar, lost his head, swam inlets *while wearing his overcoat,* waded through marshes until at last he fell face down and perished from utter exhaustion. He was, however, in no danger after landing until the panic of the lost seized him and drove him frantic. The life-saving station was near by and he passed between telephone poles and under a telephone wire in his mad struggle to reach the distant lights of the village. Had he sat down and kept his composure he would be alive to-day, for help was near at hand. It is such people who shout for help at night, and if you start out to succor them, there is not one chance in a thousand of finding the lost party. Still it is one's duty to try to save the lost one. Remember that a camp-fire in the dark woods is not difficult to discover, and that if the fire is built on a hill or elevation of some sort a smudge of smoke may be seen a long distance in the day time.

However, if you are careful about taking observations of the "lay of the country" and marking your trail, there is little danger of being really lost.

Camp Life is not Dangerous,

but accidents will happen to people on the play ground, at home, abroad and in the wilderness where one is out of reach of the ambulance. While it is impossible to tell the reader what to do in every possible emergency, every one should know how to pick up and "pack" an unconscious comrade to camp or some safe place where his injuries may receive attention or where restoratives may be applied.

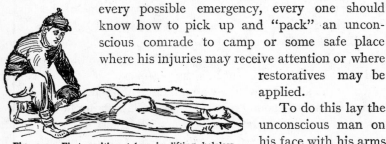

Fig. 241.—First position taken in lifting helpless companion.

To do this lay the unconscious man on his face with his arms in front of him, his chin resting in his hands (Fig. 241). Then kneel on your left knee in front of and facing him so that your right foot is placed along-side of his elbow, grasp his left wrist with your right hand, extend his arm full length and duck your head under it so that his arm pit fits on the back of your head; now raise the helpless man gently up until you can grasp the back

Fig. 242.—Second position in lifting a helpless man.

of his right leg between the knee and the hip with your right hand (Fig. 242), then assume an upright position and bring his left hand down in front of you, thus throwing his head over your back and the weight of his body on your shoulder (Fig. 243).

In this book are given plans of all manner of camps, shacks and cabins, but even more essential than a roof for shelter is

The Camp-fire,

and a man or boy who can build one in the forest, without the aid of matches and when everything is sodden and water-soaked,

is entitled to wear fringe on his leggins and wamus, for he has earned for himself the title of the "Real Thing," the true Buckskin Man.

Somewhere about 1827, the very first box of friction matches was sold, and it brought over five dollars; the same amount of money now would buy enough matches to stock a store.

It was many years before these almost indispensable little fire-sticks came into general use, and even as late as the sixties it was not uncommon in rural districts to see upon the mantel a combination tin tinder box and candlestick enclosing flint, steel

Fig. 243.—Packing a helpless comrade.

and punk, while below the mantel, in a sheet-iron cylinder, hung a lot of "sulphur matches"—*i.e.*, pine slivers, about the dimensions of slate pencils, which had had their ends dipped in melted sulphur. These sulphur matches could only be ignited by contact with a flame or live coal.

It is well to know these things, for accidents on the trail are liable to put one back to the primitive position occupied by our grandparents, in which case remember that striking the back of your knife against the sharp edge of a flinty stone will produce sparks. What next concerns us is how to make a flame from a spark after the latter is produced. All who have experimented with flint and steel know that the sparks are of no use unless we have

Good Punk

Charred cotton rags, raw cotton, paper soaked in a solution of black gunpowder and water, baked rotten wood and baked fungus, when perfectly dry, make good punk, and should be kept in tightly corked bottles or horns, otherwise these things

are liable to absorb moisture and become worthless.

When you catch a spark in a charred rag, fold the rag over and over and blow the spark into a flame, as in Fig. 244. From the flame you can ignite a match made

KINDLING
Fig. 245.
Woodsmen's
matches.

Fig. 244.—Blowing on the folded rag to make fire.

of a sliver of a pine knot (Fig. 245), and with this "match," taper or kindling ignite similar ones piled up tepee form, with larger sticks outside (Fig. 246), and thus start your fire. Punk must be blown into a flame, and from the flame a candle, or the pine match, or a bunch of dry leaves can be used to light the fire. But even after one has secured a flame one must know

How to Build a Fire

Every man and every woman in this whole broad land thinks that he or she knows how to build fires, but sad to relate, there is not one in a hundred who can do it successfully without a

Sunday edition of the newspaper, a can of kerosene and an armful of kindling wood. Even then they frequently fail. It is safe to say that all domestic servants are ignorant of the first principles of this art.

After a fire has a good start it will burn under very unfavorable conditions, *but it must be started properly.* Fig. 246 shows the wood so heaped that there will be a draught. As soon as the pitch-pine kindling in the centre is ignited larger wood can be gradually added to this, until you have a fire of any size you choose. Fig. 247 shows a diagram of

PITCH-PINE TO START A FIRE

A CAMP KITCHEN RANGE

CROSS SECTION OF GROUND

Fig. 246.   Fig. 247.

A Camp Kitchen Stove

There is nothing new in this for the accomplished and seasoned camper, but it may be of service to the real tenderfoot, and for his information it may be well to explain that the wind break (Fig. 247) piled against the stakes is green wood. The ash-pit need not necessarily be as deep as the one shown in the cross section. The flattened logs each side of the pit are arranged thus: >, a wide space at the one end for pots and pans, a small space at the other end for the coffee or tea pots. With such a fireplace, anything cookable can be prepared for your table.

Charcoal will ignite by contact with

A Glowing Ember,

and if you have but one live coal and can rake from the ashes a handful of bits of clean charcoal (Fig. 248), by carefully heaping the dead black embers over the live coal you will soon have **a fire.** The combustion may be hastened by blowing on the embers.

Two smouldering logs can be made to burst into flames by pushing them together so that each glowing side is warmed and encouraged by the other.

If you have candles in camp,

Candlesticks

can be made of "any old thing." Take a potato or a turnip, cut one part flat for the bottom, make a hole for

ONLY ONE LIVE COAL TO START THE FIRE!

Fig. 248.

the candle, thrust the ends of a bent twig into one side for a handle (Fig. 249). Drive three nails into a block of wood for a candle stick, or if you want

A Chandelier,

it may be made as shown by Fig. 250. You may use a wad of clay or mud (Fig. 251), or cut a cross in the top of a tin can (Fig. 252), push the points down and fit in the candle (Fig. 253). If you have no candles and need a light, a torch can be made by binding slivers of pine knots over the end of a stick, with a bunch of moss for a spreader (Figs. 254 and 255). Or the old Indian birch-bark torch (Fig. 256) may be used.

But if it is

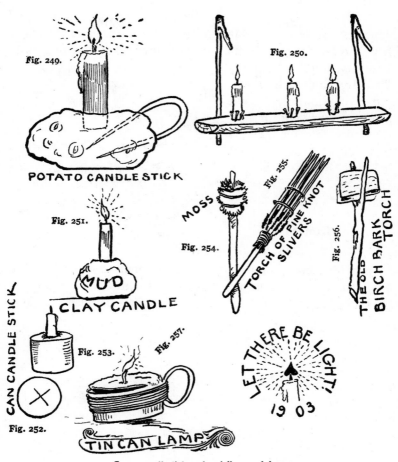

Fig. 249.

POTATO CANDLE STICK

Fig. 250.

Fig. 251.

MUD

CLAY CANDLE

CAN CANDLE STICK

Fig. 253.

Fig. 252.

Fig. 255.

MOSS

Fig. 254.

TORCH OF PINE KNOT SLIVERS

Fig. 256.

THE OLD BIRCH BARK TORCH

Fig. 257.

TIN CAN LAMP

LET THERE BE LIGHT!
19 03

Camp candlesticks, chandeliers and lamps.

233

A Lamp

you wish, make one by binding, with wire, string, or thongs, a handle on a tin can; fill the can with almost any sort of grease.

Use ravelling of canvas, the dry inner bark of cedar or chestnut, an old grease-soaked rag or un-ravelled string for a wick, and pull it through a nail hole in the top of the can (Fig. 257).

A very pretty

Lantern

can be made of birch bark

Fig. 258.   Fig. 260.

Fig. 259.

by punching holes through it with a wire nail as shown by Figs. 258, 259 and 260, and now, if you suffer with cold feet, eat raw food and stumble about in a dark camp, it is because you do it for the fun of the thing.

CHAPTER XX

CAMP COOKING AND HOW TO BUILD AN ALTAR CAMP STOVE AND A CLAY OVEN

The word camp has of late been prostituted so that one is often at a loss to know what it means; but when I refer to a camp, the reader may understand that it is the real thing, and not one of those grotesque palaces in the woods, veneered with logs, and filled with an army of missing links dressed in livery. Such things are profane and a sacrilege to nature. Not only are they all of that, but their very presence is degrading to the real forester and hunter; they sap his manhood and transform a self-reliant, manly sort of fellow into a cringing, tip-taking degenerate. But, it was not of this that I intended to write; this story has naught to do with the effete luxury of degenerates, but is written for all those wholesome beings who love to sleep on sweet-smelling balsam, hear the music of the sizzling bacon and watch the gymnastics of the acrobatic flapjack.

In the previous chapter various sorts of camp-fires have been described, and over the blazing logs or the hot embers of these fires all sorts of delicious dishes may be cooked.

In the present article are given some camp stoves for permanent camps; by the latter term is meant the shack, shanty or hut, built to last from season to season, and not a temporary summer shelter in the woods.

The Altar Camp Stove

is so called from its form and appearance, and the altar of the ancients was probably evolved from the camp-fire on the ground for the same reason that caused this invention, that is, to prevent the necessity of the priests bending their backs over the sacred fires. To the real lover of the woods the camp-fire is sacred; but the altar stove is not made for fire worship, it is a practical device to save the cook's back.

Fig. 261.
GROUND PLAN

PLANS OF CAMP STOVE
ALL RIGHTS RESERVED
BY DAN BEARD 1905

Fig. 261 shows the foundation plan, Fig. 262 the top plan, and Fig. 263 the finished stove. Build the altar in the form of a log cabin, and fill the inside with stones, sods or dirt of any description, then take clay and build the fireplace on top the altar. If clay is not obtainable use any sort of mud mixed with stones, or stones alone; in fact the whole altar, fireplace and all, may be built of stones. It is then called a "Matasiso," after a man who

TOP PLAN

FIRE PLACE

Fig. 262.

writes under that *nom de plume.* But all camps are not situated in stony countries, and the altar camp stove may be even built entirely of sods when the camp is on the prairies.

The Fireplace

is an open stove without top or front and narrower at the rear than at the front, for the convenience of small and large cooking

Fig. 263.—The altar stove saves your back.

utensils. A couple of forked sticks support a rod from which pots and kettles may be suspended.

After a few hot fires have been built the clay will harden and retain heat for a considerable time, and if the fireplace is made of stones, they will often become so hot that things may be cooked by resting the cooking utensils upon the heated stones.

The fire-pit is also a most excellent bean hole for cooking baked beans, and baking biscuits or bread in covered dishes—"Dutch ovens"—buried in the hot embers. But a real

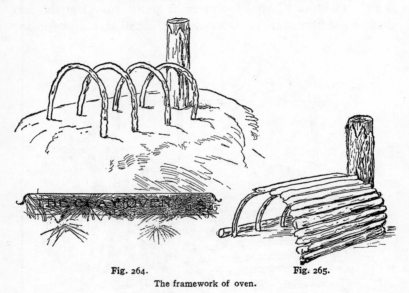

Fig. 264.

Fig. 265.

The framework of oven.

Oven of Clay

may be easily built by covering a barrel or keg with clay and earth, then building a fire inside, burning out the woodwork and baking the surrounding mud, or, lacking any product of the cooper's art, a good oven can be made by setting up a number of elastic sticks bent into loops of equal size, with the sharpened ends of the sticks forced into the ground as shown by Fig. 264. A small log or stick of firewood is next set on end at the rear as the core for a chimney, and then sticks are laid over as in Fig. 265, and the whole daubed over with mud or clay as in Figs. 266, 267 and 268.

After the clay is modeled into form, the core stick is pulled out, leaving a chimney hole, over which a box without bottom or top is placed, or a log cabin stick and mud chimney is built. After the clay is baked and the woodwork burned away, the oven is ready for use.

Fig. 266.—Half-finished oven.

How to Use the Clay Oven

Build a raging fire of split birch wood or of hemlock bark, and keep it going until

Fig. 268.—A stone will answer for a door.

Fig. 267.—The wooden door is a good one.

the oven is good and hot, then rake out the ashes, put in your baking, and with a stone or wooden door close the opening of the oven and also the chimney opening; the heated clay will do the rest. As to the

Novel Food Used in Camp,

it may be well to state that there are numerous creatures of the wilderness which, when properly prepared, make good and wholesome food, but which the novice would never think of choosing for such a purpose. I have had country people tell me that various turtles were poisonous, but after experimenting with mud turtles, sliders, snappers and even the lively little turtle with the pungent musk-like odor, vulgarly called a "stink pot," but more politely termed musk turtle, I have come to the conclusion that, when well cleaned and washed, they all make excellent material for delicious stews and soups.

According to such high authority as Mr. C. Hart Merriam, the American puma's flesh as an article of food excels all other game; while Lewis and Clark and many travellers, unknown to fame, are enthusiastic in their praise of the meat of dogs. Rattlesnakes and puff adders appeal to some appetites, but horse meat is said by others to be repellant and unwholesome, yet Mr. Frederic Vreeland, the eminent electric expert, botanist and hunter, tells me that horse meat is not only palatable but wholesome food and he has at times lived on horse beef. Wolf meat is said to be sticky and disagreeable.

The truth is that there is little need of starving in the wilderness, even when game is scarce. Almost every stream has its supply of muskrats, and I have eaten them in Delaware served as a delicacy at the hotel table, and also at the Hotel Astor in New York City.

To prepare a musquash or any other small fur-bearing animal for the table, first make

A Skinning Stick

of a forked stick about as thick as your finger. Let the forks be about one inch to each branch, and the stick below long enough to reach up between your knees when the sharpened lower end is forced into the ground. If you squat on the ground the stick should be about a foot and one-half long, but longer if you sit on a camp stool, stump or stone. Hang the muskrat on the forks of the stick by thrusting the sharpened ends of the forks through the thin spot at the gambrel joints of the hind legs; that is, the parts which correspond with your own heels. Hung in this manner (with the one and one-half foot stick), the nose of the animal will just clear the ground. First skin the game, then remove all the internal organs, and if it be a muskrat, not only remove all the musk glands, but cut into the inside of the fore-arms and the fleshy parts of the thighs, and take out a little white substance you will find there which resembles a nerve; this done and the meat well washed, it may be cooked with little fear of the food retaining a musky flavor.

How to Cook a Muskrat

The muskrat may be broiled over the hot embers, with sliced bacon so arranged that the drippings run over the musquash as it cooks. Or it may be made into a stew with vegetables and pork, and in this case the longer it simmers over the fire the better will be the results.

Only seasoned campers ever have an opportunity to feast on the delicious nose of a moose, or know the delights of marrow bones of deer split and mixed with parched cornmeal and cooked all night, or broiled wood rats, or dried venison pounded to fragments and cooked with rich bear's fat, musk turtle soup, porcupine steaks, with hellbenders as a side dish; and, although thousands of muskrats are killed and eaten every year in Maryland and Delaware, probably but few of my readers in the Northern states will experiment with this rodent. However, there is no one with his heart in the right place who does not love

Flapjacks

and baked beans. Flapjacks are simple things to make, yet it requires some aptitude on the part of the novice to learn to cook good ones. To one quart of flour add two tablespoonfuls of baking powder and a pinch or two of salt, mix with water until the mess is of the consistency of cream. Have your frying-pan good and hot, and grease it with a dauber made of a rag fastened in the form of a wad to the end of a stick and soaked with hot bacon fat. Remember that it is only necessary to have enough fat on the dish to prevent the batter from sticking to the metal. When the surface of the cake begins to have bubble holes in it turn it over with a wooden paddle until you acquire sufficient confidence in yourself to lift the frying-pan from the fire, toss the cake so as to turn it in the air, catch it in the pan, brown side up, and cook the other side.

Baked Beans

Beans baked with a good hunk of pork suit my palate, but many people, especially in the East, like them sweetened with molasses, and the lumbermen enjoy them with sliced onions. Baked beans are always good when well cooked. First we will tell how to do it with all the "fixin's." The onions and even the molasses may be left out by those who do not like them cooked that way. Fig. 269 shows a cross-section of a bean hole and a bean pot; also the arrangement of the inside much more graphically than I can describe it.

But it may be well to state that these notes of a confirmed camper are not written for cage-birds or indoor people, but for those lusty souls who love the free open air, yearn for the perfume of balsam boughs and the romance of camp-fires. For such hearty people there is, perhaps, no dish which meets with greater favor than "good old pork and beans," and here is a way to cook it so that the very aroma arising therefrom will cause you to thank Providence for the emptiness of your stomach.

CELEBRATED CAMP-FIRE DISHES

How to Bake Beans Lumberman Style

Parboil two quarts of beans until they are almost soft; then peel and slice one large onion, or two small ones, and put half of the slices in the bottom of the pail. Next empty half of the beans on top of the onions and spread the remainder of the onions over the top of the half lot of beans. Now cut two "hunks" of salt pork, each about 5 inches square, and place them on top of the last layer of onions, and over this pour the remainder of the beans.

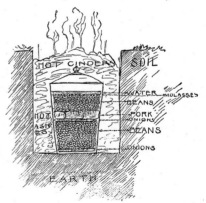

Fig. 269.—Showing a cross-section of bean pot and fire hole.

On top of the whole, spread a tablespoonful of molasses, and pour in just enough water to cover the beans.

The Bean Hole

While the beans are being prepared, some one must dig a pit to serve as an oven and line the hole with flat stones. With small sticks of split birch wood or hemlock bark, build a brisk fire in the bean-pit, or oven, and keep it blazing until the hole is filled with red-hot cinders. Next rake all the embers from the pit and, after placing the pail in its centre, pack the hot coals all around and over the bean pot and cover the surface of the hot cinders with a layer of ashes, as shown in the diagram (Fig. 269). If you do all this before retiring for the night, the beans will cook while you sleep. In the morning when you remove the lid you will be rewarded with a dish fit to set before a king.

The Open Fireplace,

wherever it may be, offers a most excellent opportunity for the novice to practice camp cookery and perfect himself or herself in the art. Over the hot coals at home one may broil a bird or rabbit, transfer the smoking game to a hot plate, put on some salt, pepper and butter, and serve the smoking dish before the fire. One may also cook a fish before the open fire at home; however, it is a different proposition to cook one in camp.

But it is not at all difficult to successfully

Plank a Fish

if you are the fortunate possessor of a piece of hard wood, oak, hickory or ash, $1\frac{1}{2}$ or 2 inches thick and several inches broader and longer than the fish. In truth, it should be of sufficient length to allow one end to be sharpened and yet leave enough space above to tack the fish.

Before building the fire it is best to drive two stout stakes in the ground just back of a small fire-hole or pit, and pile up some green back-logs against the stakes; then build a brisk fire of split birch wood, and keep it going until you have secured a fine heap of glowing red embers in front of the sizzling green logs. Now take a scaled, cleaned and thoroughly washed fish, and with a hunting-knife split it open in the back (the flatter the fish the better it is for planking). Be careful not to cut the fish in half, but to cut deep enough to enable you to spread the fish out as flat as possible. Before the fish is tacked to the plank, set the latter in front of the fire until it is almost charred upon the exposed side, then, with small nails or tacks, securely attach the opened fish with its back next to the scorching hot side of the board. Also tack some salt pork or bacon just above the fish, in such a manner that the melting fat can run down over the fish as it toasts before the genial heat of the embers. Drive the pointed end of the plank into the ground so that the belly of the fish is best exposed to the heat of the fire. Catch the drippings in a tin cup and "baste" the cooking fish by pouring them over it as it browns, and when it is thoroughly cooked no dish you ever ate will taste better.

When game is brought into camp, cut the wings and legs from the grouse, the fore and hind legs from the rabbits, and the tough parts from the big game, and keep them until you have enough for the camp kettle; then put them in the pot as the first step in that delectable thing,

A Log Cabin Stew

To the various bits of game add a lot of salt pork cut into little cubes, and to this a portion of all the vegetables obtainable, excepting beets; cover with water and allow it to simmer all day long over a slow fire. If there is such an effete luxury as a bottle of olives in camp, add some of the liquid to the simmering stew; salt and pepper to the taste; strain and serve scalding hot in tin cups, in each of which you have previously placed an olive.

Bullfrogs and fresh-water turtles add greatly to the quality of the stew; however, there is no one thing absolutely necessary to its perfection, but all who have eaten it forever after treasure in their memory the ravishing delights of A Log Cabin Stew.

CHAPTER XXI

HOW TO KEEP GAME AND FISH IN CAMP

Dampness, heat and blow flies are all enemies to fresh meat; nevertheless butchers often wrap their meat in wet cloths to preserve it; but, after the cloth is adjusted they are careful to place the meat in a cool spot, where the damp cloth protects it from the flies, and at the same time helps to retain a low temperature. There are other people who immerse meat in water and seal it by a coating of melted butter, lard, or tallow on top of the water; the jar is then placed in the coolest available spot. Few campers, however, carry stone jars to the woods with them, and none have jars of sufficient dimensions to hold a haunch of venison, a saddle of big horn, or a large hunk of bear meat. Personally, I have never tried either of the above methods, but at my permanent camp in the Appalachian highlands of Pennsylvania, I have had great success with some old barrel hoops and a piece of mosquito netting. By the way, the latter should form part of the dunnage of every camper, it takes up but little space, and is useful as a minnow net for securing live bait, as well as a bar to keep flies from meat and mosquitoes from the campers. The construction of

The Big Tink Meat Safe

is very simple. The stick A (Fig. 270) is cut, leaving the stumps of branching, from which to hang the provisions, protruding; a bit of twine is tied to the A stick at B (Fig. 270), and then knitted on by a series of half hitches, as shown by B (Fig. 270), and fastened to a support (B, Fig. 270). Several hoops are now fastened to a piece of mosquito netting, and the netting gathered at top and bottom, where it is secured with a bit of string.

I always hang this in the shade, high enough to be out of reach of predaceous animals, and where the wind blows the hardest.

To get the meat or fish, it is only necessary to unfasten the "pucker" string at the bottom, reach up, unhook the meat and remove it. For the benefit of the helpless fellow one always finds in every group of men and boys, I will add that barrel hoops are not necessary although very convenient, and if there be no such material in your camp, hoops may easily be made of slender branches bent into the form of a circle and bound in that position with a piece of string. The camper who goes into the woods without a supply of twine and string will be likely to go shooting and leave his shells at home.

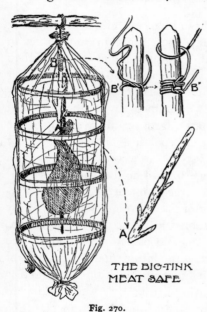

THE BIG-TINK
MEAT SAFE

Fig. 270.

Accidents on the trail sometimes deprive one of many things which were thoughtfully provided for the convenience of camp life. The man who goes supplied with string in his luggage, will have odd pieces in his pocket, and if these fail him he will be sufficiently resourceful to manufacture his own twine from tamarack roots, the inner bark of trees, rawhide or similar material as described in a previous chapter of this book.

The Big Tink Safe protects its contents from the attacks of blow flies, allows a free circulation of air around the meat, which soon drys the outer surface and forms a paper-like coating or skin that preserves the inside meat from decay.

Never allow two pieces of meat to hang touching each other, for the point of contact will remain moist, be sought by flies, and be the part that first becomes tainted. Cut away all bloody portions and pieces where the juices of the meat collect; such places invite decomposition and blow flies.

The small boys are our most practical naturalists, and when an urchin wishes some large blue bottle flies for his pin and cork cage, he seeks his prey down the area-way of the outside cellar steps; he knows that these flies avoid the upper air. If you have no mosquito netting in camp take a hint from the small boy and hang your meat as high as possible where there is wind and shade.

Nature is full of apparent contradictions, but they are only apparent and are caused by the modifying influence of unconsidered trifles; an instance of this apparent contradiction is

The Macdonald Lake Meat Safe

which, in place of being high and dry, is low and necessarily damp, for it is suspended over a mountain stream. A framework, representing in form a cubical box, is covered with mosquito netting, and hung over one of these cold mountain streams of the Macdonald Lake country, just as the Big Tink Safe is suspended in a dry, windy place, but in the former case the water is so cold that it chills the atmosphere immediately above it, forming a cool and even temperature. At some of the lumber camps in the State of Washington, a regular little shanty of boards is built over the water and the meat for the camp is hung in this dark, cool place.

In a hunter's or fisherman's camp, however, one seldom has boards or planks with which to construct shanties, and Fig. 271 shows a simple method of building a meat safe of the rustic material furnished by the forest. See Figs. 271 and 272.

Such meat houses when finished should also have thatched floors, which shut out the flies, but admit a free circulation of air.

Fig. 271.   Fig. 272.

Fig. 271.—Frame of Macdonald Lake meat safe.
Fig. 272.—Same partially thatched.
Floors in each diagram omitted better to show construction.

Hot Air

Up in the north woods the campers are wont to suspend their meat about 6 feet above the camp-fire (C, Fig. 273), where the smoke dries the outside and preserves the inner meat. A and B show a simple arrangement for this purpose, but the overhanging branches of a tree are often handy and save trouble.

An expert in discussing the philosophy of smoked meats says that:

"Smoke is not absolutely required. Indeed, smoke was not the original object of the farmer; rather it was fire or hot air, and the meat incidentally became smoked as it was being dried in the big fire places (a method still used in curing the 'Cumberland Cut,' as it is called).

"When we have a fresh side of bacon or ham the problem is to extract the water; or, in short, to dry it. Salt will remove or displace the water; but we don't want to salt the meat until all

Fig. 273.

the water is driven out, as that would make the meat too salty. So it is dried. Fire is used. In England the meat is hung in the big fireplaces to dry, where it sometimes may get some smoke.

"In Wales meat is hung up in a hot draft or kitchen and gets no smoke. If the meat has been salted too long, it is hung in a warm place and some of the salt will be removed with the brine and crystallized on the outside.

"In Ireland the one hog—'the gentleman who pays the rent'—after being finished upon barley meal and duly salted, is hung up in the cabin to dry. Hot air is the final curing agent. If the cabin smokes, the ham gets smoked. Irish hams always bring the highest price in London.

"For twenty-five years in curing pork I followed the lesson I learned in my boyhood, and used no smoke, but hot air; but now, as I am preparing bacon for the public market, I use a smoke-house. I cater to the taste for smoke, but I cure the meat, after is has been duly salted, with fire or hot air; this is what really *cures* the meat."

Fig. 274.

Another instance of the use of cool air produced by cold water is shown in

The Kootenay Fish Safe,

or Kootenai, as it is often spelled, which consists of nothing more than an ordinary packing box set in the bank of a stream, where the cold spring waters trickle through and chill the soil. The diagram (Fig. 274) shows the box without a lid and with the front removed to display the interior. The box should be set in the ground only at spots where the water will drain off without filling the box, as it will in the sloping bank of a stream.

In some parts of the South, the market fishermen dig holes in the beach and bury their first catch in the cold, wet sand, and there allow it to remain until they have secured a sufficient number of fish for the market, but the Kootenay method is neater and better, and is used successfully by the group of market fishermen at Slocan Junction near the outlet of Kootenay Lake.   These men catch all their trout with a fly and ship them to Nelson, B. C., for the consumption of the citizens who do not fish.   Slocan Junction is a wild spot, with ripping, booming waterfalls, and is one of the most picturesque fishing spots on the continent.   It is too bad that the market fishermen should have settled there, but since they have, the sportsman proper can at least be benefited by adopting the market man's idea for keeping trout fresh in camp.   One will probably not have a packing case to use as a cold storage room for one's fish, but a box is not necessary, for

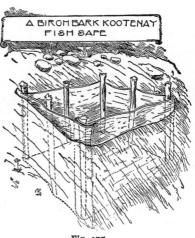

Fig. 275.

A Birch Bark Kootenay Fish Safe

will answer all purposes and be sweeter than an old packing case which has been knocked about in dirty freight cars and dirtier depots.

To make a fish safe of birch bark is simplicity itself (see Fig. 275).   After the excavation is made line it with a carpet of birch bark, then drive in the stakes, as shown in the diagram, then wind a piece of bark around the outside of the stakes, make a cover of a flat stone or another piece of bark, and the cold storage room is finished.   The fish, as may be seen in Fig. 274, are strung on sticks, and the latter are laid in notches cut to receive them. The trout are first cleaned and then strung on sticks. When hung in a cold receptacle of this kind, separated from each other so as to allow a free circulation of air, they will keep fresh and sweet a remarkably long time.

Should there be no convenient birch trees, the green bark from some other tree will answer, although it will probably be more difficult to handle.

But one may be fishing in a country devoid of big trees, or where they are so scarce that it would be almost a criminal act to mutilate or kill one, and in that case

A·KOOTENAY·OF·
ROUGH·STONE.
A·FLAT·STONE.
WILL·DO·FOR·A LID.

Fig. 276.

A Stone Kootenay

may be constructed in a few moments after the plan shown by Fig. 276.

Every angler knows that heat and flies are not the only dangers to which his catch is subjected, for the woods are full of little creatures which delight in stealing the angler's fish. Probably the worst thief among the camp prowlers is the mink, and therefore your fish safe should be built mink proof. If the lid to the box is of light material, it must be held down by stones or logs of sufficient weight to keep out trespassers.

I have seen water snakes carry away fish which exceeded the dimensions required by the game laws. The American white-footed mouse will steal a fish much larger than itself, and do it out of pure mischief, for I have proved by experiment that he does not eat them. In the Western mountains, along such streams as dash down the canyons and gulleys which furrow the almost perpendicular sides of Lake Chelan, there are many large wood rats with squirrel-like tails, known to the natives as "pack rats." These mischievous mountain brownies will not hesitate to steal anything from a revolver to a set of false teeth, and, as may be imagined, one's fish should be securely housed in a country where the pack rats abound.

It is a mistaken idea that fish are not good unless eaten fresh from the water.

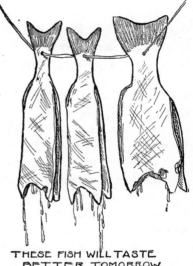

Black bass, pickerel and perch are improved by keeping from twelve to twenty-four hours. Under favorable circumstances I have kept them three or four days, and found that it had improved their flavor. There is a muddy, dead leaf taste frequently present in black bass which even onions will not conceal, but if the bass are cleaned immediately after being killed, and then hung by *their tails* (Fig. 277) and allowed to

THESE FISH WILL TASTE BETTER TOMORROW THAN TODAY.
Fig. 277.

drain for twenty-four hours, the muddy flavor is removed. The same treatment will remove the mucous-like slime so abundant in pickerel, and leave the white flesh firm and dry, giving it a flavor suggestive of lake white fish.

Wash the fish well, string them through a hole made in the roots of their tails, and hang them in a dry, shady, but windy place. If the wind blows with force, the place need not even be particularly dry.

Prepared in this manner fish keep well, and in cold, windy weather they keep a remarkably long time. I have little doubt that the treatment will work equally well with the spotted beauties as with alligator-like pickerel and the gamey black bass.

The reader must not suppose that any one of these preservative methods will keep meat as long as does ice, but neither will it incur the same danger that the cold storage does of supplying an unhealthy amount of ptomaine poison. It is

A Notorious Fact

that game kept by dealers in cold storage is very dangerous to eat, and that many cases of ptomaine poisoning occur each year from banquets where cold storage game is served to the guests.

I once suffered severely from this insidious poison which was contained in some delicious canned goods that we had at camp, but I have yet to hear of a case of ptomaine poisoning caused by eating fish or game preserved by any of the methods here suggested.

I have omitted to mention the fact that fish should be scaled before they are allowed to dry.

Tne practice of hanging birds with their entrails unremoved is disgusting, and not at all essential to produce a gamey flavor.

CHAPTER XXII

HOW TO PACK AND UNPACK IN THE WOODS

In the first place, remember that square parcels are more easily packed than cylindrical or round ones, and that food is now put up, especially for campers and packers, in cans with rectangular sides.

In the second place, do not forget that a piece of cloth, a fragment of a blanket, or any similar covering for a parcel, or box,

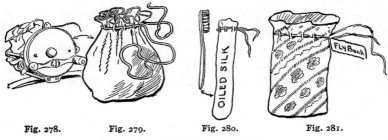

Fig. 278.   Fig. 279.   Fig. 280.   Fig. 281.

Manner of packing small articles.

is essential; a rope that will slip from the bare box will fit close and hug the same box, when it is covered with cloth, in such a manner that it is next to impossible for it to slip.

Even small parcels pack much better when covered, but it would take too much time to wrap each separate parcel in a separate wrapper; so go to the woods with these things in small bags of buckskin, canton-flannel and duck, with an oil-silk bag for tooth-brush (Figs. 279, 280 and 281). You will notice that a wad of paper is packed against the line on the reel in Fig. 278.

When you unpack, if some such arrangement is not made, you will often find your line so loose on the reel that the loops are interwoven in such a manner that it sometimes takes a good half-hour to untangle them.

Fish Rods

should be packed in a stiff leather case made for the purpose. I lost four expensive rods in a trip across Horse Plains, from Selish to Flathead Lake, because I thought it more economical to carry the rods in their own cases than to purchase a leather trunk for them. The delicate rods were ruined by chafing and rubbing against other baggage. I have since carried rods from the Atlantic to the Pacific, in camp, on horseback and on Indian wagons, without injury, because I had first provided a stout leather case lined with plush for their protection.

Your spare socks pulled over your reels will protect them from injury, and your change of underclothes are an excellent thing in which to roll up your toilet articles and personal belongings.

A Pillow

would be the last luxury one would think of taking with him on the trail, and yet if you have a good, clean flour bag in which to put your extra clothing, toilet articles, etc., you can use this for a pillow.

There should be a little spare ammunition, a private supply of matches, your fly-book and reels in this bundle; in fact, it should contain all your personal necessities, and when your bed roll is rolled up your pillow should be inside. By this arrangement you have all the things you need as soon as your bed is unrolled for the night.

The Kitchen

at first is often the source of more or less bother and trouble; packs are untied for a pinch of salt or a spoonful of sugar, tents unrolled for a block of matches; but small sacks will prevent this difficulty. Secure a number of bags, each to hold about five or ten pounds of coffee, tea, sugar, salt, rice, beans, prunes, etc. Put them all in one pack, or box, so that when in camp you can put your hand on anything you want. Put your flour in waterproof sacks, and don't forget when you have a pack-horse that before you throw the diamond hitch the pack-cover goes on.

After all the smaller stuff has been systematically and carefully arranged,

The Big Packs

are not difficult to make, although the novice may find some trouble in so adjusting the duffle that the side packs are of equal weight. The necessity of one pack balancing the other can be seen by even a very, very tenderfoot, but accurate judging of the relative weight of pack comes only with practice, and the beginner must guess it—make two guesses and strike an average until practice makes him proficient. An old hand can tell within a pound or two.

Another important item to remember is to make the packs of the most convenient form for the pack-horse and the peculiarities of the proposed trail, and to rope them tightly.

Roping Packs

First tie a slipnoose in the end of your rope, using a knot that may be easily undone, and yet will not pull out or give. Make the loop A (Fig. 282), then bring the line up and over and under the B end, making the loop C, as shown by Fig. 283, next bring the end B through the loop A, under it, double back and pull it out through the C loop, as shown in the diagram, Fig. 284; pull tight, and you have Fig. 285, a knot that will hold, won't slip

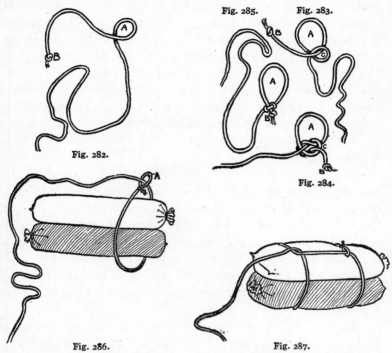

Fig. 285.   Fig. 283.

Fig. 282.

Fig. 284.

Fig. 286.   Fig. 287.

Diagrams showing the slipnoose and the first two steps in cinching the bags.   White bag is flour; tinted bag is beans.

and may be undone should you wish to use the rope for some other purpose.

Now that the rope is prepared, let us suppose that you have a 50-lb. sack of flour and a 60-lb. sack of beans, and you desire to rope them together for a side pack.   First experiment with the two sacks until you find a position in which they fit perfectly together, and then make a slipnoose (Figs. 282, 283, 284 and 285)

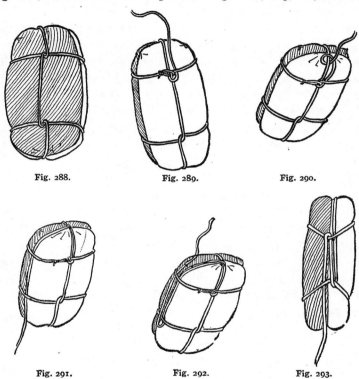

Fig. 288.   Fig. 289.   Fig. 290.

Fig. 291.   Fig. 292.   Fig. 293.

Diagrams showing the final steps in cinching up the bags.

of your rope by slipping the free end through the A loop, and slip the noose around the ends of both sacks, as shown by Fig. 286.

Draw the slipnoose tight, bring the line down the middle of the pack and take a hitch around the other end of the bags, as shown by Fig. 287. Next pass the rope under the pack, taking a turn around each rope, as shown by Fig. 288, to the place of beginning, where it is slipped under the cross loop, over the other and under the cross loop again, as shown by Fig. 289.

Now make a half-hitch on the rope, over the end of the pack, as shown by Fig. 290; bring the loose end of the rope down along the side of the pack, poking it under the two loops, or cross ropes, as shown by Fig. 291; coming back over, as shown by Fig. 292, then down again and under, as may be seen in Fig. 293, and cinch. While doing this with a large pack each of the two men throwing the hitch has a stick with which he pries up the cross ropes, in order that the loose end of the rope may be passed under, when required, without loss of time.

Now follow the pack with the rope around to the other side and cinch again, as in Fig. 293 ; make fast the loose end of the rope, and you have a pack which will not come undone.

For a large pack it is really a two-man hitch, and two old-timers will throw it in no time. One fellow takes a couple of turns, pulls tight, the other fellow lifts end of pack and passes rope under, the two working together as with the diamond hitch. When one man attempts to throw this hitch alone, unless it is a small pack, it is apt to be sloppy in execution.

The Shape of Packs

is of very great importance, while the packs themselves must be as compact as possible; they must also lie close to the horse; that is, the horse and his pack must be as near one as your skill can make them; this will prevent jutting rocks, brush or trees from scraping the pack from the animal's back. The exact shape of the packs cannot be given, but the general rule is to make them oblong. This form takes the hitch best, and can be easily adjusted to the sides of the horse's body, as may be seen by referring to the chapters on throwing the squaw hitch and diamond hitch.

Man Packing

The time to do your thinking is before you begin to pack; while packing you should work like an automaton; the nearer that you can come to packing with your eyes shut the closer do you approach wise packing.

The brain work shows in the arrangement of the pack, the animal work in the endurance displayed in carrying it, and when it is once on your shoulders, if you can get your mind entirely off your pack, you will shift more than half the load; that is why I say the animal work begins with the toting of the pack. The tenderfoot with his first pack is "a sight to sun your back on," as a North Wilderness man said to me. He looks as if he were carrying a ton, and evidently thinks that his pack weighs even more than that; this is because his mind is on his pack.

It must be remembered that there can be no cast-iron rules for this sort of thing until men are all turned from one mould, and as long as we differ mentally and physically rules can be only general. The following suggestions are the results of many backaches, and must be taken for what they are worth to novices; old hands possibly know even better rules, but they will all agree on this:

Don't Take More than You Must

to insure the necessities of life. As in animal packing, so it is in man packing.

The Shape of the Packs

is of vital importance. An oblong pack resting across the shoulders is usually a comfortable load, but a pack which extends out beyond the shoulders on each side of a man means trouble for him in brush or timber, and in crossing a wind-fall may even mean serious danger. Make your pack to conform to the nature of the trail, and modify it as much as allowable to conform to your own comfort.

Portage Packing

Where the dunnage is taken from canoes and packed over, the portage differs from wilderness packing in many important respects. The first and most important is that, be the portage long or short, difficult or easy, it has a definite beginning and a definite end, hence much heavier loads may be carried by each individual. After an ordinary man has toughened his muscle by a bit of outdoor work he may carry a 200-lb. load over a portage, but in

Wilderness Packing

the weight of the pack must be very much less than this, for here a man must carry his load indefinitely, and much depends upon the skilful arrangement of the pack. Grub, clothes, guns, ammunition, axe and frying-pan are the actual necessities, with a few small extras, such as matches, knives, tooth-brush, comb, etc.

For a Two Months' Trip

a man's personal duffle should not weigh over 50 pounds. Two 8-lb. blankets, two suits of underclothes, two flannel shirts, one light and one heavy pair of trousers, two pairs of shoes, four pairs of socks, one knife, one pocket comb, one tooth-brush, a gun, ammunition and a light waterproof cover for his

Bedroll

Make a neat bundle of all the small articles which you need every day and put them in a bag for your pillow. Spread your waterproof with your blankets in the middle (Fig. 294). Fold as in Fig. 295, the other side over now, and then begin at one end and roll it into a snug roll, but not a hard tight one; fold the ends in as in Fig. 296.   Now divide your grub and make it fit the pack; don't make a hard bowlder of your bean bag, as

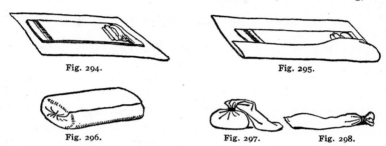

Fig. 294.   Fig. 295.

Fig. 296.   Fig. 297.   Fig. 298.

Figs. 294, 295, 296.—Show the bed roll.   Fig. 297.—Improperly packed bean bag.
Fig. 298.—Properly packed bean bag.

in Fig. 297, but give them plenty of room, and make an easily adjusted pack, as in Fig. 298.   When your pack suits you, try it on and see if it hangs well.   Keep it well up around.   When a pack begins to hurt you stop right where you are and readjust it; often a tilt this way or that or even reversing it, will make things comfortable.   It sometimes happens that a man who has been played out with a light pack recovers his strength under a heavier one.   In conclusion, if you always think of the unpack while packing, things will run smoothly in camp.

CHAPTER XXIII

THROWING THE SQUAW HITCH

How to Make a Pack that Will Stay on a Horse

Every follower of the trail should know how to pack an animal with his camp dunnage in such a manner that it will not slip or fall off on the trail, and this he may learn at home without even having a real animal to pack; for instance, if you take a stick of wood with a branch left upon it to represent the head of the horse, as in Fig. 299, then put a piece of cloth or a folded pocket handkerchief, to represent the horse's blanket, and tie it on with two strings, as in Fig. 299, you will have a good substitute for the real animal upon which to practice, but it is necessary to have a substitute also for an aparejo (as pronounced it would be spelled ah - pahr - ai - ho). Capt. Mayne Reid calls it alpereja. It is really a sort of pad for the pack (see Fig.

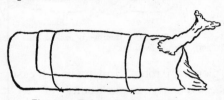

Fig. 299.—The wooden horse blanketed.

Fig. 300.—The bark aparejo.

266

319, Chap. XXIV). This can be made out of pieces of green bark, as in Fig. 300, which is placed over the blanket, as in Fig. 301; then you must have a cincha; on the real horse there is a ring at one end of the cincha and a hook at the other end of it. Make a loop of string and tie it on a small forked stick, as

Fig. 301.—The wooden horse with aparejo.

in Fig. 302, and allow the loop to answer for the ring and the fork for the hook. Now, then, tie another piece of string, which answers for the 33-foot lash rope of the packer, to the loop end of the string and put the cincha underneath the horse, as in Fig. 304.

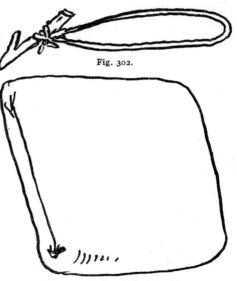

Fig. 302.

Take a cloth or any other object and fold it up in a handkerchief, as in Fig. 303, and place that upon the back of the wooden horse, as in Figs. 304 and 306, then a knot can be tied as it is in Fig. 307.

We will now refer to diagrams of a real horse with the real cincha trap-

Fig. 303.—The handkerchief pack.

pings: Fig. 306 shows a horse with real cincha trappings hanging loosely under it, and Fig. 307 shows the cincha. When the line is thrown over the horse, as in Fig. 306, you run it through the hook as in Fig. 308, cinch up, then bring it up alongside

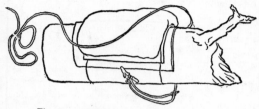

Fig. 304.—The first throw for squaw hitch.

of the pack as in Fig. 309; slip the loop of the string that is in your hand under the one that crosses the pack, as it is shown in Fig. 310; bring the loop back as in Fig. 311, then under again as in Fig. 312. "A" in all of the figures represents the loose end of the line. Fig. 313 shows the opposite side of the horse, and you may see that the loose end of the line there is brought down over the pack under the aparejo. In Fig. 314 the line is brought forward and under the aparejo, then up through the loop as shown in the diagram. In Fig. 315 it again shows the other side of the horse and also how the line of Fig. 314 is brought forward again and under the corner of the aparejo; then back and again under the rear corner of the aparejo and then up to the loop, or diamond, on the pack, pulled tight and made fast. Fig. 316 shows a diagram of the squaw hitch. Fig. 317 shows

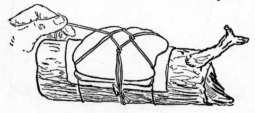

Fig. 305.—Packed for the trail.

a diagram of the diamond hitch. The hitch first described is not the regular diamond hitch, but one known as the squaw hitch and much used by packers and travellers. Study this out so that you may be able to throw this hitch, and if you have a horse you can practice putting a pack on its

Fig. 306.   Fig. 307.

Fig. 308.

269

back in this manner and see if you can fasten it tightly so it will
not fall off.   Then if the occasion requires that you at any time

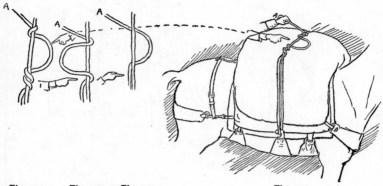

Fig. 312.   Fig. 311.   Fig. 310.   Fig. 309.

have to pack a horse, even if you cannot throw the celebrated
diamond hitch with the celerity of the United States scout packer,

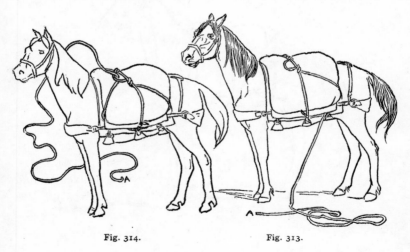

Fig. 314.   Fig. 313.

you can, at least, make the squaw hitch which will hold your dunnage on the animal's back.

The Diamond Hitch

cannot properly be called an invention because it is evidently a product of evolution.   However, it reached its present approved state several hundred years ago, probably among the Arabs, be-

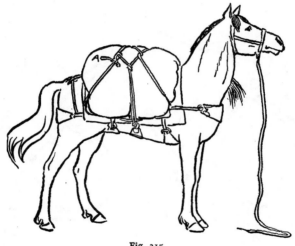

Fig. 315.

fore it reached old Spain, where the ass and the mule were the only freight trains known in the picturesque, romantic country of Don Quixote and Sancho Panza.   When the Spanish free-booters landed in Mexico to pillage and rob the natives of that country, as was the fashion of the day, they made their loot fast to the backs of animals with the diamond hitch, and the diamond hitch has been the hitch in use in Mexico ever since the Spanish first visited that country. It was undoubtedly from the Mexicans that some of our prospectors and pioneers learned the use

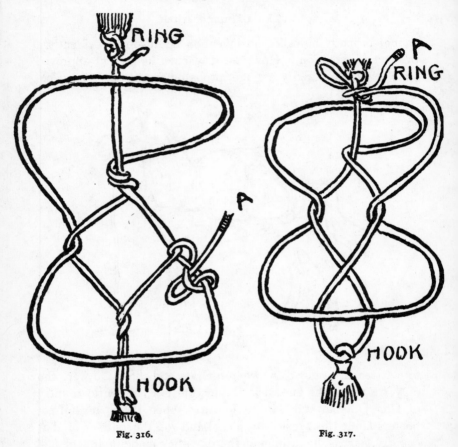

Fig. 316.

Fig. 317.

of the lariat and also to throw this hitch, and it was from some of these old veterans that Capt. A. E. Wood in 1879 gained his knowledge and introduced it into the United States army. It was the 4th Cavalry which first became proficient and now you will find the diamond hitch in the cavalry drill of the United States Army. Thus the Yankee soldiers are to-day packing their animals by the hitch they have learned indirectly from the Spaniards, and this is the reason that the saddle bags and the pad still retain the Spanish names of alforjas and aparejo.

The following chapter will tell you how to throw the diamond in the most approved style, and it is illustrated with diagrams invented by the author which are so simple that a small child may understand them.

CHAPTER XXIV

HOW TO PACK A PACK HORSE AND HOW TO THROW THE DIAMOND HITCH

In the previous chapters I told how to pack and unpack one's duffle for wilderness travel, and explained a squaw hitch. The next thing in order is to tell how to secure the dunnage on a pack animal's back.

In the first place the pack animal should be blindfolded. If it is never led nor forced to move while blindfolded it soon learns to stand perfectly still as long as the bandage is over its eyes.

We will suppose you have the pack saddle, lash-rope, cincha, aparejo, and all the needful accoutrements of a pack animal (Figs. 318, 319, 320, 321, 322 and 323). The aparejo, by the way, consists of two pieces of leather or canvas fastened together at the edges and across the middle and stretched over a light, springy framework of willow and stuffed with straw or moss, so as to form pads fitting the shape of the pack horse on each side of the back bone. It must be stiff at the edges and corners where the pull comes. Willow sticks fitted in shoes, across the width of the aparejo, at the bottom edges are used to stiffen it.

How to Use the Sling-Rope when There is no Top Pack

Fig. 324. Head packer throws sling-rope across aparejo with loop on right side.

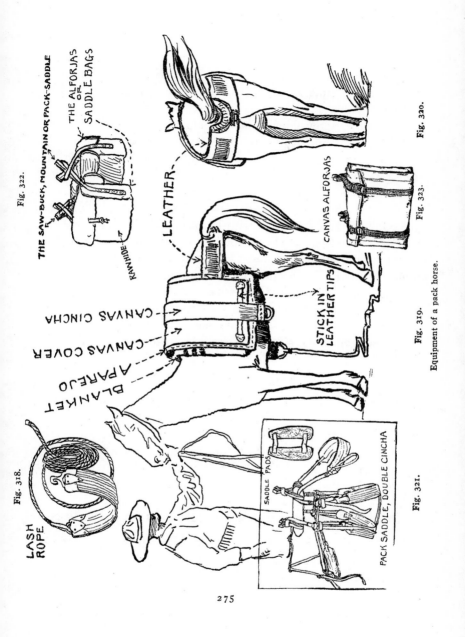

Fig. 318.

LASH ROPE

Fig. 322.

THE SAW-BUCK, MOUNTAIN OR PACK-SADDLE

THE ALFORJAS OR SADDLE BAGS

RAWHIDE

LEATHER

Fig. 320.

CANVAS ALFORJAS

Fig. 323.

STICK IN LEATHER TIPS

Fig. 319.

CANVAS CINCHA

CANVAS COVER

APAREJO

BLANKET

SADDLE PADS

PACK SADDLE, DOUBLE CINCHA

Fig. 321.

Equipment of a pack horse.

275

Fig. 325. Head packer throws first side pack on top of sling-rope and on the right side of horse where it is held in place by second packer.

Fig. 326. Shows how packer should stand and support pack with left hand and forearm. The heaviest pack can be held securely in this way while the free hand is used for fastening the sling-rope. Upper sketch shows the improper method of holding pack on horse.

Fig. 327. Second packer holds loop A (Fig. 325) of sling-rope in right hand, holding pack with left arm (see diagram 326).

Fig. 328. Head packer throws on second side pack over the sling-rope on left side of horse. Second packer holds loop A in right hand until the second pack B is in place.

Fig. 329. Head packer passes one end of sling-rope through loop A, which is thrown to him by second packer.

Fig. 330. Head packer knots loose end of sling-rope. Both packers shake down side packs and are ready for the diamond hitch.

After the Sling-Rope is Tied

Fig. 331. The head packer says "Break your pack." Then each man taking the pack (on his side of the horse) by both ends, pulls down hard with a sawing motion. This takes up all the slack on the sling-rope. As a horse's back is broader near the hind quarters than at the withers the packs should be farther apart at the hind end (as in Fig. 331) to better fit the horse.

How to Tie Your Sling-Rope when You Have a Top Pack

Fig. 334. Head packer, standing on left side of animal, throws sling-rope across horse, so that loop A hangs across aparejo, and the two loose ends across horse's neck, on left side.

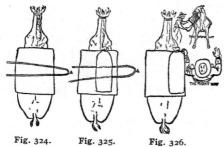

Fig. 324.   Fig. 325.   Fig. 326.

First moves in placing the load.

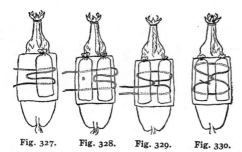

Fig. 327.   Fig. 328.   Fig. 329.   Fig. 330.

Final moves in placing the load.

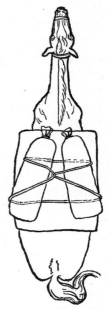

Fig. 331.—After shaking down. These bags fit the horse.

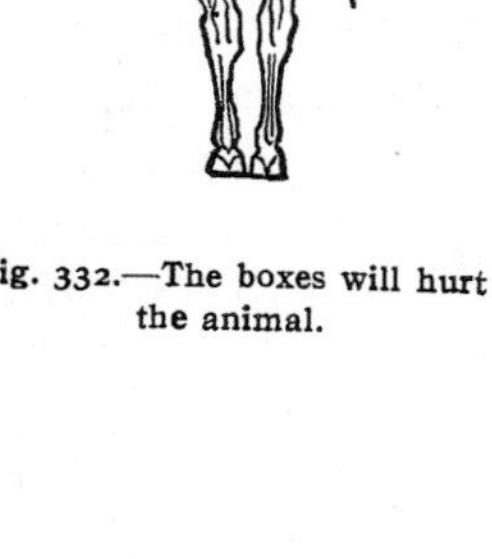

Fig. 332.—The boxes will hurt the animal.

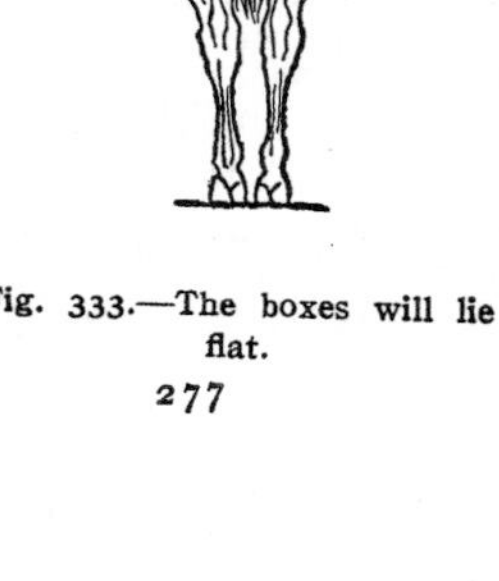

Fig. 333.—The boxes will lie flat.

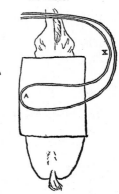

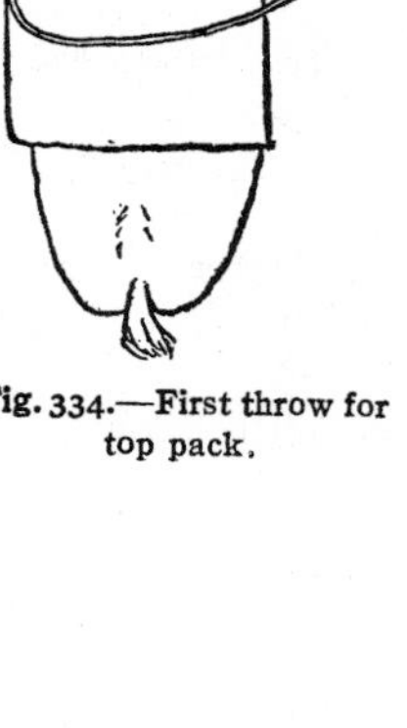

Fig. 334.—First throw for top pack.

Fig. 335. Head packer throws first side pack on horse on right side where second packer holds it in place (see diagram 326). Second packer then throws bight of sling-rope over side pack. Head packer throws loop of sling-rope to second packer who holds it in right hand.

Fig. 336. Head packer throws on left side pack—over sling-rope.

Fig. 337. Head packer passes one loose end of sling-rope over left side pack and through loop of sling-rope which is tossed to him by second packer.

Fig. 338. Head packer passes second end of sling-rope over

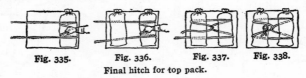

Fig. 335.   Fig. 336.   Fig. 337.   Fig. 338.
Final hitch for top pack.

left-side pack and knots it to first loose end. Packers then shake down packs (see Figs. 331, 332, and 333).

Fig. 339. Head packer throws on top pack, which fits in hollow between side packs, and now you are ready for the dia-

mond hitch. Of course the top pack will settle down on the horse's back, but the better to show position of ropes the middle pack is not shown resting on horse's back in diagram.

Fig. 332. When the pack is composed of boxes they often jam the sling-ropes and hang in this position, with nothing but a small piece touching the horse. As can be seen the boxes in this case have a tendency to act as a lever and press in. This is very bad for the horse's back.

Fig. 339.—The top pack will settle down on the horse's back.

Fig. 333. To remedy this "break the pack" by lifting the

box with your chest and pulling the top away from the horse with your two hands. Then the boxes will lie flat.

How to Throw Sling-Rope for Mountain Pack Saddle for Side or Top Pack

Fig. 340. Mountain pack saddle—sling rope way over.

Fig. 341. Packer takes a turn with loose ends of sling-rope around horns.

Figs. 342 and 343. Packer puts right side pack on inside of loop and takes up slack, pulling one end of sling-rope.

Fig. 344. Packer puts on left pack, and ties sling-rope, and you are ready for diamond hitch.

But before throwing the diamond, cover load neatly with the piece of canvas, which is made for that purpose. This is not fastened in any manner before throwing the hitch, because the diamond will hold it and everything else securely in place.

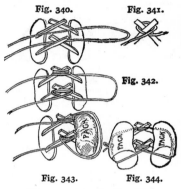

Fig. 340.   Fig. 341.

Fig. 342.

Fig. 343.   Fig. 344.

Sling rope on sawbuck saddle.

How to Throw North Rocky Mountain Diamond

First blindfold horse.

Head packer stands on left side of horse, second packer stands on right side. Head packer throws cincha under horse to second packer (Fig. 345), and throws loose end of rope on the ground to second packer. Second packer takes cincha and loose ends F in his left hand, head packer throws loop C D (Fig. 346) to second packer, making twist X. Second packer hooks loop C D

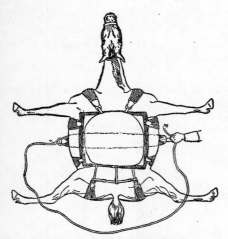

Fig. 345.—First throw for diamond.

Fig. 346.

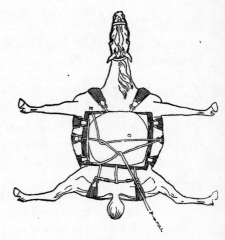

Fig. 348.—The first half of diamond.

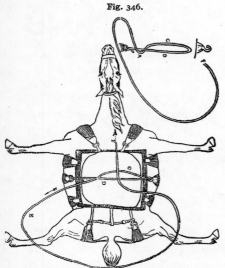

Fig. 347.
Second throw for diamond.

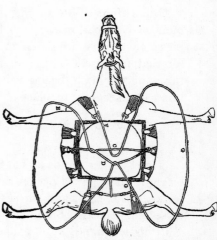

Fig. 349.—The left side is cinched, but is shown loose in diagram so as to be better understood.

(Fig. 346) into cincha hook and passes the loose end F under D (Fig. 347). Both packers cinch; second packer pulls up on rope, head packer takes in slack on E (Fig. 347).

Head packer passes loop E under aparejo and second packer pulls loose end F toward rear of the horse, taking in slack (Fig. 348). While second packer pulls the bight G, he throws loose end **F** over horse on the top of pack to head packer who passes it under C (Fig. 349). When a packer is cinching, packer on opposite side should hold down his side of pack to prevent shifting of load. While head packer holds down pack he slips loose end F under C (Fig. 349). (Diagram made with loose loops so as to be better understood.) While second packer pulls bight G under aparejo and pulls

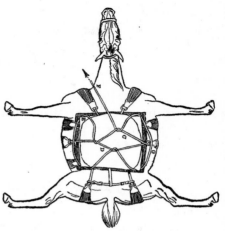

Fig. 350.—Head packer pulls in slack.

Fig. 352.   Fig. 351.

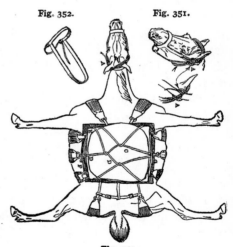

Fig. 353.

Finished diamond, also showing how to fasten up halter rope.

from the head of the horse, head packer takes loose end F and pulls in the slack (Fig. 350).

Head packer makes loose end A fast with hitch to rope D (Fig. 353). While head packer is making fast, second packer winds halter rope around horse's neck behind left ear and in front of right ear (Fig. 351), making end fast by weaving under halter and over rope (Fig. 353), then pulling the loose end under bight where rope crosses halter. Fig. 352 shows useful type of halter for pack-train work.

The U. S. Cavalry Diamond

The celebrated diamond hitch is thrown in many different ways. In the previous chapter I have shown how to throw a squaw hitch, which is really one form of the diamond hitch, and have just told how the diamond is thrown in the Northwest by the packers who penetrate the wilderness as far up as the wild regions around Mt. McKinley in Alaska, but for the end of this chapter I have selected the hitch thrown by the United States army packers.

To learn to do this or any of the hitches it is not necessary to have a pack horse.

Take a Sofa Pillow and Fold It

up until it resembles the rounded back of a pack animal; tie it in that position; for the aparejo you can use a piece of pasteboard or anything which is stiff enough to hold the lash-rope when tucked under its corners. Take an ordinary belt for a cincha and strap it around the stiff cushion and the aparejo to hold the latter in place.

Poke an Umbrella in One End

of the cushion to represent the head of a horse.

Then take another sofa pillow, or fold up a piece of cloth or a coat, or anything to represent

The Load or Pack

Now you must have a piece of thick twine, a window cord or even a clothes-line for the lash-rope. You need another cincha to attach to the lash-rope and this must have some substitute at one end for a ring and at the other end for a hook. Put this cincha under the dummy horse so that the top of the ring comes on the nigh or left-hand side of the horse at the bottom edge of the aparejo, and the hook on the off or right-hand side of the horse, also at the bottom edge of the aparejo, and then proceed to throw the hitch as here described.

I have made many diagrams to illustrate the diamond hitch, and I have discovered that the difficulty one finds in understanding the diagrams has been caused by the fact that practically each throw must be represented by two drawings: one showing nigh side of the horse and the other to show the off side of the same horse. To remedy the confusion arising from the duplication of diagrams I invented the manner of drawing the horse so that the two sides and the back are seen at a glance.

In the army they have three men to pack a horse, but hunters and campers need only a head packer and a second packer. The pack horse sometimes has a cloth to throw over his back before the folded blankets are placed on him. Then the folded blankets are put on its back about $2\frac{1}{2}$ inches in front of where the pummel end of the saddle is to rest, and over this the aparejo is placed. The mountain saw-buck or pack saddle usually used is represented by Fig. 340. Hanging to the pack saddle on each side are the alforjas (Fig. 323), consisting of two stiff canvas or raw-hide saddle bags which are suspended by means of straps from the saw-buck saddle. Over this the pack is placed, and over that a pack cover and then the diamond hitch is thrown to bind all in place, but

For Practice in Throwing the Hitch

there is nothing necessary except a substitute for the aparejo, a pack, the cinchas and the lash-rope. Now that you have your dummy animal before you, make fast one end of the lash-rope to the ring of the cincha. Throw the free end of the rope to the rear of the pack animal, convenient to the second packer. The head packer now takes the lash-rope in his right hand about 3 feet from the cincha and passes the hook end (H, Fig. 354) under the animal to the second packer. The latter takes the hook in his left hand, while head packer with his left hand grasps the rope about 3 feet above the right, raises it and passes it along the centre line (P P, Fig. 354) between the side packs from the rear to the front, as shown in the diagram. He then pulls the slack to the front until it forms a loop long enough (A, Fig. 354) to throw over the cargo and fasten in the hook H.

The right hand shown in the diagram with the palm upward holds the cincha end of the rope and the loop A falls outward over the right forearm (Fig. 354). The left hand, with the palm outward, holds the rope half way between the loop A and P P, the middle of the pack. The head packer next throws the loop A across the pack and then lets the left hand drop on the animal's neck, thus forming another loop, shown in Fig. 355 by A'. The second packer passes the rope through the hook and pulls the cincha end of it until the hook is drawn up so that when

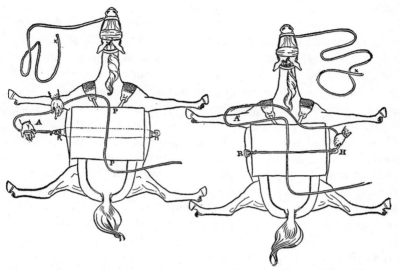

Fig. 354.—First throw for U. S. diamond.   Fig. 355.—Second position of rope.

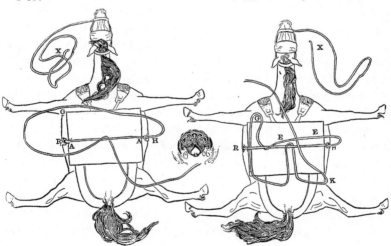

Fig. 356.   Fig. 357.

Third and fourth diagrams for U. S. diamond.

tightened it will be near the lower edge of the off side of the aparejo. The head packer now takes the rope at G (Fig. 356) and tucks a loop from the rear to the front under the part A A (Fig. 356), over the centre of the inner side pack G (Fig. 357). The second packer passes the loose end of the rope under the part marked E E (Fig. 357) and throws it over on the nigh side of the pack animal's neck; head packer now draws the tucked loop forward and tucks it under the corners and lower edge of the nigh side of the aparejo and hauls it taut from above the rear corner; second packer takes hold of the rope at I (Fig. 358) with his left hand and at K (Fig. 357) with his right and passes the rope under the corners and lower edge of the off side of the aparejo (K L, Fig. 358), and hauls taut at the front corner, head packer taking in slack at the loose end of the rope.

The lash-rope is now ready to be cinched up for the final tightening. The second packer now removes the blind from the pack animal and leads it forward a few steps, while the head packer in the rear is examining the load to see if the packs are properly adjusted. The animal is then again blinded. In making the final tightening, while the second packer is pulling the parts taut the head packer takes up the slack and keeps the pack steady; the tightening should be done in such a manner as not to shake the pack out of balance or position. The second packer takes the lash-rope above where it leaves the hook, and below the edge of the aparejo, right hand below left, places the knee against the rear corner of the aparejo, and head packer grasps with the right hand the same part of the rope where it comes from the pack on the inner side, and with the left hand at G (Fig. 358) places his right shoulder against the cargo to steady it. He then gives the command to PULL! With steady pulls the second packer tightens rope without letting it slip back

through the hook, and gives the slack to head packer, who takes
it up by steady pulls.   When the second packer thinks it is all
right he cries, "ENOUGH."   Head packer holds steady with his
right hand, slips the left hand down to where the rope passes over

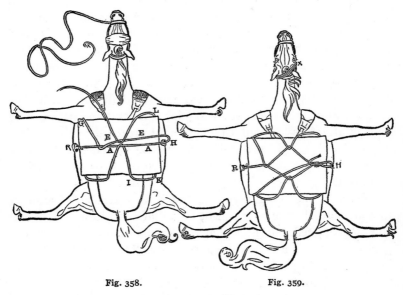

Fig. 358.   Fig. 359.

Final throw and finish of U. S. diamond.

the front edge of the aparejo, and holds steady; the right hand
then grasps the continuation of the rope at the rear corner of the
pad and pulls taut; then with both hands, placing his right knee
against the rear corner of the pad, pulls hard until the rope is well
home.   Second packer takes up the slack by grasping the
rope I (Fig. 358) where it comes over the rear end of the off
side pack with both hands.   Head packer steps to the front and

steadies the pack. The second packer pulls taut the parts on his side, taking up the slack; this draws the part of the lash-rope A A (Fig. 358) well back at middle of the pack; he then with the left hand at the rear corner K pulls taut and holds solid, while with the right hand in front of L he takes up slack. He then with both hands at the front corner and with his knee against it pulls well taut, head packer taking up the slack on his side, and then pulls steady, drawing the part E E (Fig. 358) of the rope leading from the hook well forward at the middle of the pack, then carries the loose end under the corners and ends of the aparejo, draws taut and ties end fast by half hitch near the cincha end of the lash-rope (Fig. 359). In case the rope is long enough after passing under the corners to reach over the load, it can then be passed over and made fast on the off side by tying around both parts of the lash-rope above the hook and drawing them well together.

There is one thing very essential in the packing of animals that we have before mentioned, and that is to have the weight equally adjusted. It is a common saying that an experienced packer will "heft" a jack-knife to see if it will balance the compass in his opposite pocket. A lopsided load will cause no end of trouble both to the man and beast, but it sometimes happens that owing to the form of the objects to be packed the side packs are necessarily of unequal bulk or weight. In a case of this kind the larger or heavier object should be placed on the nigh side and so arranged as to lap over the off side sufficiently to make the packs balance.

When the Blind is Finally Removed

and while the head packer is making the loose end of the lash-rope fast, the second packer winds the halter rope around the horse's neck behind left ear and in front of right ear, making end fast by weaving under halter and over rope (Figs. 351 and 353) and then pulling the loose end under the bight where rope crosses halter. This will keep the halter rope out of harm's way and at the same time there will be no danger of the animal choking itself.

CHAPTER XXV

HOW TO PACK A DOG AND HOW TO MAKE THE PACK SADDLE

Every time that I see a guide loaded down with an immense pack of camp duffle, staggering along the trail, I wonder that

Fig. 360.—A dog's pack saddle.

dogs are not used in our woods as pack animals by the guides, fishermen and hunters as they are used in the far North. It is not necessary for the thermometer to be at 70 degrees below zero to make it feasible to use dogs to carry camp luggage. A man starting out to spend a few days' fishing, with the aid of a strong dog, could lessen the labor of the trip to such an extent as to make the portages or long tramps through the woods a pleasure instead of a pain.

Let it be understood to start with that

Any Sort of a Dog May be Trained to Carry a Pack

It is not necessary that the dog should be exported from the North for this purpose, nor is it even desirable, for in the more southern countries these big, shaggy dogs suffer greatly with the heat; but any good native dog will do, a stout cur, shepherd dog, bull terrier, St. Bernard, Newfoundland, Great Dane, all of them, or any one of them, can carry a pack of considerable weight if it is properly adjusted.

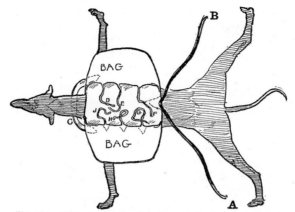

Fig. 361.—Diagram showing how the pack is placed on the dog.

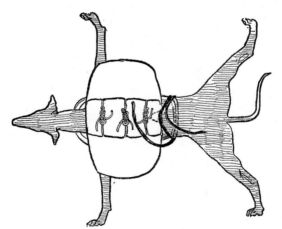

Fig. 362.—The cinch around the waist.

A Dog's Pack

consists primarily of a pair of saddle bags. These may be made of canvas or any stout material, and should be so arranged with strings (D E F G H J, Fig. 360) that they may be laced up securely after the duffle is stored. There should also be a cincha strap, rope or band attached to the middle of the rear end of the

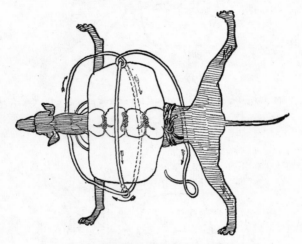

Fig. 363.—First throw of lash-rope.

saddle bag, as shown by A B (Fig. 361) and at the forward end a yoke band to fit across the front shoulders of the dog (C, Figs. 360 and 361).

To Pack the Dog

slip the breast band in place, adjust the bags well forward upon its front shoulders, and then cinch it up securely by passing the cincha straps around under its body and bringing them up again upon the back where they may be tied. The cincha is made with dark line in the diagrams (Figs. 361, 362, and 363). Reference to the diagrams will show that the cincha is back of the ribs, and when thus placed a dog may be cinched up remarkably tight with no injury or apparent inconvenience to the animal. This arrangement will hold the bags in place, but the pouches will stick out on each side unless further secured, so you must have a lash-rope for this purpose.

The Lash-Rope

should have a ring attached to one end, or the end tied in a loop or halter knot. As every one does not know

How to Tie a Halter Knot

it may be best to explain. Make the bend A in the string B C of Fig. 364, then make the bend D in the C end of

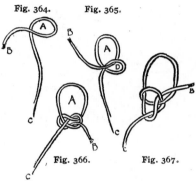

Fig. 364.   Fig. 365.

Fig. 366.   Fig. 367.

A halter and a bow-string knot.

the string and bring the end B through the D bend (Fig. 365). Then take the end B and run it under the bend A down and under the C end of the string and under the lower part of the bend D out and over as in Fig. 366. Pull this tight and you have got the halter knot which will make a loop that will not slip. Or you can make the old bo'line shown in Fig. 367. Either of these knots will be secure and not slip up under a strain.

To Lash the Pack

in place throw the ring over to the left side of the pack, then pass the free end of the lash-rope under the pack, as shown by the dotted lines in Fig. 363. Bring it up through the ring in the end of the rope, then around across the dog's breast to the right-hand side, and here pass it over and under the top rope as shown by Fig. 368, then continue around the pack and under the dog until the end comes around towards the ring. In these diagrams the lash-rope is shown loose to better explain the method, but of course it is necessary to cinch them up tightly, as in Figs. 369 and 370. Now bring the end of the lash-rope under the top rope and secure it with a simple slip knot, as shown by Figs. 371, 372 and 373. With this pack a dog can travel many miles and carry a burden equal to about half its own weight.

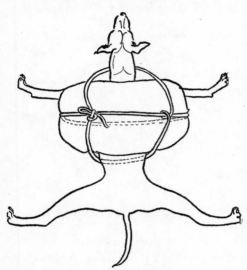

Fig. 368.—Lash-rope in position. Shown loose in diagram so as to make it explain itself.

The Bags

in the diagram are shown without any cover, but each bag may have a flap made for it, as shown by Figs. 360 and 374, and these flaps may be snugly tucked in over the duffle before the bags are tied up, but you may have a little square of waterproof stuff with which you can cover the duffle and tuck into the bags before they are laced, or as a cover, as in Fig. 375.

There is no reason why pack dogs should not be used for a

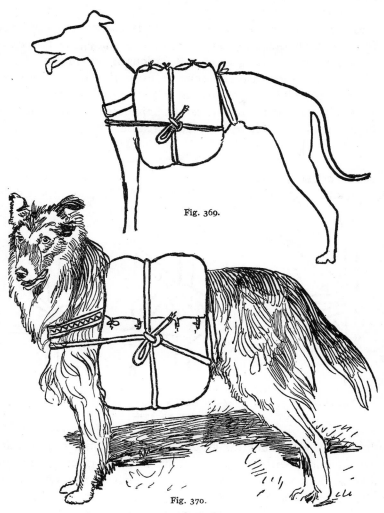

Fig. 369.

Fig. 370.

All ready to hit the trail.

great variety of purposes. If the dog is packed properly, well forward upon the fore shoulders, even a small dog can carry one's luncheon, fishing creel and various knick-knacks of that kind, with greater ease and comfort to itself than can the man if the same stuff is put in a basket and hung on his arm.

Nor is the dog the only domestic animal which might be used in this manner. There is no good reason why

Goats

should not be used at mountain resorts. When an Alpine climber is making a difficult ascent, neither he nor his guides want to be

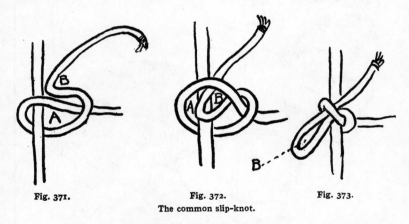

Fig. 371.   Fig. 372.   Fig. 373.
The common slip-knot.

hampered with much duffle, but there are a lot of things which would add greatly to a mountain-climber's comfort after he had made the ascent which might be safely packed on goats or dogs and the animals left to follow their masters in their own way. Of course this does not apply to extremely difficult climbs, but it does apply to ordinary summer mountain work.

Picnics and Summer Outings

Pack dogs could also be used for picnic excursions in the woods, or for any sort of pedestrian trips they would be found of great advantage. A horse requires a certain amount of time devoted to its care and comfort. It needs fodder and water and

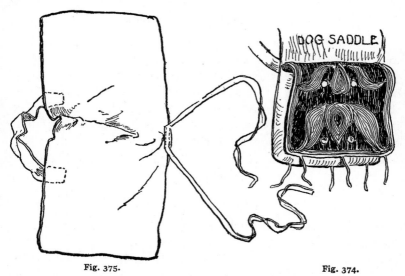

Fig. 375.   Fig. 374.

Make your own dog saddles to fit your dogs.

it must be tethered out at night and led to water and fed. This all occupies a great deal of time and costs money, but a dog does not have to be tethered out; it will feed from the scraps of its master's table, find its own drink and act as a watch dog at night and cost nothing for keep; besides which, the companionship of a dog does away with the loneliness of a trip into the woods when one has no other companion.

In the Far North

where dogs are regularly used as pack animals the huskies are frequently allowed to forage for themselves, and live well upon the small mammals which they capture near camp, and a dog will live and grow fat where a horse will starve to death.

How to Make a Dog Saddle

Inasmuch as dogs vary in size, a dog saddle built for one dog may not fit another. Consequently when you are going to make your pack, take the dog which you propose to use and a piece of any sort of cloth. Cut the cloth out in rectangular shape, like that shown in Fig. 375, and lay it over the dog's shoulders. When it is in place, make a yoke band of a strip of cloth, fit it around the dog's chest just under its throat and pin it to the cloth on the dog's back on each side. Before you remove the cloth cut it so that it will be of the proper length.

The Pack Should Not be Too Long

as it may interfere and catch upon brush and other obstacles in the trail. When you have got the pattern cut to the proper size, pin the cincha on to the saddle, as shown in Fig. 361, tie it on the dog and make sure that it fits like the one in Fig. 369. After you have fitted your pattern and pinned it in shape, remove it from the dog, cut your saddle cloth according to the pattern just made and stitch the yoke on at the points where it was pinned and the cincha at the point where it was pinned.

It is not necessary for ordinary work to have the pack bags arranged like those shown in Figs. 361, 362 and 363, but you can, if you desire, make the bags with a cover to them, like the one shown in Fig. 374, and sew these bags to the saddle. When you make a bag with a cover to hang over the side, as the one in Fig. 374, the strings for securing it should be attached to the bottom of the flap and another set to the bottom of the bag, as shown in the diagram. Now, if you have leisure time, and fancy that sort of work,

The Cover to the Bag May be Decorated

with beads, as the Indians decorate the bags which they hang at their saddle bow. This will give a very festive appearance to the dog pack, although it will add nothing to its durability or usefulness. Away up North where dogs are the only beasts of burden, the half-breeds and Indians have most beautiful pack covers made of beaded work, with tassels and bells and all the little trinkets which appeal to the Indian's heart, but these covers are not used in ordinary travel. They are carefully stowed away until the time when the driver is approaching a camp or a Hudson Bay station or some settlement. Then all the finery is brought forth and the dogs decorated in gala attire, and, with a crack of the whip and a whoop and a yell from the driver the dogs dash into the settlement. Now, since the white man and the white woman and the white boy in the bottom of their hearts are as fond of display and of creating a sensation as any copper-colored son of America, there is no reason why they should not please their fancy and their inborn love of art by making decorated covers for their dog packs to put upon the dogs when they are returning from a fishing excursion, a tramp in the hills or a hunting trip. This sort of a thing would be a novelty and tend to lend interest to the guests at the camp in the Maine woods, for instance; besides which, even the outdoor man, explorer and prospector loses something of value if his life is deprived of beauty and beautiful things, even if it is expressed only in the pack cover of a dog train.

CHAPTER XXVI

MAKING DIFFICULT CAMPS OVER THE WATER OR ON A SWAMP

There are few, if any, real "outdoor" people who are not capable of using the material wild nature affords, to construct for themselves a comfortable camp which will protect them from sun or rain. But it frequently happens that there is no solid earth in the immediate vicinity of the vantage ground, and the sportsmen are compelled to locate their camps long distances from their blinds or favorite fishing pools. Such a state of affairs necessitates long all-night journeys over the worst of trails, in order that the gunners may be at their blinds in the gray dawn, or the anglers reach the fishing place before the sun is too high and brilliant. All this may be obviated by a camp built on the spot. Besides the great convenience of such camps, they often possess other unlooked for advantages; I have slept over a salt meadow when the rank grass was blackened with millions of mosquitoes, and not an insect touched me, although my face and hands were unprotected.

There seems to be an almost constant breeze blowing over the long stretches of flat, open marshes, and the mosquitoes can make no headway against even a mild summer's zephyr and seek protection of the long grass, leaving persons a few feet above them free from the attack of their poisoned lances.

The only

Real Difficulties

to be encountered in building camps over marshes, bogs, swamps and the water is the transportation of the building material and securing a foundation on quaking ground of sufficient stability to support the shack. A house on the marsh or over the water itself requires little or no more labor than is demanded of one to build an equally substantial camp in the woods, and wherever it is possible to secure small timber and brush you may sleep in as dry a bed as can be procured in the forest itself.

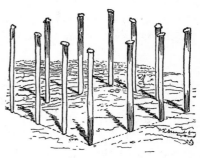

Fig. 376.—Drive your stakes on shore.

It is a simple matter

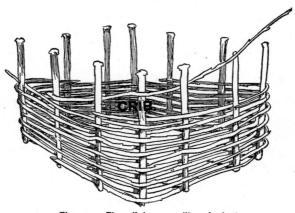

Fig. 377.—The crib is woven like a basket.

To Build Huts Over the Water

in flooded forest districts by fastening timbers horizontally between the trees and erecting a platform upon them, as whole tribes of aborigines do in some parts of South America; but to build the shack over open water is another proposition. However, this, too, may be done provided the water is shallow.

Mark Out the Site of Your Camp

by thrusting four temporary poles in the bottom at the four corners of the proposed structure. Make a measurement of the depth of the water at these four points and build your cribs according to this measurement.

Fig. 378.—A nodule of hummock grass.

If the bottom is soft enough to allow you to drive in stakes, make your cribs with the uprights projecting a couple of feet or more; this may be done by selecting a soft piece of ground on shore and driving the stakes in the earth the required distance, being careful to so drive them that when

The Crib

is finished it may be easily removed without wrenching it apart (Fig. 376).

The crib is woven basket fashion in and out of the stakes (Fig. 377). Use stout stakes, not thicker than your wrist at the big end for the uprights and split "hoop poles" of any sort of pliable wood for the basket weaving. If the proper sort of hoop-pole wood is not available, vines, roots or long strips of bark can be made to answer the purpose. Make the crib about 3 x 4 feet and of a depth to correspond with the depth of the water. In weaving use judgment and care; do not leave the joints open; that is, allow no space between the end of one woven piece and the end of the next piece to follow; overlap their ends by beginning with the next piece back of where the last one ends.

When the four basket cribs are finished, carefully redraw from the soft earth the stakes, which may be done without injuring the crib; transport the baskets to the site of your proposed camp. Set the cribs at the four corners, and with a stone, club or axe drive the stakes into the bottom as they were first driven into the ground before the basket work was begun and as they stood when it was completed.

In the middle of each of these cribs you may now erect

A Corner Post

for your camp by forcing its pointed end as far in the bottom of the water as it will go, and then securing it in place by filling around with stones; small stones make a more solid pier than the larger ones, they pack better and are less liable to work loose.

In case there are no stones handy, then there will certainly be sugar-loafed or hemispherical nodules of the roots of the hummock grass growing along the shores of marshes (Fig. 378). If these are cut off with a sharp hunting knife, they will make ex-

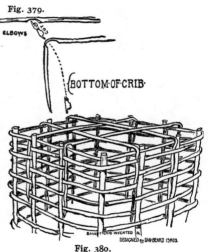

Fig. 379.

ELBOWS

BOTTOM·OF·CRIB

Fig. 380.

A basket crib with a bottom to it.

cellent ballast for the cribs and pack even better than small stones.
If the bottom is too hard or rocky to admit the driving of stakes,
a bottom to the crib must be made as shown by Fig. 380.
Fig. 379 shows how to cut a hoop so that it may be bent without breaking.

Before putting any stones in the crib, cover the bottom with

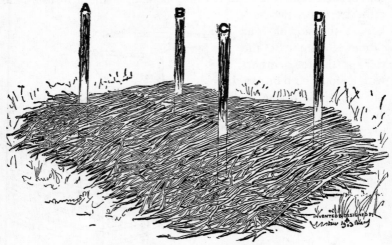

Fig. 381.—The snow-shoe mattress of brush.

A Layer of Small Boughs

to prevent the smaller fragments of ballast from falling through,
then sink your basket to the bottom.   The corner posts must now
be each held in position by one of the party, while the others fill
up the cribs with ballast, after which brace the posts with two
horizontal poles running above the water diagonally to the
corner posts, thus ✕.   They may then be further braced as the
uprights C and D are in Fig. 383.

If the water is liable to be rough, greater security is gained by filling the space between the piers with brush weighted down by heavy stones.

When your platform is erected several feet above the water you are free to erect a tent, an Indian bark wigwam, a wickiup, an Adirondack shack, a frame shanty or even a log house, according to the facilities and time at your disposal.

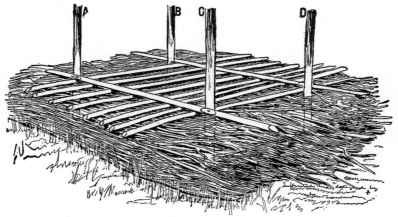

Fig. 382.—By this arrangement the posts cannot sink unless the whole mattress sinks.

A Camp on the Marsh,

even though the bog is practically bottomless, will not sink if the well-known principle of the snow-shoe is adhered to in the structure.

It is a simple act to erect the four corner posts A B C D (Fig. 381) in the soft ground, for if their ends are pointed the posts may be forced into the yielding earth without the aid of maul or hammer. The real difficulty often is not in forcing them into the ground, but in preventing them from sinking out of sight.

The Posts

should penetrate the quaking earth only far enough to support them in an upright position.

Before proceeding further, it is necessary to collect

A Great Heap of Small Boughs

of spruce, pine, cedar, hemlock or almost any other tree; those having the thickest mass of small branches are the best for the purpose. Make a mat of these branches by laying them on the ground as you would the shingles of a house, with this difference: the sides as well as the ends should overlap each other. Do this by placing them close together, a row at a time, until the green mattress extends several feet on all sides of the four posts (Fig. 381).

Spread your next layer with the direction of the rows and stems at right angles with the rows and stems of the first layer; use care in selecting branches which will lie flat and not tangle up in an unsightly mass. At right angles with the rows of the second layer, and on top of them, spread the third thickness, and continue in this manner (Fig. 381) until you have a mattress which will be 2 or 3 feet thick when compressed by the weight it has to sustain.

Parallel to each other, and at right angles to the direction of the top layer of brush,

Lay a Number of Lodge Poles

for binders (Fig. 382). At right angles with these place the two top binders E G and F H (Figs. 382, 383, and 384).

With the help of any heavy objects and the combined weight of the campers, press E G and F H firmly down on the brush mattress and hold them there until they are securely nailed to the upright corners posts A B C D (Figs. 381, 382, 383 and 384).

It will now be impossible for the uprights to sink deeper into the mire, no matter what weight they may be called upon to support, unless the mattress goes with them or the posts are torn

Fig. 383.—It is now a simple matter to build the shack.

away from the binders E G and F H. These binders may be made much heavier than shown in the diagrams, and for a structure similar to Fig. 384 this might be necessary.

A well-constructed marsh camp will not sink until time rots the structure.

The snowshoe principle will not apply to some stretches of

liquid mud and quicksands, which are too fluid to support anything not built like a boat, but it will be found to work with satis-

Fig. 385.

Fig. 384.

Figs. 384 and 385 show a bark-thatched camp and a mud fireplace.

factory results on all ordinary bogs, swamps and marshes which
have a surface crust of sod, roots or hummocks.

Fig. 383 shows the framework suitable for a canvas, board

or bark covering, and Fig. 384 shows an adaptation of the bark hut to the brush shoe foundation.

Fig. 385 shows how a fireplace may be made in front of the shack, with a hearth of clay and a frame of green hemlock, which will minimize the danger of burning your camp down while you sleep.

CHAPTER XXVII

HOW TO MAKE JACK-KNIFE DOOR LATCHES

The deeper one goes into the wilderness the less necessity there is for bolts and bars to the door of the cabin or shack, but some sort of latch is necessary in order that the door may be closed, and to keep the varmints out during the absence of the owner of the forest home.

Fig. 386 shows the Trapper's Catch which is

The Most Simple and Primitive Latch

known to the writer. As may be seen by the diagram, it consists of a notched peg for a catch and an elastic bit of hard wood for a latch. The latter is fastened with two nails, or two wooden pegs at one end, and the other end is left free to spring into place when the door is closed. The advantage of this latch is the fact that a push on the door from the outside will cause the latch to be forced up over the notch and the door to open, while a slam of the door will reverse the operation and the door will be closed. With this trappers' catch the latch-string does not hang on the outside, but the hospitality is just the same, for a push opens the door. However,

The Pioneer

latch-string does really hang upon the outside; as may be seen by reference to Fig. 387. The pioneer latch consists of a flat stick of hard wood fastened at one end by a nail or screw, upon which pivot the stick moves freely.

The catch is simply a notched stick nailed to the door jamb; a string fastened to the latch is run up and through a small hole in the door and hangs outside. There is often a button or stick fastened to the outside end of the string for a handle (see diagram in upper part of Fig. 387), but this is not always used, for it prevents the occupants from pulling the string inside when they retire for the night.

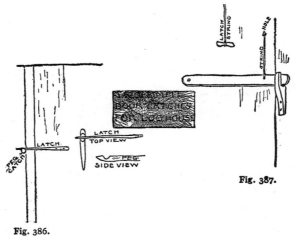

Fig. 387.

Fig. 386.

The Maine woods and the pioneer door latches.

Hunters often return to their forest home with heavy packs on their backs and guns or axes in their hands and then

A Foot Latch

is most convenient. Fig. 388 shows how such a latch can be made to work. The latch itself may be made like Fig. 387, but in place of a string a shaft (Fig. 388) is fastened to the latch and extended down to a trigger, which is projected through the door, where it is pivoted to a block outside. Fig. 388 shows first an end or edge view and then a flat or face view seen from the inside of the house.

The Gunner's Latch

(Fig. 389) is somewhat more crude than the foregoing one, but it is a practical latch and is made with the aid of a hatchet from a block of hard maple, moosewood or any other hard wood. The trigger is flattened to fit the foot, swelling out to the natural thick-

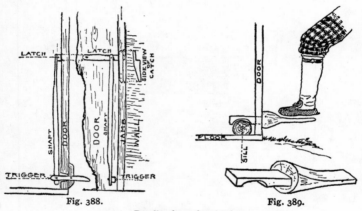

Fig. 388.   Fig. 389.

Details of two foot latches.

ness of the wood where it comes against the door. Here it is suddenly cut down to a rectangular form and then notched on the under side to fit over the log door-sill as shown in the diagram.

The flattened end with the notch underneath is pushed through a hole in the door and it often has neither nail nor peg to pivot it, but of course a pivot of some sort will prevent the latch from being knocked out-of-doors by accident.

If such crude affairs as the gunner's latch do not appeal to

your refined taste you may test your skill with a jack-knife by
making a

Tippecanoe Latch,

which is worked with a wooden spring and, when well made,
is almost as durable and serviceable as one of metal; in truth,
if the wood is well seasoned and the house dry, the Tippecanoe
latch will probably outlast a metal one, for wood will not rust.

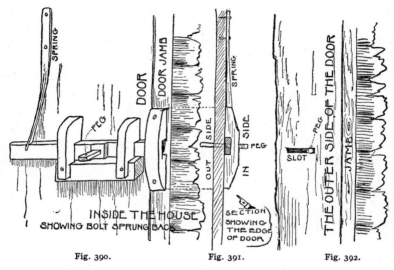

Fig. 390.   Fig. 391.   Fig. 392.

Fig. 390 shows the latch with the bolt sprung back, as the
position of the spring shows, as well as the fact that the bolt hole
in the latch is empty. In Fig. 392, which shows the outside of
the door, we know that it is fastened from the position of the peg,
and to open the door we must push the bolt back by sliding the
peg to the opposite end of the slot. Fig. 391 shows an edge or
sectional view and also how the peg protrudes on the outside of
the door.

While the Tippecanoe is a very simple device, it is made of quite a number of parts, and to make it perfectly plain to the ambitious rustic locksmith I have drawn all parts, excepting the spring stick, natural size (Figs. 393 to 397), but inasmuch as the original diagram is drawn too large for this page I have made a scale of inches at the bottom which here appears reduced in the same proportion as in the diagram.

It is understood that there are no fixed dimensions for this or any other lock, latch or catch, but the proportions here given are conservative ones and probably the ones you will want. Fig. 393 shows the foundation block upon which the latch rests and is securely nailed or screwed to the door. Figs. 394 and 395 are two wooden clamps which are fastened to the door and also to the foundation block (Fig. 390). These clamps must be notched, as in diagrams, to allow for the movement of the bolt, but since the bolt (Fig. 397) is thicker at the butt, the notch in Fig. 394 is made just a trifle larger than the butt end of the bolt, and in Fig. 395 the notch is made just a trifle larger than the opposite end of the bolt. The object of the offset on the bolt (Fig. 397) forward of the peg is to make a shoulder to stop it from shooting too far in when the spring is loosened.

Fig. 396 shows the catch which is to be securely fastened to the door jamb. The spring must of course be made of well-seasoned elastic wood—hickory is the best. This stick may be quite long, say half again as long in proportion as the one shown in Fig. 390. It must be flattened at the upper end and secured by two nails, and it must be flattened at right angles to the upper part and somewhat pointed at the lower end so as to fit in a notch in the bolt. A well-made lock of this sort is a source of constant joy and pride to the maker, and he will never tire of springing it back and forth and extolling its virtues to his guests.

Secret Locks

are more useful than strong ones for a country house which is left closed during the winter months, for it is not so much cupidity which causes such houses to be broken into, as it is the curiosity

Fig. 393.

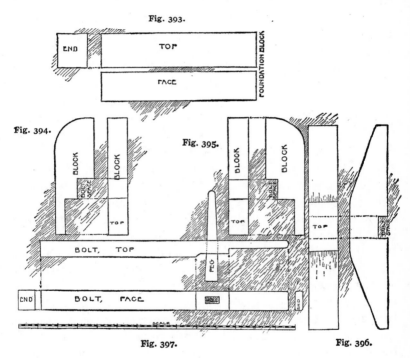

Fig. 394.   Fig. 395.

Fig. 397.   Fig. 396.

of the native boys. But while these lads often do not hesitate to force or pick a lock, they will seldom go so far as to smash a door to effect an entrance. Hence, if your lock is concealed, your house is safe from all but professional thieves, and such gentry seldom waste their time to break open the shack which contains nothing of value to them. The latches shown by Figs. 387, 388, and 390 may be made very heavy and strong, and if the trigger in 388, the latch-string hole in 387 and the peg hole in 390, are adroitly concealed, they make the safest and most secure locks for summer camps, shacks and houses.

If a large bar be made of a 1 x 4-inch plank, bolted in the middle of the plank with an iron bolt through the centre of the door and fastened on the inside by a nut screwed on the bolt, it will allow the bar to revolve freely on the inside of the door. But if a string is attached to one end and the bar is long enough to extend a few inches beyond the door jambs on each side, it may be fastened by pulling the string up through a gimlet hole in the jamb.

To conceal this lock is a very simple affair; draw the string through the gimlet hole and fasten it to a nail at a point on the string so that when it is drawn, the door bar is horizontal and the door consequently barred. Then push the nail in the gimlet hole so that only the head appears on the outside and no one, not in the secret, will ever suppose that the innocent appearing nail is the key to unfasten the door. When you wish to open the door from the outside, pluck out the nail, pull the string and walk in.

There are a thousand other simple contrivances which will suggest themselves to the camper and which he will find entertainment for rainy days, in planning and enlarging on the ideas here given. In the real wilderness, however, every camp is open to all comers, but the real woodmen respect the hospitality of the absent owner and replace whatever articles of food they may use with fresh material from their own packs; wash all dishes they may use, and sweep up and leave the shack in "apple-pie" order after their uninvited visit, for this is the law of the wilderness, which even horse-thieves and bandits respect.

CHAPTER XXVIII

HOW TO BUILD A REAL LOG HOUSE

The log house in which I am working and making these diagrams is one that I built myself, is two stories high, 40 feet front, with an ell that runs back 52 feet; there are six bedrooms upstairs, a large dining-room, kitchen and passageway separating it from the dining-room, an open gallery of 10 x 16 feet through the middle, and a grill room of 16 x 15 feet at one end. It has two stone chimneys and two open fireplaces and is made of pitch pine logs. Any man with

Ordinary Gumption

can build a log house. The logs should be selected from sound and straight trees, and after being cut should be snaked to a

Fig. 398.—Logs on skid-way.

skidway, where a man peels them. The skids are made by resting the ends of several logs upon a cross log and the opposite ends upon the ground, so as to form an incline from which the logs may be rolled without any difficulty (see Fig. 398).

The Joints of the Logs

in my house are made as shown in the southeast corner of Fig. 399, where it is marked "Pike Joints," but the usual method is to cut notches like those marked A and B (Fig. 399), and then the ends of logs may be fitted together as they are in D and C (Fig. 399). F, of the same figure, shows four key logs which are supposed to be laid upon a dry stone wall foundation. The foundation wall should be built in a trench dug below the frost line; otherwise the freezing and thawing of the ground will heave

Fig. 399.—Joints, notches and splits used in building log houses.

and settle until it throws the building out of plumb. The reason for using a wall built without plaster or cement of any kind is that such a wall allows a free passage of air beneath, and prevents the accumulation of moisture and the consequent decay of the floor and key logs.

The log house was once the common house all through the East as well as the South and West, and in " Evan's Pedestrious Tour" (1818) he speaks of them in New York and New Hampshire and says that they were sometimes without floors, had wooden chimneys, and adds that they were "the abode of virtue, health and happiness."

In Maine they use

Straight Spruce Logs

for their permanent camps and they make a beautiful house; but the universal custom appears to be to build these houses upon the bare ground, and the consequence is that the bottom logs absorb the moisture, and soon decay, extending gradually up to the adjoining logs, sets in; but if the logs were placed upon dry stone walls, and the roof built to overhang at the eaves about 2 feet, the life of the houses would be indefinite.

Where Straight Logs Cannot be Procured,

it may be necessary to use a broad-axe to make them even; in which case the house should be chinked up with clay and moss, or, if procurable, with ordinary mortar. While the mortar is soft, chink from the outside with logs, quartered as the one shown in Fig. 399, marked V and W. This will make a tight, warm house in the winter and a cool one in the summer; but where they have the straight spruce logs the chinks are very small as in E, in Fig. 399, and, in this case, the narrow crevices are calked up with oakum, like a boat.

After the Logs are Peeled

and notched, ready to be rolled in place, the house may be begun. It is a simple matter to roll the first logs in place,

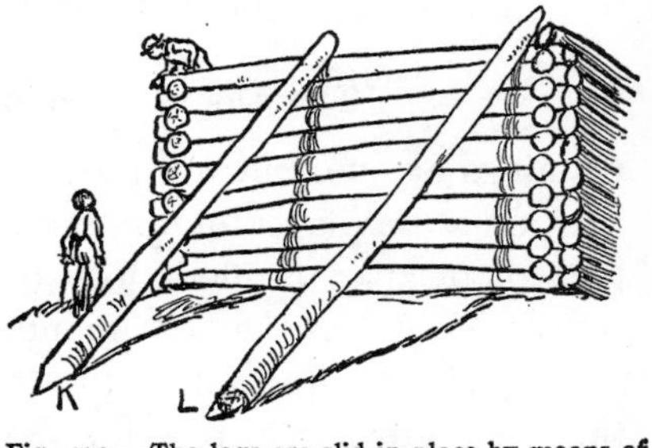

Fig. 400.—The logs are slid in place by means of the skids K and L.

but as the house increases in size (Fig. 400), it will be found necessary to use the skids K and L to slide the logs into place. Even then it may be beyond the strength of the men employed to push these logs up the steep incline. In which case, the block and tackle

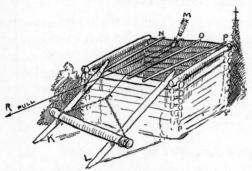

may be attached to the logs on the opposite side of the house, and two log chains fastened to the log to be hoisted and connected with the tackle rope, like the belly-band of a kite, as shown in Fig. 401. The line running in the direction of R is attached

Fig. 401.—For heavy timber use block and tackle.

to a team of oxen or horses, and as they pull away from the house the log slips up into place.

You will notice on this diagram there are a lot of poles, N O P, lying across the top of the unfinished house. These are to support the logs after they are hoisted up until they are fitted properly in their places in the wall.

The Doors, Windows and Fireplace

openings are not cut until after the logs are erected. The floor joist must be placed across the key logs. I once made the mistake of putting the floor joist on the stone foundation, and the consequence was that the foundation settled unevenly and gave a decided wave formation to the floor. This will be avoided if the joists are laid across the key logs, for even should one side of the house settle and not the other, it would give an even slant to the floor, and not a wavy, uneven surface.

It is a good idea to saw one log for the top of the window and other openings before the next log is placed over it. This will leave you room to work your saw to cut down through the remaining logs when the time comes to make the windows, doors and fireplaces; but before making a cut in any of the logs, nail on inside and outside strips or planks as shown by S and T, in Fig. 403. These are to hold the logs in place until the framework of the opening has been nailed to the ends. Do not drive the nails or spikes all the way in when nailing these strips to the logs, but leave their heads protruding, as shown in the diagram (Fig. 402), so that they may be readily withdrawn when no longer needed.

Fig. 402.   Fig. 403.   Fig. 404.

These drawings explain the construction of window openings.

If You are Using Heavy Logs

to build a house, use 2½ or 3 inch planks to nail on the ends of the logs before door or window-frame or fireplace is built in (U, end view, Fig. 404). If you use light boards for this purpose the weight of the logs has a tendency to bow them out and throw your opening out of plumb, causing all manner of inconvenience, besides spoiling the looks of the house.

In all old-time log houses

The Chimney

is built on the outside, and if you will ask the reason why, the builder will answer with a smile, "There is more room out there than inside the house" (Fig. 405).   This outside chimney gives a picturesque look to the edifice, which we all appreciate, and, as the building of log houses for summer homes is largely a matter of sentiment, we should adhere to the old-time style of building as closely as possible.

A chimney and

Fireplace

may be made of any sort of rough stones laid in cement, but I would advise that the fireplace itself be lined with rough fire

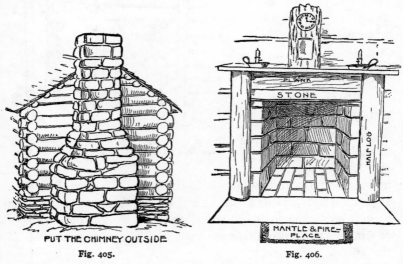

PUT THE CHIMNEY OUTSIDE

Fig. 405.

Fig. 406.

brick, for both the stone and ordinary red brick crack and crumble away when subjected to the constant heat of the fire.

A fireplace in a log house should be no plaything, such as one sees in flats, with asbestos logs on the hearth burning gas, but it should be a real thing where one can pile in great logs of birch, and send the flames roaring up the chimney without the uncomfortable feeling that the heat is going to spoil the masonry.

Fig. 406 shows one of

The Plainest Forms of Mantels

which can be made for a log house. This mantel consists of two half logs which have been peeled and maybe stained or varnished, and two planks, one above the stone, which reaches across the top of the fireplace, and one to form the shelf itself. It may be that your country mason does not possess sufficient skill to build an arch over the top of the fireplace, and, in that case, a couple of flat iron bars may be set in the masonry with a flat stone resting upon them to form the top of the fireplace under the mantel. There should be at least an inch space between this stone and the log, which space should be filled up with cement. This is to prevent the heated stone from endangering the wood above it.

Oiled Clay as Cement

By experimenting with mud and clay I discovered that the latter may be used, even for inside chinking, and when almost dry, if it is painted with linseed oil the surface becomes as hard as Portland cement, and may then be painted with any sort of house paint.

The Roof to the Log House,

as a rule is now made like the ordinary shingle roof of any farmhouse or wooden building, and the triangular portion above the eave logs is often planked up and shingled, but it is much better for sentiment's sake to adhere to the old style, and make the rafters of small logs, between which other small logs run up to the apex of the roof, as shown in Fig. 405.

In Furnishing the House,

use hickory chairs, with splint bottoms, which may be obtained from department stores and the firms who manufacture this sort of furniture, and which I know from experience to be well-built, comfortable and appropriate to the surroundings; they are in fact almost exact duplicates of the pieces of furniture used by the early pioneers.

General Jackson, who is credited with being the first white man to smoke a corncob pipe, was very fond of one of these hickory splint-bottomed chairs, but in this instance he was not unique, inasmuch as the popularity of this sort of furniture was shared by all the people who settled in the new country. For the benefit of those who would like to make their own furniture, I have given some designs and detail drawings in the next chapter.

In Conclusion

It may be said that if you are an amateur at this sort of work build first a simple, cube-shaped log house with a shed roof and add a lean-to for a kitchen. This will serve you to camp in for the first season. Then, as you grow ambitious for a larger house, build a duplicate house 10 or 15 feet away and in line with your first structure and extend the roof over the two houses. This will give you what is known in the South as "the saddle-bag house," with an open gallery between the two compartments, which is a most delightful place in which to sit on the hot days of summer. In the South the gallery is used during the warm weather as an open-air dining-room.

CHAPTER XXIX

HOW TO BUILD AND FURNISH A SURPRISE DEN IN A MODERN HOUSE

Of late years our people have come to realize the fact that a man's room or a boy's room is as necessary to the properly conducted household as the lady's boudoir. These rooms, by common consent, are known as "dens."

A den usually consists of a small space, sometimes nothing more than an alcove, where the men or boys of the house may retreat. The den is usually decorated with an abundant display of yachting flags, college colors, trophies of the hunt and athletic field, fishing-rods, guns, etc., with probably a desk and an easy chair. But, as the wealth of the country increases, and luxuries multiply, the den gradually assumes a more and more primitive condition. This is the natural result of the reaction against the surrounding effete luxury of the household.

The Surprise Den

is designed to supply a want suggested by many letters requesting ideas on how to decorate and fix up a den in one's house. The surprise den is constructed so that one may open the door from the dining-room, the drawing-room, or the library, as the case may be, and usher the guests into a primitive pioneer cabin.

Fig. 407.

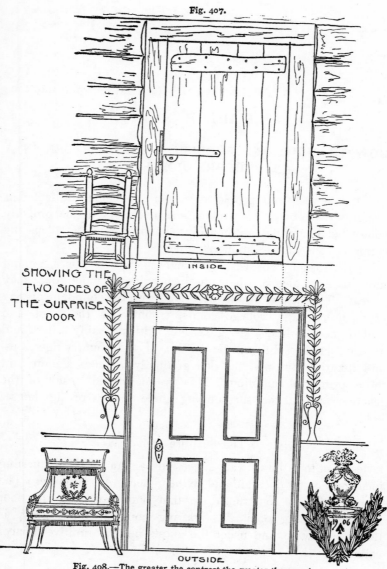

INSIDE.

SHOWING THE
TWO SIDES OF
THE SURPRISE
DOOR

OUTSIDE.

Fig. 408.—The greater the contrast the greater the surprise.

If Your House is Located in the Country,

where there is plenty of room, a small addition, say 15 x 15, may be added to one side or the other and this addition built into the form of a regular log cabin; but the outsides of the logs concealed by shingles, clapboards, bricks or stone to match the side of the house, so that the presence of the log cabin will not be suspected; but if your house is in the city you will probably have to take some room in that house for your den, and in that case the walls and the ceiling may be covered with slabs, which, if neatly done, will have all the appearance of real logs.   Slabs are inexpensive, their cost being nothing more than the cost of transportation, for wherever saw-mills exist the slabs are burned, thrown away or given away; consequently, they have no market value.

The first important thing to a surprise den is

The Doorway

Of course, the side of the door which faces the drawing-room, parlor or library must give no indication of the other side.   It must be, in all respects, similar to the other doors in the house. But the opposite side, or the side facing the den, must resemble in no respect the modern finished doorway.   (Figs. 407 and 408 are supposed to be, first, the side facing the den; second, the side facing the drawing-room of the house.)   The first problem which confronts us here is

How to Make a Door Latch

which upon one side is the original knob and lock face, but on the other a wooden latch.   Fig. 409 shows the glass knob and brass escutcheon sketched from one on a library door.   Fig. 410

shows the same knob unscrewed and taken from the door. Fig.
411 is an ordinary door-knob. By reference to these figures you
will see that the knob itself is attached to a square iron bar in the
end of which are several threaded holes. These holes are for
the screws that secure the knob upon the opposite side of the door.

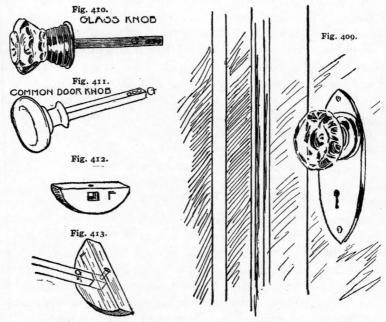

Fig. 410.
GLASS KNOB

Fig. 411.
COMMON DOOR KNOB

Fig. 412.

Fig. 413.

Fig. 409.

Details of wooden latch attached to glass and brass door-knob.

Now, then, if you will cut from a piece of hickory or other hard
wood a block of the form of F (Fig. 412), and make a square
hole in this block to admit the end of the square iron bar of the
knob, and then fasten it in place by a screw (as in Fig. 413), you
will have something with which to lift the wooden latch upon

the opposite side of the door. There should be an iron washer, such as comes upon common doors, fastened in place upon the den side of the door before the wooden latch lifter is put in place. The latch itself is simply a straight wooden bar H (Figs. 414 and 415), which fits into the wooden catch K (Figs. 414, 415 and 416) and slides up and down through the guard L (Figs. 415 and 417). In Fig. 414 the guard is omitted so as to better show the working of the latch. You can see from this figure that when the knob upon the drawing-room side of the door is twisted, the half disc F turns with the knob and lifts up the wooden latch as it is in Fig. 414. Fig. 415 shows the latch, guard and catch all in place.

But to return to the door itself. Upon the den side of this door some very thin planks must be nailed to cover all signs of the mill or

Fig. 414. BY WHICH YOU MAY SEE HOW A TWIST OF THE DOOR KNOB WILL LIFT THE LATCH

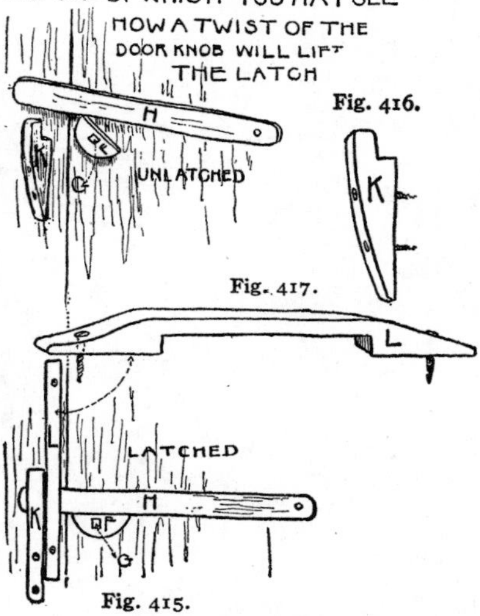

Fig. 416.

Fig. 417.

Fig. 415.
The den side of the door.

skilled workmanship. These strips of wood while apparently planks, are in fact nothing but weather-beaten boards which have been carefully sawed in half at the mill so that they are, in reality, only a thick veneering to the door; to which they can be nailed without any serious injury to the latter. After these are fitted to the door, two battens, one at the top and one at the bottom, can be fastened in place by a few small screws and afterward a number of short, hand-made rough-headed nails are driven in for appearance's sake. These nails need not be of sufficient length to enter into the real doorway.

Fig. 418 is a rough sketch of

The Interior of a Den,

showing a fireplace and the slab sides and rustic furniture of the room also, the effect of heavy logs supporting the rough board

Fig. 418.—Simple, primitive, American and comfortable.

ceiling. The ceiling of the room should be covered with rough, unplaned boards. To produce the effect of heavy log rafters puncheons may be nailed to the planks, and to further add to the quaintness of the den the floor may be sanded.

For the benefit of the effete city mortal unacquainted with

the language of the pioneers, it may be well to state that a puncheon is a flattened or halved log.   It differs from a slab only in

Fig. 419.

possessing greater thickness.   But if puncheons are difficult to
secure, and there are no discarded telegraph poles or piling pro-

curable, slabs will answer the purpose very well, and may be used to represent the log rafters shown in Fig. 418.

Any Boy with Ordinary Skill

in the use of carpenters' tools can cut these slabs so as to fit neatly upon the walls and so place them that they will, to all appearances, be genuine solid logs.

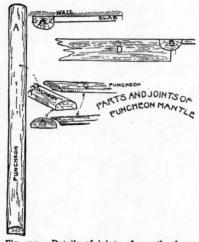

Fig. 420.—Details of joints of mantle shown in Fig. 419.

The bark should be removed from all the timber used in the den, as it will not only hold dust but serve as a retreat for various pests well known to the housewife, which are liable to enter into any house, but which are difficult to drive out of a room whose walls and ceilings are covered with loose bark.

It isn't everybody who can indulge in

The Luxury of an Open Fireplace

in his den. But there is a charm about an open fire which has been so often described by writers of prose and poetry, that I will not attempt to enter into any dissertation upon it here. It is only necessary to state the fact that we all love an open fireplace, and that it adds greatly to the charm, comfort and fascination of a den; but if we have an open fire in the surprise den it must be in keeping with the rest of the room.

Fig. 419 shows one which has been in working order now for

two decades. The beauty of the design is its simplicity.   The hearthstone is a rough slab of bluestone from the Pennsylvania mountains.   The bricks are large, rough fire-bricks.   The mantel itself D (Fig. 419) is a 2-inch plank which rests upon the puncheon C (Fig. 419).   There are two other puncheons (A and B) which run up the sides of the fireplace, to the ceiling.   This produces a very simple pioneer effect, with none of the affectation of so-called rustic work.   Fig. 420 shows the puncheon A, which is flattened on the two edges as it is shown by the sketch, which also shows the top of the mantel D and the

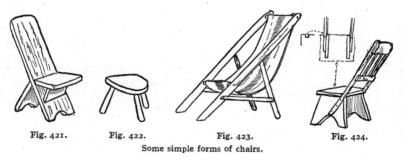

Fig. 421.   Fig. 422.   Fig. 423.   Fig. 424.
Some simple forms of chairs.

manner in which it is cut out at the corners to fit the upright puncheons A and B.

The upper drawing (Fig. 420) shows the manner in which the slabs of the wall fit up against the flattened sides of the puncheon.   The lower right hand drawing

Shows How the Puncheon is Cut

to make a snug fit upon the edges of the puncheons A and B.

E E, etc., of Fig. 419 are the rafters of the ceiling.   S S S are the slabs of the wall.

The furniture for the fireplace should not be modern.   Wrought-

iron andirons are much to be preferred to brass, for the reason
that our pioneers' andirons—when they indulged in such luxuries
—were made at the blacksmith shop, and not imported from
the brass foundries. There should be a farmer's almanac

Fig. 425:—Place the three-legged stools each side of the hearth.

always hanging at the corner of the mantel. The Farmer's
Almanac of to-day is practically the same almanac that our grand-
fathers used, the difference being only in the date, and not in the
make-up of the book.

Furniture for Den or Log Cabin

Two three-legged stools, one for each corner of the fireplace,
adds greatly to the primitive effect of the room, as shown in the

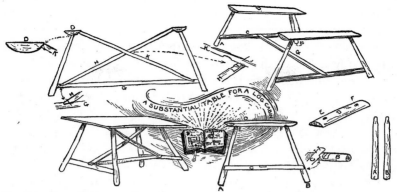

Fig. 426.—These drawings are made from an oaken hand-made table in the author's possession which has now done duty since about 1650, and is still in use.
D is the batten holding the legs A and B in the holes E and F.
H and K are braces which cross each other under the table.
C is the end rung.
G the centre rung.

Fig. 427.—A simple and dignified bedstead made of peeled logs and a common wire mattress.

335

illustration 425 drawn from the author's own log den. A rag carpet rug is better than a sanded floor, for the reason that the sand from the den may track into the other rooms to the great annoyance of the housekeeper and servants. Fig. 421 shows how to make a chair of a plank. Fig. 422 is a three-legged stool. Fig. 423 is a lounging chair made of six sticks and a piece of carpet, tent cloth, or any other strong fabric. Fig. 424 is a bench chair. Fig. 426 gives the details of a hand-made oaken table which was much in vogue in the seventeenth century, and it is bot[1]. sturdy and picturesque. Fig. 427 is a bedstead made of natural lumber, slabs and a wire mattress; this last is for a log house, but a divan for the den may be made on the same plan, by using shorter legs and posts.

WINTER

CHAPTER XXX

SOME NEW WINTER CAMPS, AND HOW TO BUILD THEM AND HEAT THEM

Once again we are in the grip of that grim old gentleman familiarly known as Jack Frost. He is no effete degenerate, but is forceful, lusty, strong and energetic, yet he is not unkind to those who fear not to meet him face to face in his boisterous play. To be on good terms with winter, it is necessary to take the buffets good-naturedly, and not whine when one's ears and toes are pinched, for old winter does this to remind us that we must protect those members of our body, or suffer frost bite.

However, even the toughest men care not to spend the season in one long tussle with the cold, and when they tire of the strenuous play of Jack Frost and his roaring companions, the North Winds, they find it desirable to have some place of refuge handy, some retreat where the camper may retire while the storm rages, or when an excess of vitality and exuberance of spirits on the part of Jack Frost, develops into a howling blizzard.

A Comfortable Camp

while in the woods is one which affords shelter from wind and storm. Such a camp should be built of small logs "chinked" with mud and moss, but it may be an open front, modeled on the plan of the old reliable lean-to, known as the Adirondack; to this should be added a wind shield. The ground plan of such a shack and shield may be 6 x 12 feet or larger. For elevation see the New Brunswick (Fig. 428).

The wind shield is made of green fir logs split in halves, with

Fig. 428. Fig. 429.

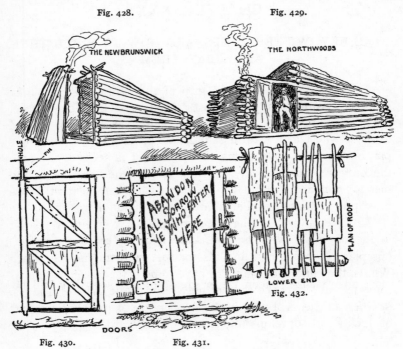

Fig. 430. Fig. 431.

Fig. 428.—The New Brunswick; no door but a wind-shield.
Fig. 429.—The Northwoods, with door to fire-yard.
Figs. 430 and 431.—Designs for doors.
Fig. 432.—Showing how to shingle roof with bark.

the bark or rounded side of the slabs outside. The slabs lean against a horizontal pole, and the latter rests in the two forks of two uprights, as may be seen by the illustration (Fig. 428).

A More Elaborate Camp

is shown by the illustration of the North Woods (Fig. 429) with a ground plan 8 x 14 feet, or as much larger as the party may demand. This is also an open camp, but there is a log fence around the open end of the shack, with a doorway.

The Door

may be made of boards, if they are to be obtained, or of slabs of wood, or even the bark of trees, properly nailed to a well-braced frame (Fig. 430).

The old backwoodsman's door hinge was made of an upright pole terminating in a long pin at the top and a short one at the bottom, the pins fitting into auger holes in the logs, as shown in Fig. 430; the hinge rod can be put in place by first slipping the long pin in the hole bored through the top log and then dropping the short pin in the short hole in the bottom log. Even a novice will understand that the pins must be sufficiently smaller in diameter than the holes to allow them to turn freely.

If the two pins at the ends of the hinge rod are well oiled with sweet oil, vaseline, bacon fat or grease of any sort they will be found to move with little friction, but then the porcupines will gnaw them to pieces when the camp is vacant. After the rod is in place nail the door to the hinge.

In case you have no tools for boring holes, make hinges of old bits of leather, soles of old shoes or folded pieces of canvas (Fig. 431). This makes a rude, crude doorway, but if my readers are of old American stock they may know that their own ancestors were content with a deerskin or an old blanket portière. The proper idea is to make the best house and doorway of which your limited time and tools will admit.

The Birch-Bark Roof

is so easily understood from the diagram (Fig. 432) that it probably needs no further description. The reader may see by the illustration that the pieces of bark are laid so as to break joints and also to overlap like shingles; it may also be seen that they are held in place by being weighted down with additional poles laid on top of the bark. Birch bark is an ideal material for the roof;

Fig. 433.—Indian log tents used for winter camps about 1820-1850 in the Northwest.

however, almost any bark which can be obtained in suitable-sized pieces will answer the purpose.

If we go to the Indians, we find that these native Americans and hereditary campers long ago devised substantial winter lodges which no boreal winds overturn, and which protect the hardy redskins from the frost of the severest cold weather.

Formerly these winter lodges were common along the shores of our northern lakes (Fig. 433), but they are now only to be found away up north in that vast country only frequented by Hudson Bay men, explorers and prospectors. These log tents are there often built of halved hollow logs arranged like tiles; that is, alternately with the convex side out and its edges fitting into the concave side of the others, thus 〰〰〰. Fig. 433 is the old form which was a common sight to the missionaries and Indian traders of this country before the reader and writer were born. The log lodge may be covered with shingles of bark, held in place by the weight of poles laid up on the logs, as in Fig. 432, or covered with sods, earth, moss and clay, or both. Of course the Indians always have camp-fires; but these log lodges are unprovided with a fireplace, such as white men are accustomed to have in their most primitive abodes. To provide one of these useful adjuncts fitted for

A Winter Camp,

one will do well to take a hint from the homely architects of the picturesque log-houses which dot the mountains in the "moonshine" districts of the Southern States, where the cabins are almost universally supplied with a simple fireplace built of stones on the outside of the house, and surmounted by a "stick" chimney; that is, a flue built with small sticks laid in the same way as the logs which compose the walls of the house, but, unlike the latter, the sticks decrease in size as they approach the top. The stick chimneys are liberally daubed with clay, which dries and is hardened by the heat from the fire below. With a few unimportant changes in the "moonshine" plan,

A Dixie

may be made to heat a log lodge, built on a modification of the ones invented by the Indians. Figs. 434, 435 and 436 show the details of the construction of the Dixie. Fig. 435 is a ground

Fig. 434.

Fig. 435.

POSTS

POST

FIRE PLOE

STONES
CLAY

CLAY
STONES POST

JOINT

Fig. 436.

Details of the Dixie.

344

plan of the fireplace, which, as may be seen, is built by laying stones up against four posts and a number of sticks that have been firmly driven into the ground. The stones are laid so as to break joints. A thick coating of mud or clay will not only prevent the fire from cracking and crumbling the stones, but also help the chimney to draw up the smoke. It is, of course, understood by all who have built fires that the less side draughts there are, the stronger is the current of air which ascends the chimney from the front, and the less liability is there to a smoky fireplace.

A glance at Fig. 434 shows that small logs have been used in the construction of the Dixie, in place of the small sticks of the moonshiner's cottage chimney. The logs make less work and require less skill than the stick chimney, besides giving the structure greater stability. The logs, however, should be plentifully coated with mud or clay, the same as the more dainty sticks. This is essential, not so much to prevent a conflagration, as to do away with leaks and insure a draught.

There is small danger from fire, otherwise the stick-chimney cabins of the South would all have been burned down long ago, in place of standing unharmed for years. There are cabins in the South to-day, with clay-daubed wooden flues, older than any of the readers of this book, and I have seen chimneys, made of unprotected flour barrels, which have been in constant use for many months. Fig. 436 shows the notches in the logs where they cross each other at the corners.

The Mossback,

one form of which is shown by Fig. 438, is built with two rafters (Fig. 437) in place of one, as in Fig. 434. This is done to prevent the rafter from interfering with the construction of the chimney. Two side logs are secured on the ground by pegs, and against these logs the lower ends of the roof logs rest, while their upper ends project above the rafters, as shown in Fig. 438. The front of the mossback may be closed with more logs laid up against the roof, with bark or with beaver mats of brush, as may be desired, or as is locally convenient for the architects.

Fig. 437.

THE MOSSBACK

Fig. 438.—The Mossback.

The Brunswick and the Northwood

These well-known camps previously depicted and described are both open-faced shacks with the opening protected by a log-fenced fireplace, or one with a green hemlock fire shield, but in both cases the snow and wind are but slightly impeded from entering the camp, and if a Dixie is substituted for the uncovered fire, as is the case with

The Red Jacket,

shown by Fig. 439, a much more comfortable and cozy winter camp is secured, with but little additional work. A tent is all the protection many sportsmen and explorers require, even when

Fig. 440.

SNOW SHEILD

THE REDJACKET

Fig. 439.

Fig. 439.—A comfortable and commodious winter camp.
Fig. 440.—In this diagram the door to tent can be seen through gate, but it should really face the blank wall.

camping in the extreme north, and a tent can be made very comfortable by surrounding it with a wind and weather shield, built of snow in the form of a wall, as in Fig. 440. In this way the whaler's ships, frozen in the Arctic Ocean, are walled in to keep the interior of the vessels warm during the long winter months.

But the city man who camps in winter for a short holiday in the woods may not find sufficient snow for this purpose, or he may find it too wet to be used in this manner. Such a man may even prefer to go without a tent and depend upon the material the forest furnishes to supply him with shelter from sleet and cold winds. In this case a light, easily constructed camp may be built on the plan of the

Pontiac,

shown by Figs. 441 and 442. This pretty little shack is built of light poles, and covered with pieces of bark, laid so as to overlap

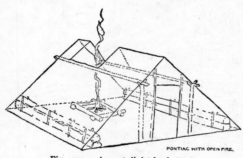

PONTIAC WITH OPEN FIRE.

Fig. 441.—A neat light bark tent.

each other like shingles. The bark is held in place by the weight of poles laid on the roof, and sticks driven into the ground, as shown by the unfinished part of the one in the diagram. Fig. 441 shows the outlines of a Pontiac arranged with an Indian fireplace and a hole in the roof for the escape of the smoke. The fireplace itself is made of mud enclosed with four green logs. Only two forked sticks for rafters are shown here, the others being omitted in the drawing of Fig. 441, the better to show the fireplace. The doorway to the Pontiac is protected by a blanket of skin, hung there for the purpose. Birch bark is very inflammable, and can be used as a torch, when it is green, hence a big fire is not desirable in a lodge of green birch bark. Still, if birch can be obtained it makes the best of natural tent material, but in winter it is difficult to peel the bark and the supply for the Pontiac should be gathered early in the season.

A Safe Heater

for a tent, or a birch lodge, can be made by digging a hole in the floor and filling it with the hot embers from the camp-fire, and then covering the hole and embers with an inverted metal pail; or stones may be used heated very hot, heaped on the floor and covered with a galvanized bucket.

THE PONTIAC

Fig. 442.—The unfinished Pontiac, also sketch showing how to pack birch bark and the way it is carried.

The objection to the Pontiac is the objection to all birch-covered lodges used for winter camp. They are difficult to build tight enough to prevent the wind from blowing in under the bark shingles; but if the campers are provided with good sleeping bags, the wind will bother them but little, even when there is no roof at all over their heads. If, however, there is a supply of sphagnum moss handy the wind can be kept out of the shack by covering the bark with moss and then putting on another lot of bark outside the moss, as many of the northern Indians treat their bark tents.

When it can be procured, there is no doubt a good, snug shack of some kind is the thing to have for a winter camp. There need be no fear that such structures will prevent the camper from getting a good supply of fresh air, for unless the reader is a much better workman than even the most skilful backwoodsman, there will be an abundant supply of ozone in any of the shacks here described.

A Camp for the Night

can be made with two forked sticks driven into the ground, a cross stick laid in the crutches, and the whole covered with brush, thus making a miniature open-faced camp of the form of one-half of the Pontiac (Fig. 441). This one-night shack need only be built tall enough to admit the camper when he creeps to cover to sleep. The small size of this shack makes little work in construction, and less work in collecting the material of bark or boughs with which to cover the simple framework.

A Big Bonfire,

built in the morning and kept burning all day, will dry and warm the earth so as to make a most comfortable place to sleep upon, after the hot coals and ashes have been carefully brushed away. A thorough baking of this kind will cause the earth to retain the heat for hours after the fire is extinguished, and give forth a most grateful warmth on a bitter cold night.

Wind Shields

A large rock, a steep bank, or the flat, upright mass of clay and roots of an overturned tree are all good wind guards, behind which one may camp with more or less comfort when the cutting north winds are sweeping through the woods.

Upon some occasion a big, hollow log is not to be despised as a bunk in which to spend a cold winter's night.

But when one expects to spend the whole winter in the woods, the ideal camp is a small, but regular built

Log House,

with side walls about 4 feet high, roof tree 6½ feet high. Make it a square structure with a Dixie fireplace and chimney, a bunk in one corner, racks on the walls for guns and traps, pegs for clothes, snowshoes, etc., and a warm welcome for the passing stranger. But all this is for big boys, so we will make the next chapter on snow houses and snow men for the younger readers.

CHAPTER XXXI

HOW TO MAKE SNOW HOUSES AND SNOW MEN

The Eskimo uses a bone-bladed knife to cut the snow into the blocks with which he builds his winter home; but our snow is seldom, if ever, hard and compact enough to admit of this treatment and we must find another way to handle it.

When the snow is damp, start with a small snowball and roll it until it has increased to the size you wish. During the process of rolling the ball, it must be frequently turned on its base, so that it will be round and solid and not a loose, oblong cylinder like a roll of cotton batting.

Make a number of these snowballs and pile them up into a heap the form of a haystack; pound and hammer the balls together, filling up all the cracks and crevices with broken pieces packed tightly in place.

After the Snowballs Have Been Welded

together into a compact mass of snow, take shovels and scrapers made of thin boards or shingles and scrape the surface of your snow mound until it is smooth, symmetrical and of the form of half an egg.

Next, Cut a Number of Sticks;

make them each exactly 2 feet in length and, after pointing one end of every stick, drive them all into the snow mound until their heads are even or flush with the surface of the snow. The sticks should be distributed over the mound at regular intervals so that the pointed inside ends may guide you while hollowing out the interior of your house and prevent you from making the walls of unequal thickness. You can now cut a doorway just big enough to allow you to creep in on all fours.

When Excavating the Inside

watch for the pointed ends of the measuring pegs, and do not dig beyond them; the walls of the igloo must be at least 2 feet thick to prevent the structure from crumbling down upon the heads of the Eskimos (?) inside, and also that it may withstand any ordinary thaw without disintegrating. If

The Site Chosen for the Igloo

be in a shady place the snow house will last longer than when exposed to the direct rays of the winter's sun, but

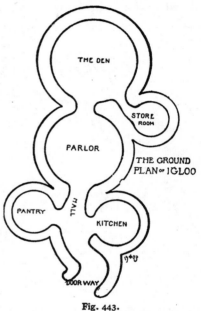

Fig. 443.

even in the sun a well-made snow house of this description will ofttimes remain intact long after the surrounding snow has disappeared.

After Building an Igloo,

as described above, if you are still ambitious to do more in this line, Fig. 443 shows the ground plan for a commodious Eskimo apartment house, and Fig. 444 shows a diagram of the outside of this compound igloo.

Although the illustration shows this snow house with the division lines as if built of snow blocks, it is nevertheless to be built of solid snow and hollowed out as already described, but to make it appear like the real thing, the snow blocks can be imitated by lines drawn with the pointed end of a measuring peg.

THE IGLOO

Fig. 444.—Finished duplicate of first igloo occupied by Dr. Hall, the Arctic explorer.

The window is made of a piece of ice set in the snow at the opening cut for that purpose.

To build this house, make the "den," or big igloo, first, as already described; from the waste snow build the little igloo marked "storcroom," then add the one marked "parlor" and from the waste snow of the last build the pantry. Next add the kitchen and the low entrance. When this is accomplished you will have a duplicate of the first igloo occupied by that daring Arctic explorer, Dr. Hall.

The Doctor slept on a snow shelf in the part we call the "den," cooked over a whale-oil lamp in the room marked kitchen, and kept his frozen provisions in the storeroom, where they were safe from the wolfish dogs.

The great advantage of all these passages and rooms in a boy's snow house is the feasibility of sealing the doorway of the storeroom or even the den itself with snow, so that a stranger entering the house will never suspect the presence of these extra rooms, but will creep out again under the impression that he has explored the whole interior.

Neither will he discover his mistake unless he makes inside and outside measurements, and by this means finds a large, unaccounted-for space; but vagrant boys do not use this much care, and are never scientific in their investigations. So the contents of the den and storeroom will be comparatively safe.

Snow Men and Animals

Since snow is easily carved and modeled, there is no good reason why statues of some merit should not replace the grotesque effigies which most men have built during the days of their boyhood. The better the work the more enjoyable the occupation, the more fun there is in the doing of it.

In place of building a figure by sticking lumps of snow on to other lumps, balls for eyes and ears and another ball for a nose, why not make a solid block of snow and carve the face from it?

Suppose A (Fig. 445) to be a snow block, B then shows the first effects of carving, C the next step, and in D we already have the semblance of a head and bust; E begins to show some likeness to a well-known American, and F and G, Fig. 446 may be passed upon an unsuspecting public as a portrait of the Father of Our Country.

In making this bust, remember and make the epaulets limp, mere bands of braid with fringe on edge, for that is the kind worn at that date—the upholstered epaulets seen upon the statues in New York City and elsewhere were not invented until after Washington's death, and like the sword of 1861, which the bronze Washington usually carries, are simply marks of the sculptor's ignorance or carelessness.

If you make a snow man,

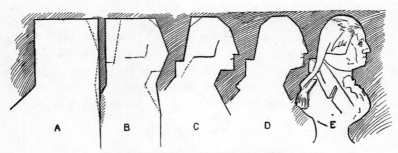

Fig. 445.—The evolution of the profile.

Make Him Right!

Of course there are many to whom these diagrams (A to G) will be of little assistance, but even untrained eyes and unskilled hands can do a thing mechanically, for that requires only care and patience. So, though you may not be able to make anything more resembling Washington than the background figure with a hat in Fig. 446, you may at least make a statue of the beast Washington drove from this country (Fig. 447).

Build a solid snow block 7 squares long by 8 squares high and 4 squares broad. These squares may be of any size you

Fig. 446.—A finished bust.   G, profile view.   F, front view.

Fig. 447.—The British lion.

find convenient, 6 inches or 1 foot, or greater or less. See the small diagram at bottom of Fig. 448. This block of snow should rest upon a rough base to elevate it above the ground. With a board and rule or string and wooden pegs divide the snow block as shown by Figs. 448 and 449. Take this book in the left hand, a pointed stick in the right hand and sketch the outline of the lion.

Placing the point of the stick a trifle to the left of the middle of the square (1, 2) and tracing a line through 1 to a point a quarter of the distance from 1 to o and half way between the line A and 1, thence perpendicularly down, crossing the line A and swinging off diagonally to a point in the line o a quarter distant between B and C, thence to a point on C a quarter distant from line 1, thence down diagonally to a point just to the right of 1 and above D, and so on as shown in the diagram.

When this is done the artist will find that he has traced out a duplicate of the diagram (Fig. 448). If he will now trace the heavy outlines of the front and rear view shown by Fig. 449, he will have something to guide him in cutting away the snow. The dotted lines show the first cuts to make on the profile view; but it will possibly be wise for him to leave the front until the last so that the outlines of front view will be there to guide him. These he may cut away on one side back to the front legs, before he finishes the profile.

A few experiments will teach him how the thing is done, and if he makes a mistake it may be rectified by plastering the snow back firmly in place and trying it again.

There is a chunk of snow left between the legs to give stability to the statue, and the legs are carved in high relief, but the snow is left under the body for support. The texture of hair on the mane and head may be reproduced by using a coarse comb.

The squares on the lion may have sides of 6 inches, 12 inches, or any dimensions the would-be sculptor may choose so long as all sides are equal.

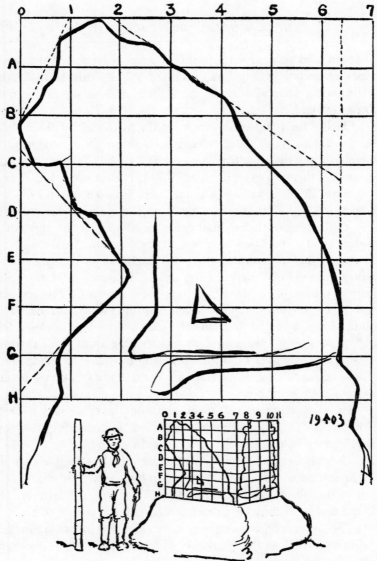

Fig. 448.—Blocked and sketched ready to be carved.

If these directions are followed, with a copy of this book in your hand for reference, the result will no doubt be a surprise to your friends and a proportional subject of pride to yourself.

Fig. 449.—Rear and front views of the snow lion.

After acquiring some skill, the beginner can take any picture of a man or woman, divide it into squares, and reproduce a creditable copy in snow.

A grotesque portrait can be modeled by marking the divisions, as described, on the picture to be copied, but making them of unequal sides on the snow block; for instance, if the sides are 16 inches broad and 10 inches high you will elongate your subject to a ridiculous degree, and if the copy is made with divisions 6 inches high and 10 inches wide, you will broaden the figure to a laughable extent. In any case you will pass a few hours in a healthy outdoor pursuit, and come indoors with red cheeks and an appetite which demands immediate attention.

CHAPTER XXXII

HOW TO PUT ON SNOW-SHOES

A review of the snow fields will reveal all sorts of appliances for binding the snow-shoes to the feet, and every expert and experienced snow-shoer, apparently, has an individual fastening of his own upon which he places the greatest reliance.

Some shoes have leather slipper toes attached to them, others broad leather straps and buckles, some simply toe straps (Fig. 453) and thongs, and others naught but the buckskin thong, the same as the American Indians were using long before Columbus came blundering around their coast in search of East India.

To prevent a confusing of terms in speaking of the parts of the snow-shoe, let us adopt nautical names. By reference to Fig. 450 it will be seen that the snow-shoe is shaped like an elongated bow kite; this is the most familiar form, and, although some shoes vary greatly from the one shown in the illustration, they all agree in their general anatomy with this diagram.

By applying nautical terms the toe (L) becomes the bow, the heel (J) the stern, and the cross stocks E and H are the thwarts. F and G are simply thongs to which the coarser net-work between them is attached. K is the hole for the toe of the moccasin. At the two lower corners of the toe hole will be found eyelets made of strengthened meshes. The framework is usually made of second growth white-ash wood, the meshes are of rawhide; from L to E and H to J the net-work is finely woven, but from F to G, amidship, it must bear the weight of the man, and the net is here made of heavier material and with much coarser meshes. It will be seen by further reference to the illustration that

a thong is so strung through the eyelets that the long ends come up b e t w e e n the wide meshes each side of the toe hole (K, Fig. 450), thus forming a loop or toe-strap into which the toe of your moccasined foot is to be thrust; by drawing the ends of the thongs, the loop may be pulled down to fit s n u g l y across the toe of the moccasin (A, Fig. 451). If your thongs be short an economical tie will be the one shown by B (Fig. 451); to make this, pass one end of the thong under the toe loop, up and b a c k over the same loop, then under itself, ma-king a half hitch on the toe loop;

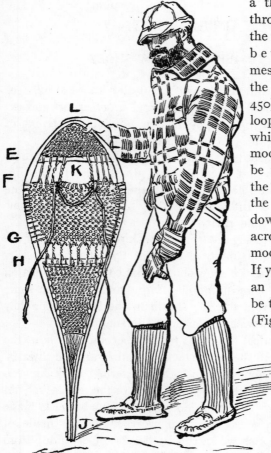

Fig. 450.—Sketch from life of a Maine woodman and his snow-shoe.

from here it is brought back behind the moccasin, where it meets the other end of the thong, which has been half hitched to the opposite side of the toe loop, as in B (Fig. 451). At the heel of the moccasin the ends pass under and over each other as shown in the diagram, then come around the ankle and tie in a square knot in front. This, as may be seen, leaves the heel free to move up and down in a natural manner (*a*, Fig. 451).

The freedom of the heel is necessary, and the toe hole (K, Fig.

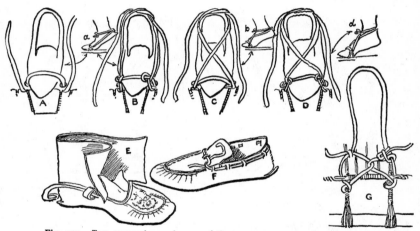

Fig. 451.—Two moccasins and some of the ways we see snow-shoes fastened.

450) permits a free movement of the toes, the foot being fastened only at the toe joints to the cross thong F (Fig. 450). It must be remembered that in using snow-shoes the latter are lifted no higher than is necessary to clear the surface of the snow; in fact, a man walking with snow-shoes scuffs along much the same as a man with slipshod slippers run down at the heels. Another way to tie on the snow-shoe is to simply pull the slack of the toe loop down to fit over the toe of the moccasin by drawing the

ends of the thongs, as in Fig. 455, then crossing them over the instep and bringing them back over the heel of the moccasin as shown by diagram C (Fig. 451), and fastening the ends around the ankle (*b*, Fig. 451). But the manifest objection to this method is that there is nothing but the friction of the moccasin to prevent the thong from slipping and sawing; this, however, can be remedied by a half hitch at each side of the toe, as is done at B (Fig. 451), and is shown with the cross bands over the instep by D and *d*, Fig. 451).

E and F (Fig. 451) show two styles of moccasins most fre-

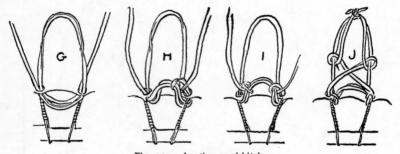

Fig. 452.—Another good hitch.

quently seen on snow-shoes in the northern United States, New Brunswick and Southern Canada, and G the one string hitch.

It is probably with good reason that the majority of men whom necessity compels to use snow-shoes, prefer a tie which brings one or more strands of the thong alongside of the foot, as shown by *a* and B (Fig. 451), and it is also evident that the cross bands over the instep give greater security to the fastening. So a method which combines the instep cross bands and the heel bands has much to recommend it. Fig. 452, G H I J, shows the evolution of such a tie with a double toe loop. The heel loop, however, is made first as shown by Fig. 454, then the double toe loop is made by passing each end of the thong through the opposite eyelet hole, as shown by G (Fig. 452). Next a half hitch is taken over the double toe loop exactly as was done with the single loop (B and D, Fig. 451) and is now shown by H and I (Fig. 452). After which the ends are crossed over the instep, half hitched on each side over the heel loop and brought back behind the foot (J, Fig. 452), where the two ends are tied in a reefing or square knot. Much of the intricateness of this last hitch may be obviated by the use of the tussle-logan toe strap, which is a permanent affair woven in through the meshes down each side astern of the eyelet holes (Fig. 453). Put the two ends of your thong down through the eyelet holes and bring them

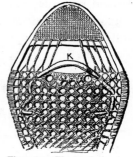

Fig. 453.—The tussle-logan toe strap.

Fig. 454.
Putting on the snow-shoe.

Fig. 455.
Sketched from life, Upper Moosehead Lake.

up between the wide meshes astern of the bow thwart, as shown by Fig. 454. Slip the toe of your moccasin under the tussle-logan, and, by drawing on the ends of the thong, pull the band snugly around your heel (Fig. 455). Next take a half hitch (O and N, Fig. 456) around the side band and draw it taut, as in the illustration. Go through the same process as shown by P R S (Fig. 457), and draw tight, as the man is doing in the same illustration.

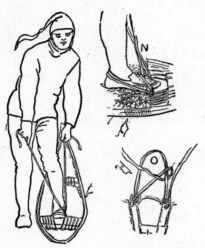

Fig. 456.—How the half-hitch is made at the side of the foot.

T is a back view of this process. When the tussle-logan happens to fit the toe too loosely, it may be made secure by passing the cross straps in and over, as shown at U (Fig. 457). Fig. 458 shows a snow-shoer bringing the free ends of the thong back behind the heel, preparatory to fastening them there with a tie. V shows the thong properly fastened (the tussle-logan omitted for sake of simplicity in the diagram). W shows the knot as tied in the Maine woods. Fig. 459 shows a man with snow-shoes on both feet, and X, Y and Z are from sketches of snow-shoers in motion, made in Michigan, Canada and the Maine woods.

A Tussle-Logan Toe Strap

on a shoe possesses many advantages for one who must needs use snow-shoes every time necessity compels travel during the winter months, and not the least of these advantages is the fact that after one's shoes have once been satisfactorily adjusted they need not be untied again until the thongs break or some similar accident renders a readjustment necessary.

The lad in Fig. 460 has one shoe on, and is in the act of slip-

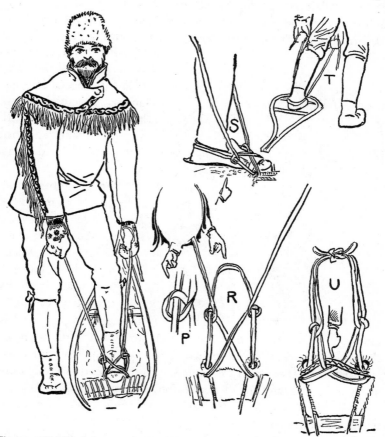

Fig. 457.—Details of the process of fastening a snow-shoe, having a toe strap, to the foot.

ping his foot into the thongs of the second shoe. It will be seen that he takes a pose like an old-fashioned dancing master, with his toes turned out; this is done so that he can slip his toes over the first side of the heel loop and under the second side, as is better explained by the empty moccasin (*a*, Fig. 460). Next he thrusts his foot so far that the heel comes under the heel loop (*b*, Fig. 461). Then, lifting his heel and pointing his toes down (*d*, Fig. 462,) he so twists his foot that the toe of his moccasin slips under the tussle-logan and the shoe is adjusted and ready to support him on drifts and fields of snow.

Three figures and three diagrams have been made of this act so that the reader may not fail to understand how it is done, but because so many pictures are necessary to make the explanation clear it

Fig. 458.—Ready to tie thongs back of the heel.

must not be supposed that this manner of putting on a snow-shoe is either difficult or intricate; it is accomplished in much less time than it requires to tell how it is done, and is really only one continuous movement of the foot like one step in dancing.

Now that you know how to put on snow-shoes, take them down from the wall where you hung them as a decoration for the library, dining-room or den and sally forth, but do not put them on in the house as did the writer in his first attempt to master the art.   There is no enacted law to prevent you from adjusting the shoes indoors, but it is better to do it outside, where there is more room and no steps to descend.

The writer forgot about the steps; his only idea was to sneak out the back way unobserved, but he did not succeed, and in going down the steps the long heels of the snow-shoes made

Fig. 459.—The snow-shoe in use, from sketches made in the north snow fields.

it necessary to step sideways. After the first step it was impossible for him to take another; he could not lift his foot more than an inch, and in spite of a struggle which nearly wrenched the thongs from the feet he stood as securely fastened to the step as if his shoes were nailed down, and it really seemed that they had frozen to the snow. The long heel of the one bearing his weight lay across the heel of the one he was struggling to lift. In regard to a

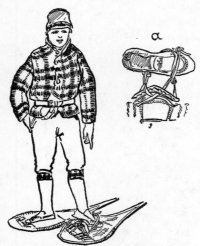

Fig. 460.—First position.

Proper Snow-Shoe Costume

it will probably be found that the mackinaw blanket coat worn by all lumbermen is best adapted to this purpose. The lumbermen also wear thick woollen stockings outside of their trousers and call them leggins. These are very comfortable, but they give the leg a thick, bulky appearance, which can be avoided by wearing knickerbockers and long stockings. Short woollen socks can be worn with advantage over the long ones, and tightly rolled down to the top of the moccasin, which will keep out the snow.

The mackinaw coats can be purchased at any outfitting establishment, and cost from $2 to $5. Some of these blanket coats are very beautiful and some as gaudy as an Indian chief in war paint. One suit in my costume chest consists of a blue and yellow striped coat and scarlet trousers with a blue plaid,

the squares of which are about 6 inches broad.   This loud dress
I bought at a lumber camp in northern Michigan.   Formerly,
lumbermen, Indians and snow-shoers wore a red silk or worsted
scarf about their middle, but now it is seldom seen, a strap,
or the belt of the jacket itself answering the purpose.

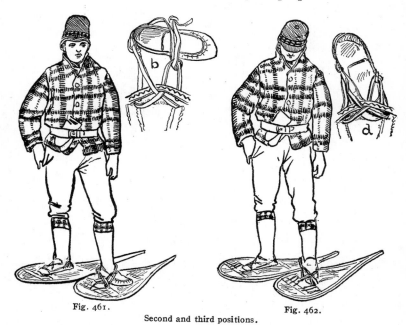

Fig. 461.

Second and third positions.

Fig. 462.

There is but one positive rule for the snow-shoer concerning
his dress and that is he must wear moccasins, but the rest of
his clothes may be anything that his taste and comfort direct.

The mackinaw coat is shown in several of the diagrams,
and Fig. 450 shows the complete winter costume of a lumberman.

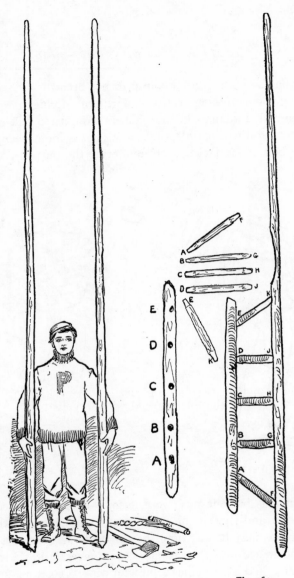

Fig. 463.   Fig. 464.

Tools used and the parts necessary to the construction of a jumper.

CHAPTER XXXIII

HOW TO BUILD A JUMPER, OR HUMPDURGIN, AND A GUMMER, IN THE WOODS

The only really necessary tools with which to work in building a jumper is an axe and an auger, but for that reason one need not throw away the contents of the tool chest.

The jumper is a sleigh made from green wood, cut in the forest for the occasion; hickory saplings furnish the proper material and the denser the forest the taller and straighter the saplings will be. These are the sort of sticks you should seek for

The Runners

of the proposed sleigh (Fig. 463). With a good sharp axe, lop off the branches, leaving no projecting stubs; then cut two more stout sticks like the one marked with large capitals A B C D E (Fig. 464) for the top rails of the runners; after which lay the top rail on a level piece of ground and the long bottom rail alongside of it at exactly the distance from the top rail which you have decided to be the height of the proposed runner (Fig. 464). Next cut the spokes AF, BG, CH, DJ and EK, and lay them along the runners, in the positions which you intend them to occupy in the finished frame (Fig. 464), and mark where they are to be trimmed down to fit the proposed auger holes in rail, at A B C D E, and runner at F G H J K. Also mark the places for the auger holes and scratch the direction, or angle, on the rail and runner of the slanting auger holes at the ends of the sleigh AF and EK (Fig. 464). This done, bore the auger holes at the points marked, being careful to make the middle ones at right angles with the rail and runner, and the end ones to exactly correspond with the diagonal scratches made to guide you. Now test your spokes and see that the middle ones are of equal length and end ones of proper length to fit holes EK, AF. Trim off the spokes so that they may be forced into the holes and then drive them in place.

Take care not to make the ends of the spokes so large as to split your rail or runner or to drive them in with such force as to produce the same disastrous result; they need to be firmly fixed in place, but not forced into the auger holes with sledge hammer blows.

The Shafts

of this jumper are the long protruding ends of the runners, and if the wood proves to be too stiff to bend properly for the correct angle of the shafts, the top of the runners may be carefully shaved off at the bending point in front of the sleigh as it is in Fig. 464. But do not do this until you have completed your jumper and tested the elasticity of the poles by lifting up the ends of the shafts, something after the manner the Yale man is doing in Fig. 465.

When one runner is finished to your satisfaction build a duplicate one as already described.

The Auger Holes

may go entirely through the top rail, but must not go through the runners, for the obvious reason that if the spokes protrude through the runners they will retard the progress of the sleigh. For ordinary purposes it is not necessary to have as many spokes to runners as are shown in Figs. 464 and 465, but the builder must here use his own judgment, as he must also do in the selection of the material. Green white ash can be split with a nail.

It requires more skill to build a light jumper than a heavy one, and the best course for a novice to pursue is to select timber heavy enough to avoid any great danger of splitting it when the spokes are driven in place.

The Frame

of the sleigh is finished when the cross braces are put in place (Fig. 465) and secured there by nails, withes or lashings of thongs,

Fig. 465.—Notice that the shafts are cut thinner near front of runners so that they may bend at these points.

twine or marline (Fig. 466). A glance at Fig. 465 will show the reader that, within reasonable limits, the greater the weight which rests on the runners, the less liability there is of the spokes working out of their bearings.

The Braces

may have log cabin joints to fit in similar ones cut in the top rail as shown by small diagrams marked "joints" (Fig. 465) or, if there is thought to be any danger of weakening the top rails by these joints, or if the builder is in haste, the braces can be nailed in place without having any notches at all.

The Gummer

is a hand sled built on the general plans of the jumper, and it is called a gummer because it is somewhat similar to the ones used by the men known as gummers who live in the forests and make

Fig. 466.—The construction and use of the gummer.

their living by collecting spruce gum for children and "sales-ladies" to chew.

The Runners of a Gummer

are lower in proportion to its size than are those of a jumper, but they are made in the same manner as the latter. The reader will of course understand that a gummer is built of very much lighter material than a jumper.

As may be seen by reference to Fig. 466 the runners are bent up until they reach the protruding ends of the top rails, when they are securely bound in place with thongs, or fastened by nails to a cross-piece which is omitted in the illustration.

If you are the happy possessor of a piece of board

The Top of the Gummer

may be made of this, but to many minds the presence of a piece of sawed lumber savors too strongly of the effete civilization of towns and cities. In the woods one likes to have

Fig. 467.—In the woods one likes to have the real thing.

The Real Thing

which, in this case, is a top made of halved pieces of spruce, pine or other wood, or of shakes, splits or clapboards, as the small, rough boards split by woodmen from quartered logs are variously called, according to the locality in which one happens to be camping. Fig. 467 shows a low sledge built jumper style, but with an elevated seat and

A Tandem Rig

This is used in narrow trails which exist in some sections where roads are wanting and where the winter snows smooth the trails by obliterating the stones and logs which impede summer travel.

The Body of a Jumper

can be finished in any style which one's time and material will allow.   A good top for a jumper can be made in the same manner as the runners; that is, by the use of spokes and a rail, as is shown in Fig. 468.   Straw or hay may be used for seats, if there is any such material obtainable, and if not, one can fill the crib with the sweet smelling balsam, upon which we all love to sleep while in the woods.   The balsam may not be so warm as hay or straw, but it is soft to sit upon, while its perfume appeals to one's poetic idea of the forest;   and blankets and wraps may be depended upon to keep out the frosts, as one goes bouncing over the "thank you marms" in the improvised sleigh, proud to be a real exemplification of

The Simple Life

It will be noticed that the jumper in Fig. 468 has the top rail of the runner prolonged into shafts and the lower rails of the runners curved up and made fast to the shafts.   This can sometimes be done when the sleigh is so light that the stiffness of the runners, if prolonged into shafts, would cause the jumper to rear up on its hind legs, so to speak.   Yet the wood may be elastic enough to be forced up to the upper rail of the runner and made fast there, as it is in Fig. 468.

When you have horses, you, in all probability, also have wagons, and in that case it may be possible to take the shafts from a wagon and attach them to a jumper, or it may save time and labor to remove the whiffletree from one of the wheeled conveyances and attach it to the sleigh, to which to fasten the traces.

Fig. 469.

Fig. 472.

Fig. 471.

Fig. 470.

Fig. 468.

Details of single horse, humpdargin and the tin-can bells.

JUMPER FOR A SINGLE HORSE

But if there are no wagons handy there will probably be no traces, and in that case ropes must supply the place of traces and reins. With ropes for traces a rude

Whiffletree

may be made of a stick notched at the end to receive the rope and notched in the middle, where it is bound to the cross-brace between the shafts, as shown by Figs. 469 and 472. In the illustrations good harness is depicted upon the horses, but that is because they are picture-horses, and good harness is always as acceptable to the illustrator as is bad, or improvised, and looks much better than either; but in the woods, with only pack-horses at one's command, improvised harness of ropes or thongs will probably be the only kind available, and a breast strap must then be substituted for the collars worn by the animals in the diagrams.

Home Made Sleigh Bells

are not a difficult proposition to one who wishes them for use and not appearances, and tobacco, meat, or tomato cans, which are to be found around almost any camp, will be as much admired by the deer, moose, wolves, coons or jack rabbits as the most expensive Russian sleigh bells. If a few round pebbles be placed inside of the cans they will make as much noise as necessary to apprise any other wayfarer of the approach of the jumper. Fig. 470 shows how the cans may be hung by strings run through nail holes, and Fig. 468 shows some such crude bells attached to the shafts of the jumper.

It is possible that one may want to build a heavy sledge on the jumper plan, for the "toting" of weighty dunnage or heavy material of some sort, and in that case the ordinary jumper runners, if made tall, even when built of heavy material, may be liable to spread, or fold up under the sleigh. Fig. 471 shows a cross-section of a jumper with braces to prevent such accidents, simple affairs nailed in place so as to stiffen the frame. As emergencies arise change the shape to suit the conditions, while keeping the real essentials.

CHAPTER XXXIV

HOW TO MAKE A SKIBOGGAN, A BARREL-STAVE TOBOGGAN, AND A TOBOGGAN-BOB

In the New England States, where the snow is seldom soft and often is coated with a hard crust of ice, the runners of the native sleds, only a few inches in height, appear very low compared with the Ohio sled; even sleds with no runners at all are sometimes used. On steep, icy hills any old thing will slide, and here it is that the

Skiboggan

is seen in all its glory. In construction this cranky sled is sim-

Fig. 473.
A stave skiboggan.

Fig. 474.

plicity itself, but its successful use requires an expert, and there will be many a tumble for the beginner in the art of skibogganing.

384

If you live in the country, go to the woodpile and find a round cord-wood stick no wider than the stout barrel stave selected for your runner. Saw the cord-wood stick so that it will stand perpendicularly when it is fastened to the stave at a third of the distance from one end (Fig. 473). If cord-wood is not available, take a piece of studding 4 x 4 or 2 x 4 and use that. With the convex side of the stave underneath, lay it over the block and nail it securely in place; reverse it, and you have Fig. 473. The comfort of the rider demands a seat, which can be made of a

Fig. 475.

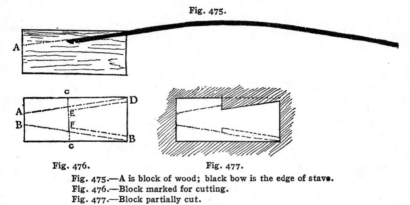

Fig. 476.   Fig. 477.

Fig. 475.—A is block of wood; black bow is the edge of stave.
Fig. 476.—Block marked for cutting.
Fig. 477.—Block partially cut.

small piece of thin board fastened T-wise on the block (Fig. 474).

With the long end of the stave in front of you, seat yourself on the T saddle with your feet on the snow on each side of the runner and start down hill. The skiboggan can be used on hills which are so steep as to make the use of an ordinary sled impracticable.

The best skiboggans are made of the staves of sugar hogsheads or oil-barrel staves, and the upright post is braced upon each side by parts of barrel staves thus ⌐|⌐, or with bits of plank thus /|\. But if you are going to put much work on the thing, you might as well build a really good

Barrel-Stave Toboggan

Winter weather frequently brings a good deal of dry, soft snow which won't pack and makes ordinary sledding laborious. The narrow runners sink through quickly, and the average boy finds himself longing for a toboggan of some sort. If he has no

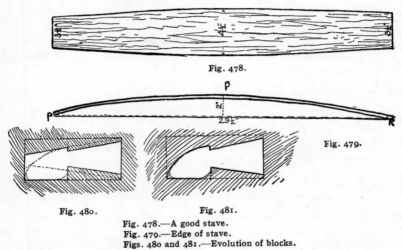

Fig. 478.

Fig. 479.

Fig. 480.

Fig. 481.

Fig. 478.—A good stave.
Fig. 479.—Edge of stave.
Figs. 480 and 481.—Evolution of blocks.

toboggan, however, it is a simple matter to nail some pieces across two or three barrel staves and thus secure a rude but very serviceable substitute.

The serious defect of a barrel-stave toboggan like this is that it has not the high-rolling front of the real American toboggan, and consequently is liable to bury itself in the first hummock of snow encountered by the coaster, or to stick its nose in the snow, "turn turtle" and throw over the boy who is using it. It was these little eccentricities of the stave sled which led the writer to produce the toboggans shown in the accompanying illustrations and diagrams, and reference to them will show you how the faults may be overcome by the insertion of bow and stern pieces cut from strips of plank nailed together or of blocks

Fig. 482.—A finished runner.

of wood sawed from the end of a 4 x 4 inch post. Such a toboggan can be used alone (Fig. 485) or joined to another (as in Figs. 494, 495 and 496) by a reach-board and thus form a unique machine which we shall call the toboggan-bob.

Any boy who can manage a saw and drive a nail can make one of the toboggans, and any boy with skill in carpentry can

Fig. 483.—A reinforced runner.

build a good bob from the material usually to be found in the back yard, cellar, or attic.

No Really Good Results

can be obtained by the use of poor lumber, but if good lumber proves too costly, excellent oil-barrels can be purchased from dealers. Casks such as are used to catch rain-water have smooth, stiff staves and are well adapted for the purpose of the sledge-builder. Again, you can buy a very good sugar-barrel at your grocer's for 15 cents, and although the wood is not so good or the staves so well made as those in an oil-barrel, still there are some of them good enough to make very serviceable bottom pieces for the runners, and the rougher staves can be used for the top parts.

As has already been suggested, the advantage of a barrel-stave toboggan-bob over the ordinary double-runner sled-bob is three-fold: the former may be used on snow which is too soft for the narrow runners of the common sled, the materials for its construction are more easily obtained, and it requires less skill to build.

The Materials Necessary Are

a plank for a reach-board, a good barrel and a small piece of 2 x 4 inch or 4 x 4 inch timber, or some pieces of one-inch plank which may be nailed together to make 4-inch stuff. Select a good, sound stave and rest it upon a block of 4 x 4 inch timber so that the centre line of the block is parallel with the bowstring line of the stave (P R, Fig. 479), and so that the outside edge of the stave cuts the corner of the block at D (Fig. 476), as shown by Fig. 475; then with a soft pencil or a sharp-pointed nail draw an outline of the stave on the wood, and with a rule or straight-edged piece of plank continue the outside line to the end of the block (A, Fig. 476). Take another stave for the bottom of the toboggan and place it so that the end extends upon the block to the line C C (Fig. 476) and the outside edge of the stave reaches the corner B just as the first stave reached the corner D. With your straight-edge continue the line B B to the edge of the block as you did in the first place with the line A D. This will give you a block marked as in Fig. 476. Now saw down through the line C C until you reach the lower outline D E of the upper stave; next begin at D and saw down to E.   This will cut out C E D and leave Fig. 477.

Saw Along the Line

A until you cut off the block A C as shown in Fig. 480.   This, as you see, leaves a place for the stave to fit.   In the same manner cut out the block C B of Fig. 476 as shown in Fig. 480.   Now take your blue pencil again and sketch the bow of the sled-runner as shown by the dotted lines (Fig. 480).   Saw off the pieces to correspond with these lines, and after trimming away the angles with a sharp knife or chisel you will have the end piece (Fig. 481).   You can probably make this piece in less time than it takes me to tell you how to do it.

If the Lumber at Hand

is 2 x 4 inches make duplicate pieces of the shape shown in Fig. 481 and nail these together, making one piece 4 inches across the base.   The average barrel stave (Figs. 478 and 479) is about 4 or 5 inches across the middle, $3\frac{1}{2}$ to 4 inches or more in width at the two ends, and about $29\frac{1}{2}$ inches long measured on a straight line from end to end—that is, if the curved stave is thought of as a bow, the bowstring would be $29\frac{1}{2}$ inches long and the arch about 2 inches high between the middle of the string and the outside of the bow (Fig. 479).

When making

The Stern Blocks

to the runners cut both sides as the top is cut in Fig. 480; then it is necessary only to round off the ends as in Figs. 482 and 483.

If the barrels you have are of too light material to support the weight they must carry, this defect is easily remedied by cut-

THE STAVE TOBOGGAN

Fig. 484.—Showing construction of two runners.

ting deeper notches in the blocks so that two or three staves together instead of single ones may be used for the upper and under side of the runner (Fig. 483).

Each toboggan may be made of two runners (Fig. 484), or

Fig. 485.—Showing how it may be used as a sled.

A Third Runner

may be put in the middle, making it almost the same as a solid board for both top and bottom. Remember that the broad piece of board which represents

The Top of the Toboggan

(Fig. 484) must be nailed on from the under side; consequently this work must be done before the lower runners are nailed on the bow and stern blocks, and the top boards must set a little back of the centres of the sledges. Fig. 491 represents the rear toboggan of the bob; the front toboggan differs from the rear one in having a longer projecting cross-piece at the bow ends to be used as a foot-rest and to help in steering (Figs. 494, 495 and 496). In making

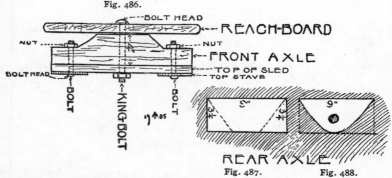

Fig. 486.

Fig. 487.   Fig. 488.

Figs. 487-488 show how to make the rear axle blocks such as are used in Figs. 494 and 496.

A Light Toboggan-Bob

it is not necessary to build it on the elaborate plan shown in Figs. 494, 495 and 496; in fact, the top board of the toboggan may be simply nailed fast to the reach-board, while the bow-axle can be arranged by fastening to the reach-board a block shaped like that shown in Fig. 492, and then dropping a bolt through a hole in the reach-board, through a hole in the centre of the block, and through another hole bored in the top pieces of the bow toboggan (Figs. 492 and 493). Fig. 486 shows

A Well-Made Front Axle

bolted through the top board and the top staves with iron bolts
and fastened to the reach-board by a king bolt secured with a
nut at the lower end.

Figs. 487 and 488 show how to make

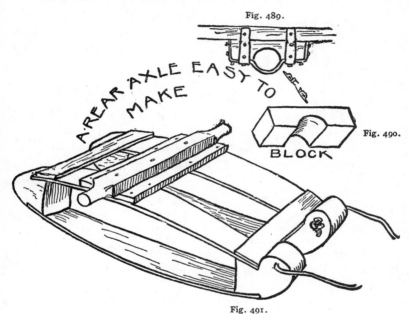

Fig. 489.

A REAR AXLE EASY TO MAKE

BLOCK

Fig. 490.

Fig. 491.

The Rear-Axle Blocks

such as are used in Figs. 494 and 496, but these may be simplified
in a light toboggan by making half-round notches in the blocks
(Figs. 489 and 490), and using a wooden axle (Fig. 491). This
axle is secured to the axle-blocks by nailing a piece of an old trunk-
strap over the axle and to the axle-block (Fig. 489) and securing

it by two other straps nailed to the reach-board and axle-block, so as to cross the first strap at right angles and extend over and around the other side of the block (Fig. 489). This will allow a free up-and-down movement of the rear toboggan and prevent sudden jolts. A line, a rope, or a chain should be run from the front pieces of the rear toboggan and fastened to screw-eyes on

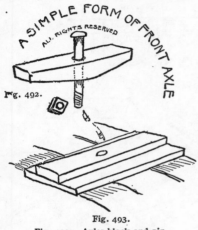

the under side of the reach-board (Fig. 494) to prevent the rear toboggan's turning from side to side.

The King Bolt

is the only part of either of these two simple toboggan-bobs which may have to be bought at a shop; the rest of the material can be found around any country or subur-ban house. But if the reader is ambitious to make a more pretentious affair he may con-

Fig. 493.
Fig. 492.—Axles block and pin.
Fig. 493.—Lower axle block.

struct the front and rear axles as shown in Figs. 486, 487, 488 and 494.

The Front Axles

have already been described; after the rear-axle blocks are securely nailed or screwed to the under side of the reach-board and flush with its edges, an iron bolt is run through a block which has been previously bolted to the top of the stern toboggan, as shown by the dotted lines in Figs. 486 and 494.

By reference to this diagram you will see the ropes attached to the stern toboggan

To Prevent its Sheering

from one side to the other and wrenching loose from the reach-board, while the axle pieces moving freely upon the iron bolt allow the toboggan to move up and down over the uneven places in the hill-side. The front axle allows free movement from one side to the other to guide the craft. The toboggan may be steered as shown in Fig. 495, the pilot sitting upright on the top piece, or he may lie prone upon the reach-board, grasp the ends

Fig. 494.

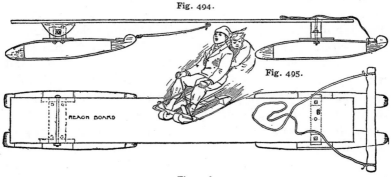

Fig. 495.

REACH BOARD

Fig. 496.
Top and side views and one method of steering.

of the foot-rest with his hands, and then steer by a movement of the arms.

If you place the boards upon which the axles rest a little back of the centre of the toboggan it will

Elevate the Bows of the Runners,

thus making it easier for them to overcome obstructions, and will do away with the danger of burying the runners in any accidental mound or lump of snow that may be found in the road.

The toboggans may be used without the reach-board as ordinary sleds (Figs. 485), but before using them the runners should be smoothed with sandpaper or rubbed with an old soft brick and coated with oil or tallow.

An Obvious Advantage

of these barrel-stave toboggans, one which adds greatly to the comfort of the coasters when sliding over an uneven surface, is that the runner itself is a spring.

Boys know well how often they are obliged to give up their sledding and coasting because the snow is not just right for it. This is not so bad when it happens during the school-term, for there is little enough time then for outdoor sports. But when the holidays come, and the snow then is light and flaky, and refuses to pack, or there is only a thin crust so that their sleds break through—then it is that boys wish they could manage the weather themselves and order their own kind of snow. In default of this, however, there is one thing they can do: make such a toboggan-bob as I have described here. It is fairly simple to make, it can be used on snow that is too deep or too soft for a narrow-runner sled, and it is perfectly safe on a steep hill which would be dangerous to coast down on an ordinary sled. And when summer comes it may be used to coast down grassy hill-sides.

Fig. 508.—The Flushing, L. I., bob-sled.

CHAPTER XXXV

HOW TO MAKE PLAIN SLEDS AND BOB-SLEIGHS

The sled with high runners looks odd to a Yankee, but it has its advantages when the snow is soft and deep, and it may be for this reason that the runners of

The Native Sleds of the Ohio Valley

average more inches in height than the sled runners of New England, where the snow is seldom slush as it is further south.

Anyone can make the Ohio sled who has access to a lumber pile, a saw, a hammer and some nails. From the inch pine board 1, 2, 7, 6 (Fig. 497) saw off the triangles 1, 2, 3 and 5, 6, 7, then with your jack-knife round off the corners at 1 and 3 as shown in the diagram (Fig. 497).

A few inches from the stern, saw two slits one inch deep and 2 inches apart, then knock out the block, leaving a rectangular notch 1 inch deep by 2 inches broad (see 8 of Fig. 497); trim it evenly with your

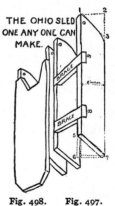

Fig. 498.   Fig. 497.

397

jack-knife and make a duplicate notch near the bow of the runner (9, Fig. 497); these are to hold the ends of the two braces shown in the diagram (Fig. 497). Lay the runner on another inch pine board and trace its outline, then make the duplicate runner in the same manner that you did the first. Now take two strips 1 inch by 2 inches, and about 15 inches long, fit them in the notches so that the runners will stand about 1 foot apart (Fig. 497); see that the ends of the braces are flush with the outside of the right-hand runner and fasten them securely in place with nails or screws, after which saw the protruding ends of the braces even with the outside of the left-hand runner. Next hunt up a piece of board long and wide enough for a top; cut it as shown in Fig. 498, and nail it to the runners, and the sled is finished.

To make it run smoothly the runners should be shod with iron; narrow strips of sheet-iron will answer the purpose, but half-round iron is the ideal thing.

On a short sled the half-round irons will be sufficiently secure if fastened only at the bow and stern of each runner, as shown in the diagram of the bob (Figs. 502, 505, and 507). The Ohio sled may be made of rough lumber, or it may be made of good planed wood and finished in the most elegant style.

In "the good old days" I have seen such sleds 7 and 8 feet long, loaded underneath with *pig-iron* to give weight and velocity.

If you desire to further test your ability by building something more difficult than a simple Ohio sled, you may try your hand in the construction of

A Double Runner, Traverse or Bob-Sleigh,

as it is variously called in different localities. When skilfully built, one of these compound sleds is enough of an achievement

to satisfy the vaulting ambition of even an amateur carpenter.
The bob-sleigh is made by joining with a reach-board two low-
runnered sleds or "bobs."

Almost any sort of tough wood will answer for the purpose,
but since we are going to spend time and skill upon this work we
will select good, strong 1¼-inch oak planks for the runners. We
shall need four pieces of the oak plank, each 5 inches broad by

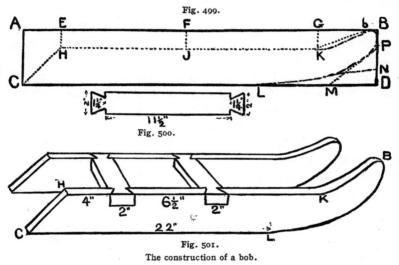

Fig. 499.

Fig. 500.

Fig. 501.

The construction of a bob.

32 inches long (A B D C, Fig. 499). From the end of one of
these pieces (A) measure 5 inches (to E), and mark the point;
from the opposite end (at B) measure 8 inches (to G) and mark
the point; from E and G measure 2 inches toward the middle
of the plank and mark the points H and K. Now take a carpenter's pencil, or a blue pencil, and rule with a straight-edge the
line H J K (see dotted line on Fig. 499); also rule the lines GK,
FJ, EH and HC. On the lower edge of the plank, 10 inches

from D, on the line DC, mark the point L.   On the line BD, 1 inch below B, mark the point P; also on the same line, 1½ inches above D, mark the point N, and on line BA, 1½ inches from B, mark *b*, and draw the lines LN, MP and K*b*.

The pencil lines which you have drawn will now show a rough outline of a sled runner (C H J K *b* B P L, Fig. 499).   Round off the angles by sketching inside of the ruled lines the curved lines of the bow of the runner, as shown in Fig. 499.

Saw slits from G to K, F to J and E to H; then cut out the block A E H C by sawing along the line CH until you meet the slit at H.   It is now an easy matter to saw along the line from H to K and from *b* to K, which removes the pieces E H J F, F J K G and G K *b*, leaving us only the triangle P M D and the small piece made by the line LN crossing MP to be sawed off the lower edge of the runner.

When all the saw work is done, the angles may be rounded with plane, chisel or jack-knife to conform to the sketched lines of the prow of the runner.   Using the runner just finished as a pattern, make each of the other three exactly like it.

The eight braces for the two bobs must now be cut from 1¼-inch oak.   Make them 2 inches wide, 11½ inches long.   At both ends of each brace make mortises to extend 1¼ inches, the width of the top of the runner (Figs. 500 and 501).   Set each pair of runners upright on their bottom edges; lay the braces in place, then carefully trace the form of the mortises on the top edges of the runners, and with saw and chisel cut out the notches, as shown by Fig. 501.   Fasten the braces securely in place with screws, and your two bobs only need top boards and half round iron shoes to finish them (see Figs. 502 and 505).

However, it takes two bobs and a reach-board to make a bob-sleigh, and so our work is really but half done.

The Reach-Board

may be any length to suit your fancy; the one shown in the diagrams, Fig. 502 (side view) and Fig. 505 (top view) is 7 feet long, 11 inches wide and 1 inch thick, which makes a well-proportioned bob-sleigh.

There must be allowance for a certain amount of independent motion in the two bobs under the reach-board; this is provided for by the use of two iron pins, a horizontal one for the rear bob (see dotted lines, Figs. 502 and 505) and a vertical one for the front bob (Fig. 506).

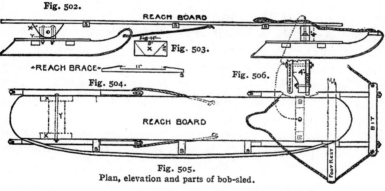

Fig. 502.
REACH BOARD
Fig. 503.
◄REACH BRACE►
Fig. 504.
Fig. 506.
REACH BOARD
Fig. 505.
Plan, elevation and parts of bob-sled.

For the rear bob take two pieces of $1\frac{1}{2}$-inch oak, 9 x $3\frac{3}{4}$ inches (X, Fig. 503), saw off the corners as indicated by the dotted lines (Fig. 503), then round off the angles as in X, Fig. 502, where the right-hand piece is shown fastened to the under side of the reach-board. Between these two pin boards fit a 4 x 4-inch oak block, which must be bolted to the top of the bob (Y, Figs. 502 and 505, dotted lines); this block must be long enough to fit snugly between the pin boards and yet allow movement to the sled. Bore a hole through the block Y corresponding to holes bored in the pin boards X—this is for the horizontal iron pin.

The second pin block is also made of oak and securely bolted to the top of the front bob, as indicated by the dotted lines (Figs. 502, 506 and 505). In Fig. 506 is shown but half of the pin block, but as one half is a duplicate of the other, it was not thought necessary to draw both ends. The same liberty has been taken with the guard rail and reach braces in Fig. 505. As may be seen these are shown on the lower side of the diagram only. Fig. 504 shows the form of the reach braces, which are screwed securely to the under side of the reach-board and have an ash or hickory guard rail fastened to their ends, as shown in the lower part of Fig. 505.

To prevent the stern bob from turning too far from side to side, ropes or chains are fastened from the bow ends of the rear runners to screw eyes on the under side of the reach-board.

A safe steering gear is the next important problem to solve and one can be made by an arrangement of a wooden bit, a foot rest or spreader and a pair of reins, as shown in Figs. 502 and 505. An iron pulley wheel should be securely fastened at each end of the spreader to hold the reins and facilitate the movement of the rope. The pulley wheel is not drawn in the diagram.

Figs. 507 and 508 at head of chapter show the details of a

Flushing Bob-Sleigh

Here you will notice that the pin block is set further back on the bow sled than it is in the one previously described; this is done to allow the driver to keep out of reach of his horse's heels. In other respects the bob-sleigh differs from the one shown in Figs. 502, 503, 504, 505 and 506, only in the addition of shafts for the horse and omission of steering apparatus. A stout plank is

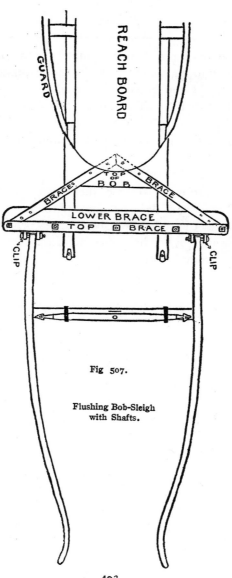

Fig 507.

Flushing Bob-Sleigh
with Shafts.

screwed fast across the front of the runners of the bow sled and a top brace bolted to it; the clips which hold the ends of the shafts are fastened to the top brace (Fig. 507).

This sort of bob-sleigh seems to be peculiar to Flushing. Moonlight nights when the sleighing is good the streets are alive with bobbing parties. If noise and laughter count as indications of fun, then is the

"Horse Bob"

truly a howling success. Many of them have two horses, hitched tandem, and the sport does not appear to be confined to very young people, for I have been on "bob parties" where the frost was thicker and whiter in the hair of some of the merrymakers than it was on the ground over which they glided.

CHAPTER XXXVI

THE VAN KLEECK BOB'

is named after the Messrs. Van Kleeck, two gentlemen of Flushing, who own a double runner of this description which was built on their own designs, and is the swiftest bob-sled of my acquaintance.

This fast bob-sled is neither so simple nor so crude as the rustic jumpers described some time ago, and it will test your skill to build it properly, but with all the plans and measurements before you the task should not be too difficult for even a boy who can handle tools.

The Sleds for the Bob'

are built entirely of good heavy oak; the runners of the sleds are $34\frac{1}{4}$ inches long, $4\frac{1}{2}$ inches high, $1\frac{5}{8}$ inches thick at the top, and $\frac{3}{4}$ of an inch thick at the bottom. To make the runners for the two sleds, one must have four $\frac{3}{4}$ inch oak planks, each 3 feet long by 5 or 6 inches wide. Trim these planks down to $4\frac{1}{2}$ inches thick, by $34\frac{1}{4}$ inches long, and $4\frac{1}{2}$ inches wide (Figs. 509 and 511). On the top of the runners measure $2\frac{1}{2}$ inches from the stern toward the bow and draw a line to the bottom corner, then saw off the triangles. At a point about 8 inches from the bow end of one of the runners, mark a point for the beginning of the curve (Fig. 510), and describe a neat and gradual curve to the top of the bow end of the plank. Saw off a rough triangle first, and then trim down until the curve of the wood corresponds with the line drawn.

Use this runner as a pattern and make the other three exactly like this one. The exact proportions are here given, not because others might not answer as well, but because this sled has proved to be a very fast one, and sleds, like boats, are fast or slow according to their lines and balance. After the runners are blocked out, trim them down on the inner sides with a plane until the lower edge is only ¾ of an inch broad (Fig. 510). The runners are set at an angle, as may be seen by Fig. 512, it being only 11

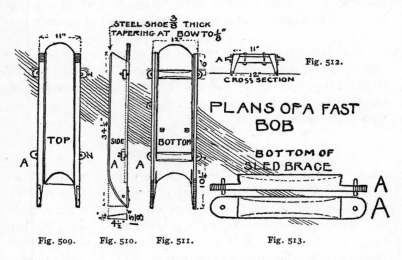

STEEL SHOE ⅜ THICK TAPERING AT BOW TO ⅛"

Fig. 512.

CROSS SECTION

PLANS OF A FAST BOB

BOTTOM OF SLED BRACE

TOP

SIDE

BOTTOM

Fig. 509.   Fig. 510.   Fig. 511.   Fig. 513.

inches from outside to outside of top of sled, while it is 12 inches from outside to outside of the bottom of the runners. There are two oak braces to each sled (Figs. 511, 512 and 513, A A A); these braces are 2 inches wide and 1½ inches thick, and cut with a bevelled step or notch to fit the slant of the inside of the runners (Figs. 512 and 513). The top ends of the braces extend through holes cut for that purpose, 1½ inches beyond the outside of the runners, and ½ inch below the top edges of runners, and are held in place by oaken pegs or pins (Figs. 509, 510, 511, 512, 513). To make the parts fit exactly and to get the porportions correctly, it is best to make on tough wrapping paper a set of plans the exact size of the proposed sled, and use these patterns to test your work by constant comparison.

After the braces are made and found by experiment to fit the runners neatly, they may be rounded off on the under side, the better to pass over lumps of snow or ice which chance puts on the tracks.

Make the tops of the sleds of ½ inch oak planks according to the plans (Figs. 510, 511 and 512), to fit between the runners and rest upon the braces, which have been set ½ inch below tops of the runners purposely, to leave room for the top plank. Secure the top board to the braces by iron bolts with nuts screwed to the lower ends (Fig. 512).

The Reach-Board

should be of selected maple 10 feet long, 11 inches wide and 1 inch thick (Fig. 514). To it are bolted five oak braces, each 1½ inches wide by ¾ of an inch thick (B, Figs. 515, 516, and 517). The centre of the bow-brace is 1½ feet astern of the bow of the reach-board, and the centre of the stern-brace is 6 inches forward of the stern of the reach-board. The bow-brace is 1 foot 1 inch long, and the others are all 1 foot 3 inches in length. To the braces hickory hand or guard rails are bolted (Figs. 516 and 517), and the bow ends of the rails are fastened with large screws to the sides of the reach-board.

Thus far I have described only a well-made bob, but when we come to joining the reach-board to the sleds we use

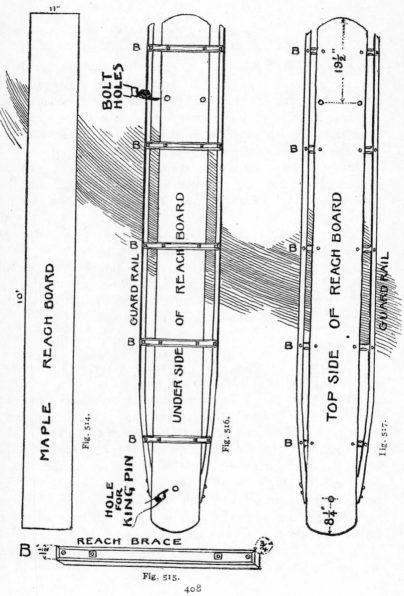

11"

10'

MAPLE   REACH BOARD

Fig. 514.

BOLT HOLES

B

UNDER SIDE   OF REACH BOARD

GUARD RAIL

HOLE FOR KING PIN

Fig. 516.

19½"

B

TOP SIDE   OF REACH BOARD

GUARD RAIL

8¼"

Fig. 517.

B   1½"   REACH BRACE   ¾"

Fig. 515.

The Van Kleeck Device,

which lets the bob over the "thank-you-marms" without the hard thud and jolt to which we are so accustomed.

Reference to Fig. 518 will show that, contrary to custom, the king bolt does not go through the top of the sled, but is fastened

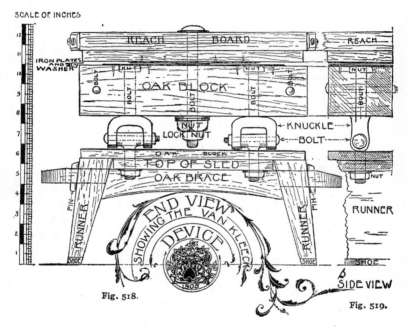

Fig. 518.

Fig. 519.

by two washers and two nuts to an oak block, and the block is itself bolted to the sled top by two iron knuckles; this arrangement not only allows the front sled to turn sidewise in any direction, but it can tip up and down, until the ends of the runners strike the reach-board, thus allowing the sled to adapt itself to

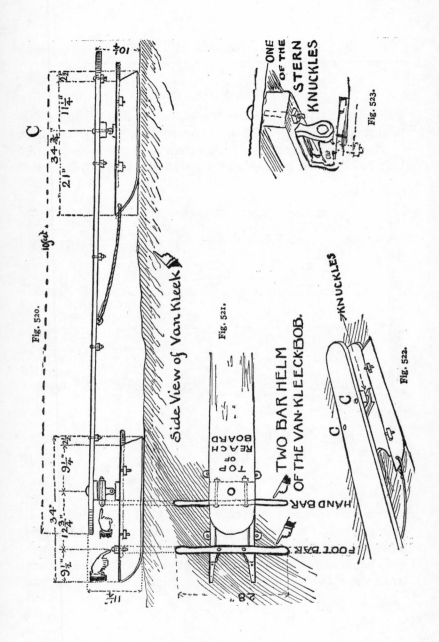

Fig. 520.

C

10 feet

2½"

11¼"

34¾"

21"

10¼"

Side View of Van Kleek

3 4'

9¼"

2¼"

12¾"

9½"

11¼"

Fig. 521.

TWO BAR HELM
OF THE VAN-KLEECK BOB.

TOP
OF
REACH
BOARD

HAND BAR

FOOT BAR

28"

ONE
OF THE
STERN
KNUCKLES

Fig. 523.

Fig. 522.

KNUCKLES

C   C

the unevenness of the track without making heart-breaking jolts. Figs. 520, 522 and 523 will show you that the stern sled is similarly provided with knuckles, but in the latter case there is no king pin, the oaken blocks being respectively bolted to the reach-board and the stern sled.

Where the king pin goes through the reach-board there is an oak block $10\frac{3}{4}$ inches long, $4\frac{1}{2}$ inches wide and a trifle over 1 inch thick, bolted across the bottom of the reach-board; to this is screwed an iron plate; another and longer iron plate is screwed to the big oak block below, and

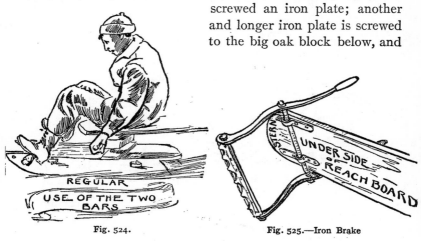

Fig. 524.

Fig. 525.—Iron Brake

an iron washer separates the two (Figs. 518 and 519) and lessens the friction. The plate on the big block is not screwed on until the nuts for the knuckle bolts are let into the holes cut for them and the knuckle bolts screwed into the nuts (see dotted lines, Figs. 518 and 519).

Across the top of the sled is another oaken piece, $\frac{1}{2}$ inch thick, $4\frac{1}{2}$ inches wide and 11 inches long, and through this and the top of the sled the lower bolts of the knuckles pass, and are held in place below by nuts and washers. The runners of the sleds are shod with steel bands $\frac{3}{8}$ of an inch thick and tapering gradually at the bow to $\frac{1}{8}$ of an inch, where it overlaps and is screwed on top of runner. Of course the hardware must be made by a smith.

The Steering Apparatus

can best be understood by examining Figs. 520 and 521, where it will be seen that there is a solid oak foot-bar bolted across the

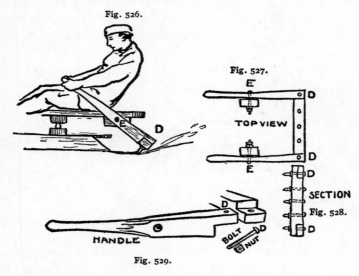

Fig. 526.

Fig. 527.

TOP VIEW

SECTION

Fig. 528.

HANDLE

Fig. 529.

bow of the sled, its centre $9\frac{1}{2}$ inches from the points of the runners, and a stout hickory hand-bar bolted to the big oaken block below the reach-board. Fig. 524 shows the proper way to steer a heavily loaded bob down a steep hill.

This steering apparatus is simple, safe and effective, and the pilot has the full strength of arms and legs available for turning the bow-sled as occasion requires. Fig. 525 shows the construction of an iron bob brake, and Figs. 526, 527, 528 and 529, the parts of a wooden brake, with teeth of iron bolts.

Before using your racing bob polish the steel shoes with emery cloth until they are as smooth as it is possible to make them, and then oil them with sweet oil; thus prepared, the heavy bob will slip down so quickly as to explain why one man calls his "The Oyster."

CHAPTER XXXVII

HOW TO STEER A BOB-SLED

Of late there has been a great revival of interest among people of all ages in the boyish sport of coasting and tobogganing. So keen has this become that we find in Europe clubs formed for coasting down the mountain side, and tracks built in deep snows with many difficult twists and turns to test the skill of the pilots on the American bobs, which they use and which are there improperly called toboggans. Also some of the New York papers have been filled with letters from bald-headed and gray-headed "boys" discussing the propriety of certain terms familiar to their youthful days and used in connection with the different methods of steering their sleds or bobs down the snowy hillside. But we will not enter into this discussion, for the good reason that the terms in question, "belly-buster," "belly-whopper," etc., are the ones used by the boys in different sections of the country, and consequently all of them proper in describing the method of coasting where the coaster lies prone upon the sled and goes down head first; but with the improvement of the sled and the bob there have crept in a number of devices for steering these crafts, the use of which

Should be Forbidden by the Authorities

because of the imminent peril the riders incur (especially the helmsman) when they are used.

There are almost as many methods of steering as there are styles of sleds.

Some people crowd on the sled with

Legs Extended on Each Side

and steer or attempt to steer with sticks held in their hands, Others steer by sitting on the front of the sled and

Vigorously Kicking Their Heels

upon the surface of the track as they go rushing down the hillside. This was the popular method in the Southwest, along the Ohio River, when the writer was a small boy, and many legs and arms were broken as a direct consequence of this style of steering. Another popular method in steering a small sled was to

Sit Sideways on One Leg

and allow the other leg to dangle out behind with the foot resting on the surface of the snow. This style of steering I have seen used by the tobogganers on Mt. Royal, up in Canada. It is comparatively safe for small sleds and toboggans, but when the foot is encased only in a moccasin it sometimes receives painful injuries in going down the steep courses, and I have noticed many bloody moccasins on the feet of our enthusiastic sport-loving Canadian brothers.

Belly-buster

Figs. 534 and 535 show the coaster going down head first. This is an exciting and exhilarating manner of coasting, but should never be used on dangerous courses where there is any liability of the coaster's head striking something harder than a soft snow bank; but on safe hills there can be no serious objection to coast-

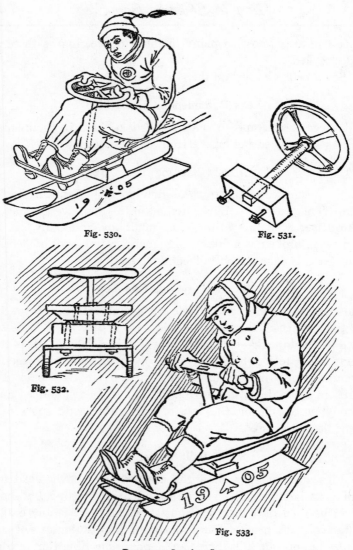

Fig. 530.

Fig. 531.

Fig. 532.

Fig. 533.

Dangerous Steering Gear

416

ing head first, unless it be that the sport itself is always strenuous and dangerous enough without unnecessarily adding to this
element.

The Wheel

(Figs. 530 and 531) which is in common use, leaves no avenue of
escape for the pilot; in case of accident he will be jammed suddenly and with great force against the iron wheel and the inflex-
ible iron upright bar, which
can but produce the most
serious results.

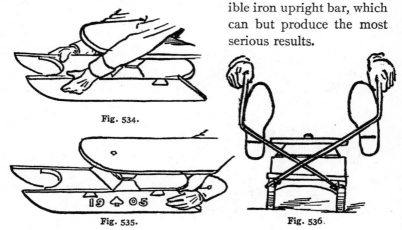

Fig. 534.

Fig. 535.

Fig. 536.

The Wheel Helm

is composed of an iron wheel fastened to an iron rod which has a
"squared" head fitting into a square hole in the hub of the wheel
(Figs. 530 and 531); this arrangement causes the rod to turn
with every turn of the wheel; the lower end of the wheel rod is
also "squared" to fit into the oaken block, which is bolted to the
front sled of the bob; thus it may be seen that every turn of the
wheel also turns the sled—an excellent plan *if no one had to sit
behind and astride of the shaft of the wheel.*

Built on the same principle as the wheel helm, Figs. 532 (cross section, front elevation) and 533 should never be used, for any sort of iron or wooden steering apparatus which extends above the reach-board contains possibilities of serious or even fatal results to the coasters. Rather than use either of the foregoing helms it is better to abandon all steering appliances and depend upon your unaided hands to control the direction of the front sled—a method often resorted to by small boys, who stretch their bodies full length upon the reach-board and grasp with their

Fig. 537.

hands the front of the runners of the bow-sled (Fig. 534), or the back part of the same runners (Fig. 535), and dart head first down the icc-coated hills.

The positions shown by Figs. 535 and 534 are those which all boys know under the forceful but eloquent names of "belly-buster," "belly-whopper," or "belly-gut." I will not stop to apologize for the use of these words, for they are now recognized as technical terms, and so used. But when one goes belly-buster, one leaves but little room for other passengers on the reach-board, and thus loses half the fun of coasting. One of the best ways to steer a loaded bob is with

Crossed Lines

as shown by Figs. 536 and 537. Fig. 537 shows a Yankee boy's way of using the crossed lines and feet without the aid of a foot-bar, while Fig. 538 shows an immovable iron foot-bar attached to the reach-board. In the last device the lines cross beneath the foot-bar, pass through smooth eyelets in the foot-bar and sometimes end in rings for the hands to grasp. The advantage of the crossed lines is apparent at a glance; it would be most difficult, indeed often impossible, to turn the sled by a direct pull, but when the line runs diagonally, a slight tug is sufficient to deflect the bow-sled.

Fig. 540 shows the bow-sled with a stout foot-bar bolted to it and extending half a foot on each side of the runners. With your feet on the foot-

Fig. 538.

rest and the reins in your hands you can brace your foot firmly against one end of the bar as you pull on the proper rein with your hand; this gives the strength of one leg and one arm to each pull.

Fortunately for us all the long solid-runner sleds are now obsolete and no longer to be seen crowded with reckless men and boys whooping down the hill. These "leg-breakers" were guided by the man in front, who vigorously kicked the snow to the right or left as required. Small single sleds are to this day often guided in the same manner, but not with the same risk to life and limb.

While Figs. 537, 538 and 540 are all good methods to use, a

Fig. 539.

Fig. 541.

better one still is to have a foot-bar on the bow of the front sled and a handle-bar attached to the king pin block of the same sled (Figs. 542 and 543). With this double helm it is an easy matter

Fig. 540.

for the pilot to sit in the front of the reach-board with his feet upon the foot-bar and his hands down at his sides grasping the hand-bar on each side of the reach-board (Fig. 524, Chap. XXXVI). In this manner he can use all the force of the muscles in both legs and arms to guide the bob-sled. This is the Van Kleeck method.

When I said that the American bobs in Switzerland were called toboggans it is to be understood that I mean they are so

called by the Americans, for it seems that the native Swiss call
their rudely fashioned sled a *handschlitten* and their double runner a *luge*. At the celebrated Cred d'y Bau run at Caux the *luge*
seems to be a term used for almost any form of sled, and coasting
down these mountains is
called *lugeing*. There are
several of these coasting
places in Switzerland, one
of them five miles long.
There is one at St. Montz
called the Cresta which is
only three and four-tenths
miles long, but the coasters

BELLY BUSTER

Fig. 542.

cover the distance in seventy-three seconds. Another place
is at the Grindinwold, and all of the American methods of
steering or guiding bobs are used at these places. But it
is not necessary for Americans to go to Switzerland to find
mountain sides upon which to coast. There are numerous places
within reach of New York, not farther from Manhattan than
Tuxedo, which might be
used by enthusiastic lovers
of the sport, and which
would afford long and steep
enough courses to satisfy
the most enthusiastic dare-
devil sportsman. Our own
Rockies in the Northwest

BELLY WHOPPER

Fig. 543.

are buried in snow each year, and adventurous spirits can find
on their steep declivities places to test their nerve and skill;
but whatever course they slide or whatever the location of
the hill, let them use common sense and abandon all

steering gear which projects above the front of the reach-board, so that when they start down hill they may not only enjoy the coasting but be reasonably certain of reaching the bottom safely, thus making the ride enjoyable from the beginning to

THE END

INDEX

A CATALOG OF SELECTED DOVER
BOOKS IN ALL FIELDS OF INTEREST

CONCERNING THE SPIRITUAL IN ART, Wassily Kandinsky. Pioneering work by father of abstract art. Thoughts on color theory, nature of art. Analysis of earlier masters. 12 illustrations. 80pp. of text. 5⅜ x 8½.   0-486-23411-8

CELTIC ART: The Methods of Construction, George Bain. Simple geometric techniques for making Celtic interlacements, spirals, Kells-type initials, animals, humans, etc. Over 500 illustrations. 160pp. 9 x 12. (Available in U.S. only.)   0-486-22923-8

AN ATLAS OF ANATOMY FOR ARTISTS, Fritz Schider. Most thorough reference work on art anatomy in the world. Hundreds of illustrations, including selections from works by Vesalius, Leonardo, Goya, Ingres, Michelangelo, others. 593 illustrations. 192pp. 7⅛ x 10¼.   0-486-20241-0

CELTIC HAND STROKE-BY-STROKE (Irish Half-Uncial from "The Book of Kells"): An Arthur Baker Calligraphy Manual, Arthur Baker. Complete guide to creating each letter of the alphabet in distinctive Celtic manner. Covers hand position, strokes, pens, inks, paper, more. Illustrated. 48pp. 8¼ x 11.   0-486-24336-2

EASY ORIGAMI, John Montroll. Charming collection of 32 projects (hat, cup, pelican, piano, swan, many more) specially designed for the novice origami hobbyist. Clearly illustrated easy-to-follow instructions insure that even beginning papercrafters will achieve successful results. 48pp. 8¼ x 11.   0-486-27298-2

BLOOMINGDALE'S ILLUSTRATED 1886 CATALOG: Fashions, Dry Goods and Housewares, Bloomingdale Brothers. Famed merchants' extremely rare catalog depicting about 1,700 products: clothing, housewares, firearms, dry goods, jewelry, more. Invaluable for dating, identifying vintage items. Also, copyright-free graphics for artists, designers. Co-published with Henry Ford Museum & Greenfield Village. 160pp. 8¼ x 11.   0-486-25780-0

THE ART OF WORLDLY WISDOM, Baltasar Gracian. "Think with the few and speak with the many," "Friends are a second existence," and "Be able to forget" are among this 1637 volume's 300 pithy maxims. A perfect source of mental and spiritual refreshment, it can be opened at random and appreciated either in brief or at length. 128pp. 5⅜ x 8½.   0-486-44034-6

JOHNSON'S DICTIONARY: A Modern Selection, Samuel Johnson (E. L. McAdam and George Milne, eds.). This modern version reduces the original 1755 edition's 2,300 pages of definitions and literary examples to a more manageable length, retaining the verbal pleasure and historical curiosity of the original. 480pp. 5³⁄₁₆ x 8¼.   0-486-44089-3

ADVENTURES OF HUCKLEBERRY FINN, Mark Twain, Illustrated by E. W. Kemble. A work of eternal richness and complexity, a source of ongoing critical debate, and a literary landmark, Twain's 1885 masterpiece about a barefoot boy's journey of self-discovery has enthralled readers around the world. This handsome clothbound reproduction of the first edition features all 174 of the original black-and-white illustrations. 368pp. 5⅜ x 8½.   0-486-44322-1

STICKLEY CRAFTSMAN FURNITURE CATALOGS, Gustav Stickley and L. & J. G. Stickley. Beautiful, functional furniture in two authentic catalogs from 1910. 594 illustrations, including 277 photos, show settles, rockers, armchairs, reclining chairs, bookcases, desks, tables. 183pp. 6½ x 9¼. 0-486-23838-5

AMERICAN LOCOMOTIVES IN HISTORIC PHOTOGRAPHS: 1858 to 1949, Ron Ziel (ed.). A rare collection of 126 meticulously detailed official photographs, called "builder portraits," of American locomotives that majestically chronicle the rise of steam locomotive power in America. Introduction. Detailed captions. xi+ 129pp. 9 x 12. 0-486-27393-8

AMERICA'S LIGHTHOUSES: An Illustrated History, Francis Ross Holland, Jr. Delightfully written, profusely illustrated fact-filled survey of over 200 American lighthouses since 1716. History, anecdotes, technological advances, more. 240pp. 8 x 10¾. 0-486-25576-X

TOWARDS A NEW ARCHITECTURE, Le Corbusier. Pioneering manifesto by founder of "International School." Technical and aesthetic theories, views of industry, economics, relation of form to function, "mass-production split" and much more. Profusely illustrated. 320pp. 6⅛ x 9¼. (Available in U.S. only.) 0-486-25023-7

HOW THE OTHER HALF LIVES, Jacob Riis. Famous journalistic record, exposing poverty and degradation of New York slums around 1900, by major social reformer. 100 striking and influential photographs. 233pp. 10 x 7⅞. 0-486-22012-5

FRUIT KEY AND TWIG KEY TO TREES AND SHRUBS, William M. Harlow. One of the handiest and most widely used identification aids. Fruit key covers 120 deciduous and evergreen species; twig key 160 deciduous species. Easily used. Over 300 photographs. 126pp. 5⅜ x 8½. 0-486-20511-8

COMMON BIRD SONGS, Dr. Donald J. Borror. Songs of 60 most common U.S. birds: robins, sparrows, cardinals, bluejays, finches, more—arranged in order of increasing complexity. Up to 9 variations of songs of each species.

Cassette and manual 0-486-99911-4

ORCHIDS AS HOUSE PLANTS, Rebecca Tyson Northen. Grow cattleyas and many other kinds of orchids—in a window, in a case, or under artificial light. 63 illustrations. 148pp. 5⅜ x 8½. 0-486-23261-1

MONSTER MAZES, Dave Phillips. Masterful mazes at four levels of difficulty. Avoid deadly perils and evil creatures to find magical treasures. Solutions for all 32 exciting illustrated puzzles. 48pp. 8¼ x 11. 0-486-26005-4

MOZART'S DON GIOVANNI (DOVER OPERA LIBRETTO SERIES), Wolfgang Amadeus Mozart. Introduced and translated by Ellen H. Bleiler. Standard Italian libretto, with complete English translation. Convenient and thoroughly portable—an ideal companion for reading along with a recording or the performance itself. Introduction. List of characters. Plot summary. 121pp. 5¼ x 8½. 0-486-24944-1

FRANK LLOYD WRIGHT'S DANA HOUSE, Donald Hoffmann. Pictorial essay of residential masterpiece with over 160 interior and exterior photos, plans, elevations, sketches and studies. 128pp. 9¼ x 10¾. 0-486-29120-0

CATALOG OF DOVER BOOKS

LIGHT AND SHADE: A Classic Approach to Three-Dimensional Drawing, Mrs. Mary P. Merrifield. Handy reference clearly demonstrates principles of light and shade by revealing effects of common daylight, sunshine, and candle or artificial light on geometrical solids. 13 plates. 64pp. 5⅜ x 8½. 0-486-44143-1

ASTROLOGY AND ASTRONOMY: A Pictorial Archive of Signs and Symbols, Ernst and Johanna Lehner. Treasure trove of stories, lore, and myth, accompanied by more than 300 rare illustrations of planets, the Milky Way, signs of the zodiac, comets, meteors, and other astronomical phenomena. 192pp. 8⅜ x 11.

0-486-43981-X

JEWELRY MAKING: Techniques for Metal, Tim McCreight. Easy-to-follow instructions and carefully executed illustrations describe tools and techniques, use of gems and enamels, wire inlay, casting, and other topics. 72 line illustrations and diagrams. 176pp. 8¼ x 10⅞. 0-486-44043-5

MAKING BIRDHOUSES: Easy and Advanced Projects, Gladstone Califf. Easy-to-follow instructions include diagrams for everything from a one-room house for bluebirds to a forty-two-room structure for purple martins. 56 plates; 4 figures. 80pp. 8¾ x 6⅜. 0-486-44183-0

LITTLE BOOK OF LOG CABINS: How to Build and Furnish Them, William S. Wicks. Handy how-to manual, with instructions and illustrations for building cabins in the Adirondack style, fireplaces, stairways, furniture, beamed ceilings, and more. 102 line drawings. 96pp. 8¾ x 6⅜. 0-486-44259-4

THE SEASONS OF AMERICA PAST, Eric Sloane. From "sugaring time" and strawberry picking to Indian summer and fall harvest, a whole year's activities described in charming prose and enhanced with 79 of the author's own illustrations. 160pp. 8¼ x 11. 0-486-44220-9

THE METROPOLIS OF TOMORROW, Hugh Ferriss. Generous, prophetic vision of the metropolis of the future, as perceived in 1929. Powerful illustrations of towering structures, wide avenues, and rooftop parks—all features in many of today's modern cities. 59 illustrations. 144pp. 8¼ x 11. 0-486-43727-2

THE PATH TO ROME, Hilaire Belloc. This 1902 memoir abounds in lively vignettes from a vanished time, recounting a pilgrimage on foot across the Alps and Apennines in order to "see all Europe which the Christian Faith has saved." 77 of the author's original line drawings complement his sparkling prose. 272pp. 5⅜ x 8½.

0-486-44001-X

THE HISTORY OF RASSELAS: Prince of Abissinia, Samuel Johnson. Distinguished English writer attacks eighteenth-century optimism and man's unrealistic estimates of what life has to offer. 112pp. 5⅜ x 8½. 0-486-44094-X

A VOYAGE TO ARCTURUS, David Lindsay. A brilliant flight of pure fancy, where wild creatures crowd the fantastic landscape and demented torturers dominate victims with their bizarre mental powers. 272pp. 5⅜ x 8½. 0-486-44198-9

Paperbound unless otherwise indicated. Available at your book dealer, online at **www.doverpublications.com**, or by writing to Dept. GI, Dover Publications, Inc., 31 East 2nd Street, Mineola, NY 11501. For current price information or for free catalogs (please indicate field of interest), write to Dover Publications or log on to **www.doverpublications.com** and see every Dover book in print. Dover publishes more than 400 books each year on science, elementary and advanced mathematics, biology, music, art, literary history, social sciences, and other areas.